The London and North Eastern Railway
A century and a half of progress
LNER 150
Patrick Whitehouse & David St John Thomas

The London and North Eastern Railway
A century and a half of progress
LNER 150

Patrick Whitehouse & David St John Thomas

David & Charles

First published in the UK in 1989
Reprinted 1991, 1998

ISBN 0-7153-9332-4

Book design by Michael Head

Printed in Italy by New Interlitho Italia SpA
for David & Charles
Brunel House   Newton Abbot   Devon

Frontispiece.
*The Yorkshire Pullman. The 16.45
departure from Kings Cross once
known as the West Riding Pullman
but renamed from 1935 after
provision was made for through
coaches to Hull. The photograph
was taken in 1938 or 1939 and
shows 'A1' class Pacific No 4481
St Simon of Doncaster shed. The
engine was built in very early
LNER days, September 1923, but
was originally allocated a GNR
number 1481 with an 'N' suffix
which it carried until July 1925.
The run to Doncaster (arrival 19.21
when the train divided) gave a
60mph schedule for the 156 miles.
The leading Pullman car is a 12-
wheel brake third whilst the
remaining vehicles appear to be
1928-built stock.*

*Non-stop run repeated. 1968 was
one of the years of the Great British
Rail Steam Ban when the Board
led by Henry Johnson refused to
permit any privately-owned steam
engine, bar No 4472 Flying
Scotsman (still within the time of
an agreed contract), to run over
their tracks. One event during this
period was particularly worth
noting; the 40th anniversary of the
first London to Edinburgh non-stop
run, 1 May 1968. This was re-
enacted using No 4472 and this
photograph shows the train complete
with two corridor tenders (there
were now no water troughs)
climbing Holloway Bank.*

CONTENTS

1 INTRODUCTION 7
  The Eastern Counties Main Line to 1843 24
  Tree of Growth 26
2 FREIGHT 29
  Working the Fish 39
3 AN OBSERVER REMEMBERS 45
  Soldier Enthusiast in Wartime East Anglia 54
4 STATIONS 57
  Peterborough 69
5 EAST ANGLIA 70
  LNER Personalities 82
6 LOCOMOTIVES 85
  Locomotive Stock and Allocations 99
7 SCOTLAND 105
  Named Trains Summer 1939 112
8 THE GOLDEN YEARS OF HIGH-SPEED
  TRAINS 117
  Signalling and Safety 125
9 SHEDS AND WORKSHOPS 129
  Problems by the North Circular 142
10 BRANCH LINE MISCELLANY 144
  Seen at York 162
11 COACHES: JAZZ QUINS TO
  CORONATION LUXURY 164
  Joint Lines 176
12 LNER INTO BR 179
  Publicity and Public Relations 187
13 PRESERVATION 189
  Station Interludes 193
14 BRITAIN'S NEW PREMIER LINE 198
  LNER Chronology 203
  Acknowledgements 205
  Index 206

Early days. A great Eastern Railway 0-6-0 (LNER class 'J15') takes a local freight through Gidea Park station. Note the use of white disc as headcode, a practice carried on well into British Railways' days. This is one of the later members of the class and is fitted with both dual brake and steam heating.

1
INTRODUCTION

IMAGES: Of boyhood, walking down the tree-lined avenue to the recently-rebuilt Gidea Park, exuding good-quality neatness; and along the path overlooking the quadrupled tracks, expresses (famous names among them) now given a clear run, and more modernity in the continental wagons running to London courtesy the Harwich train ferry. Pride in 'our' station, teeming with passengers at rush hours, terminus for many of the frequent suburban trains with a grand new signalbox and extensive sidings. Vivid memories of the first-ever train journey, to Liverpool Street by what must have been one of the last rakes of four wheelers. It waddled in like a goods and so full that no chance of a former second-class compartment and so endured the real McCoy of Great Eastern economy, listening to the conversation on the benches beyond the half partition.

On later journeys, always travelling in the rear and seeing the front of the train round the curves through the dismal arches into Liverpool Street, perhaps running parallel with an articulated set. Nothing like that in the toy shops. Last off platform, train out, next in seconds later, frightened by release of Westinghouse brake . . . all so quick, dark. Back home, dad undoubtedly right to have chosen GWR for Hornby layout in garage; LNER ok but everyday, even ordinary. Of course could not know just what an achievement the everyday peak service was; heard later that if the GWR had anything half so difficult its managers would have had twins on the spot.

Then to Harpenden where the joys of the Midland could occasionally be foresaken for the LNER's single-line crossing station a long way off. How could it possibly be called Harpenden? Branch-line love at first sight. How orderly, quiet; but why did the signalman cause false hope of another train by failing to restore signals to danger for half an hour?

Kings Cross: Not ordinary, at all. Too late to see the like of the *Silver Jubilee* but an unforgettable first head-on view of an 'A4' sweeping out of the tunnel depending heavily on last-minute application of brakes, and northbound expresses starting off for really interesting places with deservable commotion.

Immediately after the war, Nottingham Victoria, vast, endless trains but hardly any of them going anywhere special or carrying many people, though endless goods snaking through. Aboard for Sheffield Victoria, all stations; how sensible those island platforms seemed, but so slow – and dirty. Back by express, job to find standing room between soldiers and kit bags in corridor, equally dirty and for ever slowing (probably for mining subsidence). But a compartment to self from the platform-

Morning departure. Kings Cross station 1932–3 with four Gresley Pacifics at the head of East Coast main line trains. Centre stage is class 'A1' No 2547 Doncaster making a spectacular departure with what is possibly the relief to Flying Scotsman *whilst 'A1' No 4475 Flying Fox prepares to take that famous train north at 10.00. Both these Top Shed based locomotives have been fitted with corridor tenders for working the non-stop Scotsman. Despite the availability of the class 'A3' Super Pacifics the 'A1's were used turn and turn about with them on all top link expresses. Indeed it was as an 'A1' that No 4472 Flying Scotsman went down in the record books in achieving the first official 100mph in 1934.*

7

Foreigner on the Great Central. One of the ex Great Northern Railway Ivatt Atlantics as LNER class 'C1' No 4449 heads a York-to-Swindon (via the Banbury connection) Sundays-only cross-country express near Rugby during the mid 1930s.

Through Coaches

In LNER days many expresses served a variety of destinations with through carriages. Even the *Flying Scotsman* was divided into four on arrival at Edinburgh Waverley, as described in the company's *The Flying Scotsman: The World's Most Famous Train*, a mini-bestseller at 1s (5p):

'Part of the train, including the "Triplet" dining car set, has been drawn forward, to be put away, after all luggage has been removed until tomorrow's up *Flying Scotsman*. The Glasgow coaches, behind one of the busy little shunting engines of which a number are moving about the station all day long, are taken to the platform from which starts the 6.30pm Glasgow express. The Perth coaches are taken by another engine to the 6.38 train, and finally our Aberdeen coaches are added to the 6.32 express already partially made up [with] another restaurant car than that we have used as far as Edinburgh, equally comfortable and equipped for serving dinner.'

next-the-wall at Manchester London Road to Sheffield, still in steam days, guard checking all windows closed before going under Pennines. We passed a long goods, mainly coal, immediately before and after going through one of the twin single bores.

A 'B1' at Swindon, the Sunday cross-country neatly connecting with the GW's Devon express, again horribly crowded. Excellent journey on *Master Cutler* from Leicester but amazement at slowness of approach to London: fancy having to follow an all-stations London Transport electric between Rickmansworth and Harrow! Another occasion miserably late from Rugby Central: false hopes as signals raised, always another freight, only one seat left in restaurant car, 'The LNER never serves Yorkshire pudding *and* horseradish, sir.' All very run down, but one later learnt how high GC standards of comfort (its restaurant cars among the best) had been maintained during the 1920s and 1930s.

Edinburgh Waverley, very LNER unlike York which always had a cosmopolitan touch about it. But like Nottingham Victoria, great emphasis on bays and locals with few through platforms or trains but some of them very exciting . . . arriving through Princes Street Gardens – wonderful signals – in parallel with an 'A4' and then the first-ever sight of a Pullman, *The Queen of Scots* running in from Glasgow. But only third-class *Flying Scotsman* to Kings Cross: exciting yet even here that acrid LNER smoke and soot, ladies for ever brushing smuts (real or feared) off their dresses, restaurant car fully booked before departure.

Everywhere yards, some of them huge, being shunted by small locomotives like you did see in toy shops, more powerful machines at the head of long formations ready to follow your passenger train, porters at stations humping, lumping, pushing, pulling carts, crates, churns. Fairly friendly, ordinary railwaymen, just going about their business. Back at home, the day-a-week gardener, an LNER night fire watchman at Bethnal Green, could not understand why people got so excited by the GW. 'They've got just one thing we can't afford, a proper pension,' which did not register much at the time.

Steadily the images, memories and reports from family and friends formed a pattern . . . of a purposeful, once powerful railway doing its best to cope simultaneously with too much traffic and poverty, proud of its latest developments (leaflets about them were left around at home) but generally making do with last century's locomotives, trains, stations, restrictions.

In several ways it seemed a misty railway. Literally, if not outright fog substantially of its own making, it was shrouded in smoke and dust. It went with a kind of automation you had to understand or you would be lost: nobody helped you find your way around Liverpool Street, and dad went missing for hours because he was not warned that the train in the mainline platform at Gidea Park was not the presumed semi-fast for Ingatestone but a delayed express, first stop Ipswich. At school it was all LMS and GWR. Few people seemed to pore over the LNER timetables (issued in the same large format as the GWR's until the war) and so few were retained by the enthusiasts of the twenties and thirties that they are now the scarcest of all. Yet especially the summer issues, such as that for 1937 totalling over 500 pages, three sections of folding map, and silver-paper streamlined train supplement were endlessly full of fascination.

Was the LNER taken for granted? Were people even ashamed of it? 'Oh, the LNER . . . what can you expect?' Yet, after nationalisation, when the family occupied the front compartment of the 13.30 Paddington–Penzance, the train was seen off and watched en route by thousands, *Seagull* (this happening to be an exchange trial) seeming to be even more popular than *King George V*.

Looking back, it is now clear that the LNER did fight enormous

The viaduct at Durham. An ex North Eastern Railway Atlantic No 717 (as LNER class 'C7') heads south with a train of LNER varnished teak coaches banked by an NER class 'G5' 0-4-4 tank No 1751. Note the lattice girder NER signal gantry and the last three vehicles, a non-corridor coach, a six-wheeled van and a Gresley full-brake bogie van. The date is May 1936.

A Team

Not until January 1927 did the LNER produce an all-line magazine. In its first issue chairman, William Whitelaw, boasted:

We are already a Team. Our early prejudices have gone; we see each other's virtues now, and have forgotten the shortcomings. Great Central engines have become a standard for Scotland; the Great Eastern Musical Society has played and sung in Scotland and its four hundred members have stood looking at the Forth Bridge, saying 'This is *our* Bridge,' Great Northern permanent way will one day be our standard as it is our example, and both passenger and goods trains will run in England as punctually as they now do in Scotland; the North Eastern, to say no more, has given us the priceless heritage of being first in the world, started by George Stephenson a hundred years ago.

difficulties, being by far the most impoverished of the four of the 'grouping years' 1923–48. Its total revenues were perpetually down many millions of pounds from its starting point, itself well below what the constituents had achieved in happier years. But it is also clear that with its limited resources the railway did many things splendidly.

It was run as a business in a gentlemanly manner and tried hard to please its customers, though its shareholders were deeply unsatisfied. It had the misfortune to serve the least glamorous part of Britain. To quote one small example, when a new privately-owned hotel was opened nearer Parkeston Quay, there was no question of retaining the Great Eastern in the town centre, for the old town at Harwich like so many eastern non-resort coastal towns was a dump, attracting nobody but for the cross-channel services.

Nowhere was unemployment more widespread than in the LNER industrial heartlands, and one has to be reminded that the transition from heavy to light industry was well under way even in the 1920s and that migration of employment south is not a post-war phenomenon; even within the coal industry Scotland and the North East were already declining at the expense of the East Midlands. The decline of heavy industry, including shipbuilding (most of which was on LNER territory), the collapse of coal exports after the 1926 strike, the agricultural depression in the mid inter-war years, even the rise of imports shipped into south and west coast parts . . . they all hurt. To go back to Harwich, management complained that the Danish vessels brought in five times as much cargo as they loaded outward: 'The

North Eastern swing bridge. An LNER built 'B16' class 4-6-0 (the continuation of the NE class 'S3') heads a fitted freight over the bridge at Selby in 1950. This was the route of the old East Coast main line until 1983. Note the bracket signal with the splitting distant arms dating back to NER days and the solitary LNER or BR upper quadrant replacement.

Englishman's appetite for Danish butter and bacon and eggs is insatiable, and he is also developing a taste for Danish lager. And all such problems were before road competition began to bite. Ironically for a railway always associated with industry, yet more serious distress was averted by new agricultural traffics (discussed in detail in the chapter on freight) though most of those were eventually – in BR days – lost to road.

So while the LMS was able to replace large quantities of its inherited locomotives, and the Southern electrified, the LNER (taking over 249 different classes or variations) modernised painfully slowly, mere handfuls of new engines at a time, virtually none for a couple of years after the 1929 crash. Yet ultimately it produced perhaps the best steam express locomotives Europe has ever seen, along with expresses that set new standards of speed and reliability. That is but one tribute to the management. Another is that it could never be accused of extravagance and even less of waste. What was spent was spent wisely, and where the improvements it effected have not been obliterated by post-nationalisation decline, they have stood the test of time well. Many are of course mentioned in later pages, though it is a great shame there were not more, and that the only LNER electrification completed before 1948 was hundreds of miles from London.

If the LNER lacked the continuity and traditions of the Great Western, and the personality of a Southern's Walker to gain unity and purpose through electrification, at least it was fortunate in avoiding a Lord Stamp of single-minded determination to unify and standardise. The LNER's recipe was devolution, the avoidance of centralisation and complication. Though it was served by many exceptionally fine men (tribute is paid to several in later pages), there was no single giant of a manager, no one theory of how the railway should be run. It was all thoroughly professional.

In part this was made easier by the nature of the amalgamations that brought the LNER into being. There were the 'three Greats' running out from London: Great Eastern, Great Northern and Great Central. They had toyed with getting together years before but the then government did not like it. There was little in common between them, and merging them so far as they were merged at all gave most of such troubles as came the new company's way. Difficulties were enhanced by the coincidence of retirements; there was no natural leader. But further north, it was a matter of fusion rather than merger. The Great Northern led to the North Eastern which handed over to the North British on the East Coast route to Scotland on which joint stock had run for many years, while the GN and NE had established an East Coast conference to develop traffic with Scotland.

Headquarters in London were kept slender, and most work undertaken by the three areas: Southern (incorporating the three Greats based at Liverpool Street), North Eastern (essentially the old North Eastern but including its only major competitor, the Hull & Barnsley, voluntarily merged some months ahead of grouping), and Scottish (and even here the former North British and Great North of Scotland

Standard Revenue

Under the 1921 Railways Act, the big four were entitled to levy charges that would produce their 'standard revenue' adjusted upward for national interest on capital works. As can be seen from the table the LNER never reached its 'standard', coming closest in its very first year and suffering severely in many pre-war years. Yet only the Southern with its massive electrification had greater allowances for additional capital, the LNER's being almost exactly twice those of the LMS.

	£
Standard Revenue	14,787,733
Allowances for	
Additional Capital	429,002
	15,216,735

Net Revenue Earned:

Year	£
1923	13,184,763
1924	10,856,365
1925	9,236,237
1926	3,759,775
1927	11,268,021
1928	11,277,759
1929	13,061,250
1930	11,168,750
1931	9,424,610
1932	7,166,857
1933	7,723,120
1934	8,348,147
1935	8,371,373
1936	9,141,395
1937	10,107,442
1938	6,653,167
1939	9,271,030
1940	10,350,992
1941	10,647,027
1942	10,700,599
1943	10,655,441
1944	10,753,279
1945	11,027,813
1946	11,078,471
1947	11,387,350

AGM's Summary

The 6,540 route miles had to be supervised, and the mileage of running lines reduced to single track, including sidings, was 16,530. The company began by employing about 207,530 people, though by 1937 the number was 31,680 (or 15 per cent) less. In 1923 the stock of steam locomotives was 7,388, with 896, or 12 per cent, under repair; in 1938 the stock was lower by 870, or 11 per cent, and only 6 per cent of the fleet was unserviceable. Over the same period 23,640, or 10 per cent, of the 1923 stock of wagons were scrapped, but the average capacity of the 253,570 wagons left in traffic was almost 1½ tons higher.

The LNER was primarily a freight carrier, working in 1937 about 978,220 ton miles per route mile and producing over 500 ton miles in a total engine hour, well above the average for the other main lines. Passenger services were, however, developed in speed and comfort. Each year before the war over 70 million coaching train miles were run. A highlight of the summer timetable after 1928 was the non-stop run of the *Flying Scotsman* between Edinburgh and King's Cross. Gresley built some superb trains for the East Coast services, while his best sleeping cars were the envy of other railways and were so popular that over 15 years the number in service was doubled.

In 1935 Gresley sought authority to build a new type of streamlined train, which could run the 268 miles from Newcastle to King's Cross in four hours, with a stop at Darlington to pick up Tees-side passengers, and return to Tyneside in the late afternoon of the same day. The outcome was the *Silver Link* Pacific locomotive at the head of the *Silver Jubilee*, moving so smoothly that a passenger in the

continued opposite

continued substantially to run their own affairs). The chairman, William Whitelaw, grandfather to the present Lord Whitelaw, who chaired shadow board meetings in 1922 at which the structure was established, came from the North British and enjoyed equally setting a chairman's lead and playing trains. The chief general manager, Ralph Lewis Wedgwood, came from the North Eastern, a thorough professional, much respected. He had indeed been the very first traffic apprentice to be appointed with university education under the North Eastern's scheme which was adopted for the whole LNER and resulted in the company being more professionally managed than the other three – and in ex-LNER men claiming a large proportion of top BR posts in later times. Education was always an LNER priority; old timetables may be scarce, but one constantly comes across notebooks – usually in question-and-answer form, covering what to do in every conceivable kind of situation – kept by traffic apprentices and others anxious to further their careers. A sound promotion policy also undoubtedly helped keep up morale during difficult days. Management salaries were modest but promotion fair, the responsibility often great. Traffic apprentices included many well-known figures, and several contribute to later pages.

Not merely did the highly-delegated management make for smooth transition on the LNER's formation (except in the Southern area where the first chief appointment failed), but the pattern was hardly varied throughout the company's total life, in average times and worse. Just how successful was it?

The stiffest criticism has to be that what the LNER did best was on an all-line basis. Very few departments (not even estates and hotels) reported direct to the general manager, but the chief mechanical engineer, Nigel Gresley, undoubtedly did, and his achievements with carriages as well as locomotives are what is inevitably best remembered. Publicity (and the industrial officer who persuaded scores of new light industries to take sites alongside the LNER) was also a central function and was again extremely successful. Signalling, however, was delegated and despite scattered innovation was pretty basic, the new company pleading poverty in not pursuing the forms of automatic warning actually in use on parts of the North Eastern (its drivers were furious at losing such protection) and being developed by the Great Central. So the score is not entirely in favour of devolution, but there were many fewer frustrations and muddles than on the LMS. The LNER was ever professional and its distinct style depended perhaps more on men in the areas and districts getting on with their jobs than upon directive from on high. Local fire power was aided by the then unique area boards which, though acting mainly in advisory capacity, helped monitor performance and gave valuable identity, especially in the North East and in Scotland where most initial seats went to the former directors of the constituents not upon the main board.

Though slightly smaller than the LMS, the company was still a massive organisation, employing far more men and resources (see snippet 'AGM's Summary') than any industrial concern had yet contemplated. The railway had four major London termini, served the

East Coast almost continuously from Southend to Lossiemouth, had incursions into Wales and the West Highlands and great activity in the East Midlands and around Manchester and Glasgow. Additionally there were extensive bus, port, ship, hotel and other activities. It was indeed the world's largest railway dock owner in length of quay though its turnover was substantially less than that of the rich GW docks; and while its ships have an epic story of their own, by the outbreak of World War 2 they were making a loss. The railway workshops alone employed 50,000.

It worked. It had to make do with much antiquated equipment, including strings of gas-lit four wheelers on the Great Eastern suburban services up to 1935 and many locomotives over half a century old. But it was never divided, unhappy or as wasteful as the LMS, and the worst of its stations (Leeds Central always excepted) compared favourably with the comparable ones of the larger company. It maintained the loyalty of its staff, lobbied government harder than any of the others (it needed to, of course, but did well with grants which made possible most of the capital schemes) and – perhaps the greatest test – despite its financial situation succeeded in carrying vast volumes of wartime traffic such as to the East Anglian air bases often with real panache. On the East Coast the Pacifics and 'V2s' were expected to haul in excess of twenty vehicles weighing up to 850 tons gross.

As a business, however, it was a hopeless failure, doomed from the decline in traffic receipts (which included rate cuts 'to stimulate the economy' as well as volume reductions). It saved where it could – the teams seeking economies were nicknamed 'razor gangs' – for example controlling overtime payments with great care and running vast numbers of trains on certain dates only also to cut coal consumption. Staff were pressurised to take early retirement . . . on top of the wage cuts all railwaymen endured in the twenties and despite the lack of a proper pension fund for wages staff. (Salaried staff did have a superannuation scheme.) The railway was never in danger of going bust, for there was always an operating profit. But net revenue out of which dividends could be paid was totally inadequate, falling from £13 million in 1923 to £7 million in 1932. To begin with a compensation fund (government money paid at the company's inception) was raided, but soon payments were stopped on ordinary shares. Later dividends had to be cut on the next stock in line, the second preference, and though debenture dividends were always paid the railway lost its trustee status. Wartime memories are of how pathetically low LNER stock was compared with that of the others, notably the GW. And while the GW directors were positively proffered compensation at nationalisation, the compensation the LNER ones had voted themselves at the company's final meeting was turned down so that an extra minuscule distribution could be made to the shareholders – a sorry end to a tale punctuated by shareholder protest. And it has to be said that in the last days that MPs were allowed to raise questions about train services to their constituencies (it ceased once the nation owned them), a disproportionate number of complaints concerned the LNER, especially ailing commuter services.

continued

rear coach could read, and even write, in comfort. In 1937 there followed two *Coronation* trains, running 392 miles between Edinburgh and King's Cross in six hours. Later came two high-speed trains for West Riding of Yorkshire service. Another fine train, the *East Anglian*, was built for a high-speed service between Norwich, Ipswich, and Liverpool Street, but owing to speed restrictions at Colchester and elsewhere it ran as an ordinary express train.

These high-speed trains were well advertised and were often fully booked. They were popular with regular travellers, who did not grudge a supplementary charge for a quicker journey. The whole development aroused keen interest among the workmen who built the trains and the staff of all grades who helped to run them punctually.

In other ways the LNER was not lacking in enterprise. Total capital expenditure in 1923 was over £339 million; in the next 7 years another £8 million was spent. About £250,000 of that sum was the cost of installing Fröhlich brakes in March shunting yard – the first yard in this country to be equipped with retarders. With some Government help in raising capital, a further £8 million was laid out in 8 years to 1938. Of the aggregate expenditure to that time, no less than £25 million was spent on docks and other shipping places and nearly £3 million on steamships, so that all the company's property on land and sea was in a thoroughly efficient state.

In 1937 Mr Whitelaw was glad to improve the LNER accounts by selling Tyne Dock to the Tyne Improvement Commission for £650,000. Opened in 1859, the Dock shipped 7 million tons of coal every year in the heyday of the Durham coal export trade; but *continued overleaf*

continued
in the 1930s came a succession of lean years, and the cost of future maintenance would have been high. In 1937 the LNER held its operating ratio down to 81 per cent, but largely owing to unregulated road competition traffic fell away in 1938 and the operating ratio rose to nearly 87 per cent – R. Bell (assistant general manager), on the company's first sixteen years from *The Journal of Transport History*, 1962.

Farewell

Together, we have built up a fine organisation in the last seventeen years, and it has a fine spirit of its own. We are proud of the London and North Eastern, and none the less so that each of us thinks his own old railway, now merged in the new unity, was in its time the best of the lot. I hope the tradition of those double loyalties, each reinforcing the other, will not be lost as the date of our unification recedes.

From some other sphere of work, I shall look back on a London and North Eastern Railway, united and progressive as of old, only I trust more prosperous. I hope you will give me your good wishes in the activities, whatever they may be, to which in these anxious times I may turn my hand. To you all I wish Good luck and better days. – Two statements selected from the farewell message of the LNER's first chief general manager, Sir Ralph Wedgwood, March 1939.

Though there was much enthusiastic planning and lobbying in the two and a half years between peace in Europe and nationalisation, parts of the system were now shuddering with deterioriation, though generally the tank engines with their Westinghouse brakes still puffed smartly in and out of Liverpool Street every couple of minutes at rush hour. The LNER *had* been going to electrify and could fairly blame the war for the last part of that delay.

There have been a number of sound formal histories of the LNER and the lines that went to make it. The purpose of this final volume in the '150' quartet on the four great systems of the 1923–47 years is more to catch the flavour, to tell what it really was like being a passenger or having to organise engine maintenance. While carefully reflecting the character of the whole diverse system, we have given the work a slight East Anglian slant, celebrating the 150th anniversary of the first part of the Eastern Counties, the LNER's first trunk route out of London, in the same way that the LMS 150th was for the London & Birmingham rather than the Liverpool & Manchester. Following this introduction is an account of the Eastern Counties' first tempestuous years.

The Eastern Counties merged to form the Great Eastern which after a dreadful period of monopolistic non-caring (it indeed had a virtual monopoly but not of a rich territory) became at least a half decent railway with increasingly enterprising expresses, including non-stops (some with Pullmans or restaurant cars) to an amazing variety of destinations, some well off the main line. But they had to be lightly powered because of weight restrictions, ever a GE incubus. 'Claud Hamilton' 4-4-0s and 'B12' 4-6-0s worked the main services, 'B17' 'Sandringham' 4-6-0s (designed with the GE section especially in mind) taking over from 1928. Following the introduction of streamlined trains out of Kings Cross, two 'B17s' were streamlined to work a new *East Anglian* between Liverpool Street and Norwich in 1937, but it was little more than a gesture to a backwater region and still took 2 hours 10 minutes. The best GE section trains were the 'Continentals' from Liverpool Street to Parkeston Quay, connecting with LNER, Dutch and Danish ships. In 1924 two new sets were made for the *Hook Continental*, thirteen-car formations weighing 430 tons. Even heavier for this hard route at 443 tons was a more luxurious train with internal arrangements similar to those of the *Silver Jubilee*, which included ordinary restaurant cars for second as well as third class passengers and Pullmans for first. The *Hook Continental* at 20.30 was followed from Liverpool Street ten minutes later by the *Antwerp Continental*, while the *Flushing Continental* left the capital at 09.30 or 10.00, and the *Scandinavian* for Denmark at 16.10.

Mainly due to the difficult exit from Liverpool Street, services on the GE section's other trunk route to Cambridge were poor. But in 1932 the LNER introduced five trips each way on a new *Garden Cities and Cambridge Buffet Express* taking the slightly longer Great Northern route from Kings Cross. Generations of undergraduates nicknamed them the 'Beer Trains'. By the war there were three non-stops in 65 minutes from Liverpool Street.

Most of East Anglia remained an economic backwater even in LNER

Boat train departure. The busy platform at London's Liverpool Street station with crowds waiting to depart on the Antwerp Continental service.

Great Eastern main line. One of Holden's classic 4-6-0s as LNER No 8539 heads a train made up of eleven vehicles (some non corridor) near Brentwood in the early days of grouping. The engine is painted apple green with the number carried on the tender under the small LNER lettering. Class 'A' headcode white discs indicate that in spite of the train's make up it is classified as an express.

Great Northern local. A down outer suburban train emerges from Hadley Wood tunnel behind 'D2' class 4-4-0 No 3049 in the late 1930s.

Short, fast and comfortable. A large boilered ex Great Northern Railway Atlantic No 4458 resplendent in green livery heads the six-coach Harrogate Pullman in the mid 1920s. Note the GNR somersault signals with their spectacle plates down the lattice post from the semaphore arms.

Streamliner. The down Silver Jubilee express passes Wood Green Junction, North London on 20 June 1936. The whole train is in silver grey livery and the 'A4' Pacific No 2512 Silver Fox *is virtually brand new. It was the last of the batch built in the previous year specially for this service.*

days, and it is perhaps not surprising that the Great Eastern was a second rather than first-ranking railway, though its managers paid themselves the most handsome salaries in the business – which added to the pangs of amalgamation. As already mentioned, its agricultural freight traffic increased enormously in LNER days; and if the suburban trains for which the GE was most famous – the 'Jazz' service from colour-coding the classes – alas continued to be hauled by the same steam engines throughout the grouping era, at least riding was improved by mounting the old, cramped passenger accommodation on new bogie chassis.

More surprising, perhaps, is that the Great Northern was also not quite a top-class company. It had many excellent characteristics, notably an excellent track for the first part of the East Coast main line to Scotland. The GN itself only reached Shaftholme Junction, north of Doncaster, and expanded in Lincolnshire and westward into the West Riding and Derbyshire with a sickly branch even reaching Stafford. Jointly with the Midland, it owned the Midland & Great Northern Joint from Peterborough to Yarmouth, with branches from that route's HQ at Melton Constable to Norwich and Cromer. (Though the MGNJ remained jointly owned throughout grouping, the LNER assumed working responsibility in 1936.) The GN also owned a third share in the Cheshire Lines Committee giving it access to Lancashire and the North Wales coast.

The GN's Kings Cross–Doncaster main line was a relative latecomer; until 1850 passengers from the North East had gone to Euston. The route was built for speed, but it always suffered from bottlenecks. The GN's energy and enterprise also seemed to ebb and flow; certainly the

Romford Widening

At the present time the LNER are spending £288,000 on the Romford widening. The work is going ahead with remarkable despatch, but when it is finished the new lines will not enable us to overcome the many operating difficulties which exist owing to the dense traffic over this line, particularly in the Stratford Area and approaching Liverpool Street at busy times. Our passengers will, however, have reason to be thankful to Mr Winston Churchill for a certain degree of relief. The scheme is being carried out as part of the bargain under which he remitted the amount of the railway passenger duty when he was Chancellor of the Exchequer.

While the engineers are busy alongside the main line there is a heavy restriction on the speed of passing trains. Despite this handicap, during the week ended 8 November, over 1,200 trains were dealt with daily at Liverpool Street and the incoming trains were less than two minutes late on an average. During October the goods and mineral trains in the London Area, numbering between 4,000 and 5,000, arrived at destinations less than 15 minutes late on the average. Speaking from the impartial realm of Kings Cross, one cannot but feel proud of one's fellow railwaymen who achieve these results. Perhaps the greatest thrill comes in the evening peak hour when 108 trains come and go, carrying about 42,000 passengers. Of that number 39,000 go down from Liverpool Street, conveyed in 56 trains. When we bear in mind the limited track facilities and terminal accommodation, the despatching of a train nearly every minute must be almost a record for a steam service. During this peak hour the lever movements in the two signal boxes total over 2,000. – R. Bell, assistant general manager, in November 1930.

North Eastern was often impatient at what it saw as lack of commercial opportunism in its southern partner. But it was the GN that first brought massive quantities of coal to London, and its opening just in time for the Great Exhibition enabled a larger proportion of north eastern artisans to go south than from any other region north of the Chilterns.

The coal traffic, growing suburban traffic, and two-track bottlenecks not finally eliminated until BR days, meant strict rationing of expresses, many of which were made up into heavy trains, the *Flying Scotsman* fourteen or fifteen carriages in winter, though lighter in summer when coal traffic was less dense and the train could be run in two parts. The summer *Aberdonian* sleeper often ran in three portions, with more sleepers for Newcastle, Edinburgh and the Highlands.

One of the first acts of the LNER was to transfer Pullmans (other than those on the Harwich boat trains) from the GE to the East Coast main line, a *Harrogate Pullman* being immediately successful, though many changes were made with the running of other trains until a pattern settled, *The Queen of Scots* eventually projecting the *Harrogate Pullman* (though that still ran on Sundays) through to Edinburgh and Glasgow, and a *Yorkshire Pullman* also serving Harrogate along with Bradford and Leeds. A characteristic of the East Coast main line has always been its sheer variety of passenger services: sleepers (though BR has recently re-routed these to Euston), Pullmans, the famous LNER streamlined trains (the subject of a separate later feature) and ordinary expresses still including the most famous of all, the *Flying Scotsman*. In 1928 this (leaving Kings Cross watched by people who mattered at 10.00) ran non-stop to Edinburgh in summer, a new train set including cocktail bar, ladies' retiring room, hairdressing saloon, while the engine tenders were equipped with corridors to allow a crew change en route. The engines were of course Gresley's famous Pacifics, naturally also the subject of a later article.

Incredibly, however, the non-stop had to dawdle to occupy a minimum of 8¼ hours on the road, agreed between the East and West Coasts after the famous railway races to Aberdeen at the end of last century. Only in 1932 was this awful agreement finally abandoned, successive accelerations reducing the time to seven hours in 1937, an average speed of 56.1mph.

The third of the southern 'Greats' was perhaps just too enterprising. Had not its famous Sam Fay been of retirement age, he would have been a strong contender for LNER control. The GC lost no opportunity to boost business, though by 1923 there was already consensus that the building of the 'London Extension' to Marylebone, only opened in 1899, had not been commercially justified. The extension gave it the vertical part of its T; previously it had been the Manchester, Sheffield & Lincolnshire, formed in 1849, with access to North Wales over the Cheshire Lines (it also owned a third of the joint concern and ran the trains). The only common feature between its two parts was that everywhere it went GC was in stiff competition with other lines. Usually it was LMS constituents, so the competition continued until BR days.

The LNER generally accelerated the GCs London service, introducing new corridor stock, though as vividly reported in later pages it was many years before modern locomotives were common. The best known GC section train was the 15.20 Marylebone to Manchester, once known as the *Sheffield Special*, booked in LNER days to run to Leicester – 103 miles – in 109 minutes. Later the *Master Cutler* became the route's showpiece, though the emphasis was always on freight, especially coal.

The superiority of the LNER's best constituent, the North Eastern, was by no means threatened by the fact that all three Greats ran into its majestic headquarters station at York, beside which was its showpiece hotel which remained one of the LNER's best. Tracing its ancestry back to the Stockton & Darlington of 1825 (the first passenger-carrying public railway), the NE had developed into one of Britain's top three. It was formed in 1854 by the amalgamation of the York, Newcastle & Berwick, the York & North Midland, Leeds Northern and Malton & Driffield lines, which made York a focal railway town where tradition and legend from the days of the Railway King and Railway Mania mingle with today's tourism including the National Railway Museum and modern administration through BR's Eastern Region headquarters. The NE served resorts, ports and cliff-top coal mines, rich agricultural country and put its tentacles across the Pennines. A list of its directors might sound like a roll-call of railway history, but was ever primarily a business – a highly successful one exploiting its near monopoly situation in much of its territory and its wealth. Its shareholders were richly rewarded.

Coal of course was king. Alone among the constituents it provided coal wagons rather than relying on private-owners. They were larger, more modern wagons, too, including the first hoppers. Its stationmasters were encouraged to set up as coal merchants on the side; even individual farms wanting a coal supply might gain their own private siding. But it was built when labour was cheap and the hundreds of level crossings on

Daily bread. Freight was the LNER's main source of income with mineral traffic counting as one of its premier loadings. This photograph shows the somewhat insalubrious surroundings of the Appleby-Frodingham steelworks at Scunthorpe, Lincs. In 1932 the LNER opened a totally new shed here to serve the steelworks which were expanding at the time. This was one of the only three depots built by the LNER on completely new sites.

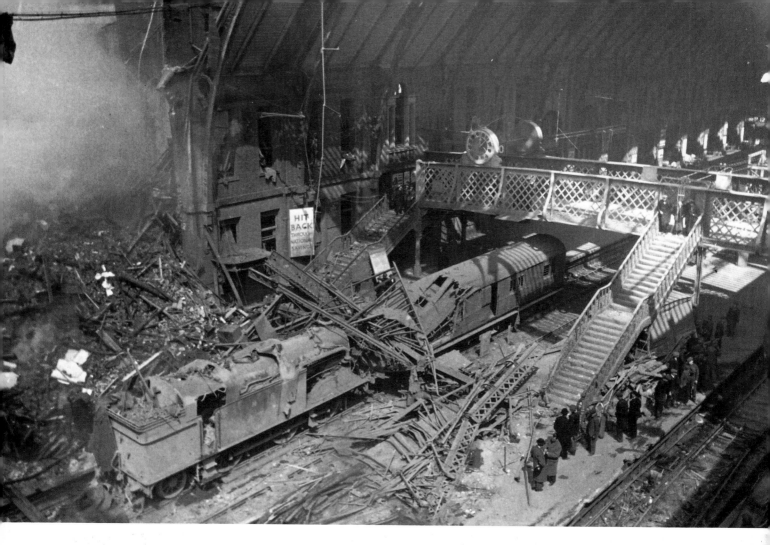

War comes to Kings Cross. World War II was to see a large number of attacks on Britain's railway system during the German bombing campaigns of the early 1940s with damage occasioned to most of the London main-line termini. Kings Cross did not escape as this photograph shows. The date was May 1941 and a whole section of the overall roof has been demolished. The locomotive under the wreckage is an 'N2' class 0-6-2 tank. The notice on the wall adjacent to the footbridge steps exhorts Londoners to 'Hit back with National Savings'.

its lines in flat territory, especially in the Hull area, became an increasing nuisance. Seeing several gates ahead being opened simultaneously and signal arms rise only shortly ahead of the oncoming train is another of those lasting LNER images. Hull was its greatest port, and it was here that it finally met its only major competition, with the Hull & Barnsley, built specially to break the monopoly. Eventually the two worked closely and the H&B was voluntarily absorbed in early 1922, ahead of amalgamation. Hull Corporation panicked and requested in vain that it go to the LMS group instead.

In Newcastle the NE retained its powerful monopoly and ran very extensive suburban services. Those to the north of the river were electrified as early as 1904, and the LNER electrified the South Shields service in 1938.

The North Eastern was at the centre of the new LNER and but for the fashionable pull of London, York would no doubt have become the enlarged company's base. As it was the NE exercised considerable influence on the rest of the system while continuing to control its own affairs to a remarkable degree. Many improvements were made in LNER days, such as buffet cars introduced in 1937 on the coast route between Newcastle and Middlesbrough. The summer *Scarborough Flyer* began in 1935, a 'Shire' or 'Hunt' 4-4-0 working the train on its 42 miles from York to the coast in fifty minutes.

and fishermen reporting for duty as well as local people going from village to town. Lossiemouth, at the end of a dead-straight branch, was the furthest that could be reached on LNER metals from London and had a weekday sleeping car on which the first Labour prime minister, Ramsey Macdonald, MP for the area, was a regular passenger.

The LNER had an extensive system of cross-country trains. For example, the 07.30 Newcastle to Bournemouth (via Sheffield, the GC, Banbury, Reading and Basingstoke) was followed two hours later by the 'ports special' also going down the GC and then across via Cheltenham to Swansea. The 12.44 from Newcastle, carrying a through coach from Glasgow and Edinburgh, ran via the Swinton & Knottingley Joint and again the GC to Southampton. The summer Aberdeen–Penzance through coach was noted for its record length of journey rather than its speed. The *North Country Continental* ran from Harwich via the GN/GE Joint to Lincoln to split for York and Liverpool. Across the centre of England three routes connected Liverpool and Manchester with Leeds, Bradford, York, Newcastle and Hull, the all-LNER one being via the Cheshire Lines (two thirds owned and LNER operated), Woodhead Tunnel, Sheffield and Doncaster. Cleethorpes and Grimsby were connected to Manchester by regular services over the Woodhead route. Summer Saturday through trains went on an ever more imaginative set of routes; even Rotherham & Masboro could be reached by through coach from Glasgow.

As already emphasised, more and more passenger business was by special workings. To finish with one example, on St Leger day in 1935, 32 up specials (mainly carrying miners) and 20 down ones (including the aristocracy) arrived at Doncaster, a key junction often under pressure with its ordinary services that were also more heavily laden that day. Over a thousand horseboxes were handled during the race week. And still the coal trains rumbled through.

Great Central cross-country express. 'C4' class 4-4-2 No 6091 crosses Barby Road bridge south of Rugby with an up express in August 1925 – probably the 08.00 Newcastle – Bournemouth. The engine has recently been fitted with a short flower-pot chimney, somewhat marring the looks of a once handsome Jersey Lily. It carries the full green livery of the period with LNER and the number on the tender sides. The basic train set is seven ex Great Central corridors plus two extra clerestory vehicles next to the engine, possibly through coaches from Leeds.

The Eastern Counties Main Line to 1843

The Eastern Counties Railway was incorporated on 4 July 1836 with a share capital of £1,600,000 to provide a 126 miles line from Shoreditch to Norwich and Yarmouth via Colchester, Ipswich and Eye. As surveyed by Braithwaite and Vignoles in 1834 it would require neither tunnels nor major works, would follow existing traffic streams and be within 'available distance' of 739,697 persons, a number that would increase as branches were added to Harwich and elsewhere. Industry would be fostered, agriculture revived (although the three counties involved already supplied half London's needs), the 'overwhelming evil' of the Poor Rates (then nearly £1 million in Norfolk, Suffolk and Essex together) reduced by the additional employment the line would stimulate, fishing increased 'ten-fold', and Harwich and Yarmouth reinstated as leading ports for the continent and northern Britain. These last two places were losing trade to London since steam navigation had reduced passage time on the Thames, but the traveller from eastern Scotland to the capital would still save up to 24 hours on the water by disembarking at Yarmouth for a 6¼ hour rail journey. As 'transmarine sources' would almost certainly cover working expenses and the line produce a general increase in traffic, a 22 per cent return on capital was probable; needless to say such calculations totally disregarded both the resilience of coastal shipping and the possibilities of north to south trunk railways.

Despite these impressive claims the company had a hard struggle. By September 1836 only 2,324 of the £25 shares remained unissued, but 'little more than one twelfth' had been taken locally even after a regional 'progress' by the chairman, Bosanquet, and two directors in November 1835. Indeed, it was only a month earlier, with six weeks left for the final compilation of the bill, that a Provisional Committee had been formed of sufficient respectability and local connections to carry the project through. This had dispelled suspicion of the promoters, including the engineer John Braithwaite and the London firm of solicitors, Dimes & Boyman, who would gain from professional services without necessarily incurring the risk of investment and who had turned to the Norwich concept only when an Edinburgh line (proposed to them in 1834 by Henry Sayer) was judged too ambitious; but it achieved little else within the region. Many were rendered cautious by never having seen a railway, others were depleted in personal resources by depression in farming, and there was widespread fear, despite the company's repeated reassurances, that the line would increase the poor rates by displacing workers in road transport, and that this, coupled with reduced demand for horses and fodder, would lead to further depreciation of land values.

There was a more sympathetic reception in Liverpool where the merchants, successful pioneers in railway enterprise, subscribed 'upwards of one third' of the required capital, and in the northern industrial areas generally. Unhappily much of the balance came from 'men of straw' (vice-chairman Rigby in 1841) so making the ECR 'little better than a bubble company'. However, when the pressure of calls revealed this the solidarity of the 'Liverpool Leviathians', who at an early stage had displaced the local men and assumed control of the board, permitted transfer of forfeited shares to 'men of substance'.

In Parliament 'strenuous opposition', backed by 'a portion of the press', was encountered from the Northern & Eastern and Great Northern companies, both seeking a line to Cambridge and the north with a branch to Norwich. 'A formidable array of dissenting owners and occupiers' had to be pacified by secret and extravagant promises of compensation. The seemingly superior merits of the ECR bill carried the day against the rival companies, although the Commons actually divided on the second reading before giving it a majority of only 74. During these anxious days the directors busied themselves in raising petitions of support within the region, but as Gladstone informed the Commons, that from Norwich at least was 'got up by the foulest means', each signatory being rewarded with a 'good lunch'.

Success attained, the confidence of the ECR knew no bounds. Characteristic of this was the curious 5ft gauge adopted at Braithwaite's behest. He argued that for adequate boiler room, steadier motion and less wear on moving parts his locomotives would require 4ft 11¾in, but in carrying his point failed to convince entirely those directors who, perhaps a little less short-sightedly, had pressed for the 7ft 0¼in of the Great Western and insisted on provision for future conversion to such if found desirable. The outcome was an expensive road-bed 30ft wide bearing a 5ft gauge track, and engines that in fact turned out to be of smaller internal dimensions than many already at work elsewhere on the 4ft 8½in gauge.

Late in March 1837 construction began, but at the London end only, incomplete land negotiations preventing the concurrent start planned between Norwich and Yarmouth. Endless troubles now beset the ECR. The marshes near Stratford, and London Viaduct both presented unexpected problems and consumed vast quantities of time and capital. Further delays ensued from the abnormally wet weather of 1838–9, and as time passed iron and other prices were rising. Landowners, great and small, set themselves to exact the uttermost penny in compensation for real or imaginary damages, and amenities disturbed, while the secret promises of 1836, made by the original local directors, had to be honoured. Lord Petre of Ingatestone Hall received £120,000 (with which he bought a new estate) and nearby Labouchère £35,000 although their combined properties affected only 6 miles of line. Like Sir Edward Kerrison, who received £20,000, Labouchère was obliged to resort to the courts when the ECR attempted evasion, but on his death, the estate not having lost value as expected, his son did remit £15,000. This was a unique occurrence, however, and by 1843 the 51.2 miles to Colchester had cost the ECR £600,000 in land and compensation alone.

Forty per cent of the capital had been called by October 1838, but only 9 miles were under construction. Creditors were pressing and each fresh call on the proprietors was serving only to provoke resistance and further depress the value of company stock. Only decisive action could avert total ruin. Hence, in April 1839, 'in accordance with the wishes of the Lancashire proprietors who have so great a stake in the undertaking' (*Norfolk Chronicle*), the decision to terminate at Colchester was made. To increase public confidence, efforts to commence operation were redoubled and, after a formal opening two days earlier, the first public trains ran between a temporary terminus at Mile End and Romford on 20 June; extensions at each end, to Shoreditch and Brentwood respectively, followed on 1 July 1840. Meanwhile, Robert Stephenson had been called in but could only confirm the estimate of £520,000 needed to complete to Colchester. By applying the brutal logic that everything spent could still be lost the mutinous shareholders were persuaded to meet their calls (one of £2 per share in January 1840 producing £148,000), and in 1840 Parliament was successfully approached for authorisation of a further £350,000 share capital; with these assets and the additional borrowing powers sanctioned in 1840 the final section could be contemplated.

Wisely this was treated as one unit so that the heavier works could be undertaken while means allowed. Prolonged rain in 1841 caused serious delay and damage to earthworks already completed, and at different times there were various mishaps such as the collapse of an underline bridge at Kelvedon and the subsidence of a timber viaduct at Mountnessing, but eventually goods services opened to Colchester on 7 March 1843, passenger trains commencing on 29 March. Altogether seven years and nearly £2½ million had been consumed in covering the 51.2 miles; works alone, at £1,631,330, had cost rather more than the total construction estimate for reaching Yarmouth.

In July 1843 the ECR gained the mail contract and from the withdrawal of the *Golden Path* coach in the November was left as the only means of public conveyance between London and Colchester. Services suffered, however, from the usual defects of ECR operation and the only progressive step in early days was conversion to 4ft 8½in when the lease and authorised extension of the Northern & Eastern in 1844 brought the imminence of contact with other lines. A third rail between Shoreditch and Stratford, to accommodate what would become standard-gauge trains from the N&E and beyond, was considered, but, on the advice of Robert Stephenson, rejected because of cost, technical problems at junctions and the undesirability of maintaining two separate rolling-stock establishments. The work of conversion, conducted in sections along each running line in turn to avoid disruption of traffic, was effected between 5 September and 7 October 1844 at a cost of roughly £1,000 a mile, a heavy but essential burden as the necessity for manual transhipment between gauges would have crippled both the company and regional development.

In January 1846 one daily service was reaching Colchester in 90 minutes, eased to 95 minutes in the summer; by this time the principal services had been extended over the Eastern Union to Ipswich and Bury St Edmunds. But then, after a period of worsening relations, the Eastern Union completed its line to Norwich in December 1849, thus establishing a rival route to that via Cambridge, wholly controlled by the ECR since taking the Norfolk Railway on lease in 1848. It now became a matter of deliberate, albeit self-immolating policy to discourage through Norwich traffic via Colchester. Slow, dirty and unpunctual trains were run at inconvenient times and by the end of 1850 there was nothing faster than 130 minutes to Colchester.

In the end the EUR was forced to concede defeat. The assumption of its working by the ECR from 1 January 1854 brought some improvement, but only with the GER accelerations of 1863–4, by which the 10 am down was timed to Colchester in 70 minutes, did the line, its ill-repute at last dispelled, recognisably become part of a major trunk route.

LNER TREE OF GROWTH

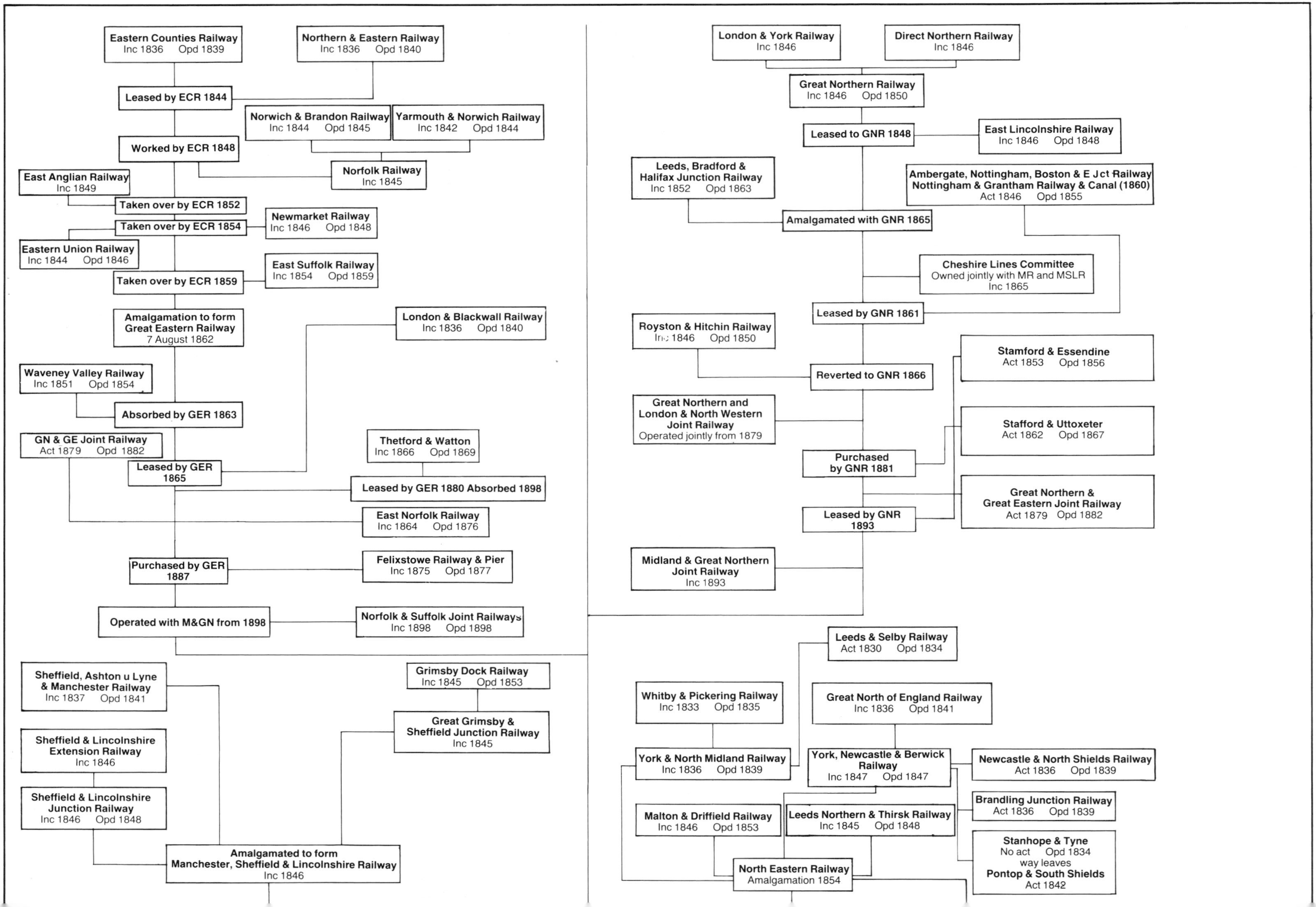
Eastern Counties Railway Inc 1836 Opd 1839
Northern & Eastern Railway Inc 1836 Opd 1840
Leased by ECR 1844
Norwich & Brandon Railway Inc 1844 Opd 1845
Yarmouth & Norwich Railway Inc 1842 Opd 1844
Worked by ECR 1848
Norfolk Railway Inc 1845
East Anglian Railway Inc 1849
Taken over by ECR 1852
Newmarket Railway Inc 1846 Opd 1848
Taken over by ECR 1854
Eastern Union Railway Inc 1844 Opd 1846
East Suffolk Railway Inc 1854 Opd 1859
Taken over by ECR 1859
Amalgamation to form Great Eastern Railway 7 August 1862
London & Blackwall Railway Inc 1836 Opd 1840
Waveney Valley Railway Inc 1851 Opd 1854
Absorbed by GER 1863
GN & GE Joint Railway Act 1879 Opd 1882
Thetford & Watton Inc 1866 Opd 1869
Leased by GER 1865
Leased by GER 1880 Absorbed 1898
East Norfolk Railway Inc 1864 Opd 1876
Purchased by GER 1887
Felixstowe Railway & Pier Inc 1875 Opd 1877
Operated with M&GN from 1898
Norfolk & Suffolk Joint Railways Inc 1898 Opd 1898
London & York Railway Inc 1846
Direct Northern Railway Inc 1846
Great Northern Railway Inc 1846 Opd 1850
Leased to GNR 1848
East Lincolnshire Railway Inc 1846 Opd 1848
Leeds, Bradford & Halifax Junction Railway Inc 1852 Opd 1863
Ambergate, Nottingham, Boston & E Jct Railway Nottingham & Grantham Railway & Canal (1860) Act 1846 Opd 1855
Amalgamated with GNR 1865
Cheshire Lines Committee Owned jointly with MR and MSLR Inc 1865
Leased by GNR 1861
Royston & Hitchin Railway Inc 1846 Opd 1850
Stamford & Essendine Act 1853 Opd 1856
Reverted to GNR 1866
Great Northern and London & North Western Joint Railway Operated jointly from 1879
Stafford & Uttoxeter Act 1862 Opd 1867
Purchased by GNR 1881
Great Northern & Great Eastern Joint Railway Act 1879 Opd 1882
Leased by GNR 1893
Midland & Great Northern Joint Railway Inc 1893
Sheffield, Ashton u Lyne & Manchester Railway Inc 1837 Opd 1841
Grimsby Dock Railway Inc 1845 Opd 1853
Great Grimsby & Sheffield Junction Railway Inc 1845
Sheffield & Lincolnshire Extension Railway Inc 1846
Sheffield & Lincolnshire Junction Railway Inc 1846 Opd 1848
Amalgamated to form Manchester, Sheffield & Lincolnshire Railway Inc 1846
Leeds & Selby Railway Act 1830 Opd 1834
Whitby & Pickering Railway Inc 1833 Opd 1835
Great North of England Railway Inc 1836 Opd 1841
York & North Midland Railway Inc 1836 Opd 1839
York, Newcastle & Berwick Railway Inc 1847 Opd 1847
Newcastle & North Shields Railway Act 1836 Opd 1839
Brandling Junction Railway Act 1836 Opd 1839
Malton & Driffield Railway Inc 1846 Opd 1853
Leeds Northern & Thirsk Railway Inc 1845 Opd 1848
Stanhope & Tyne No act Opd 1834 way leaves Pontop & South Shields Act 1842
North Eastern Railway Amalgamation 1854

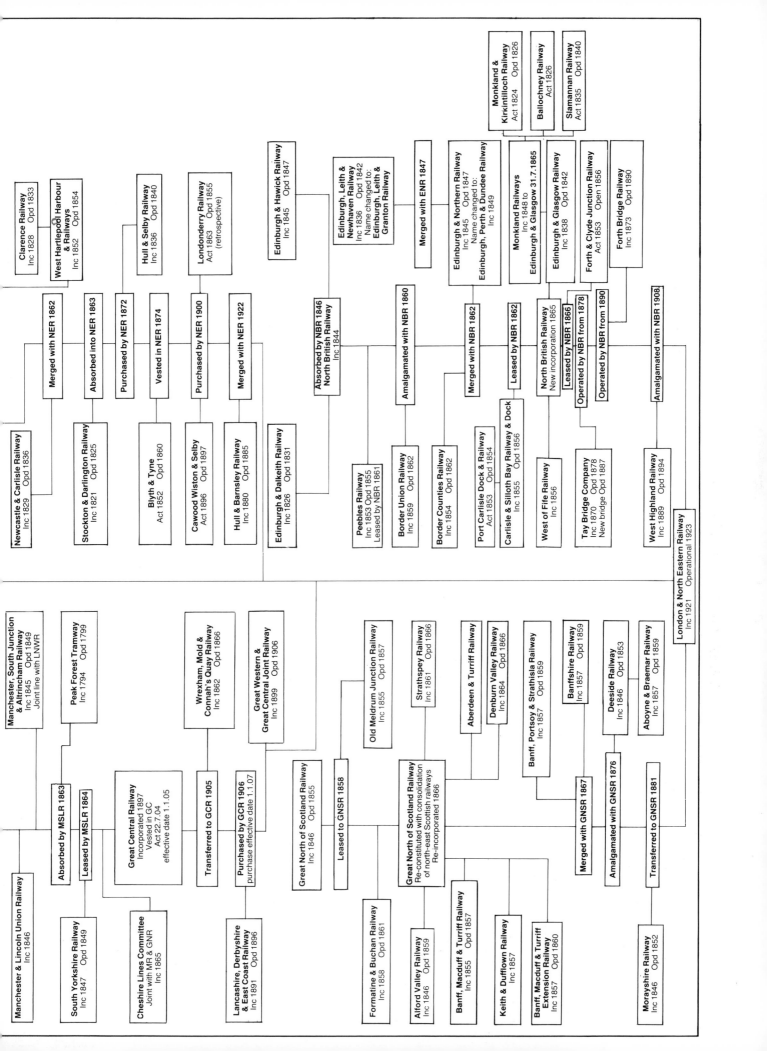

Clarence Railway
Inc 1828   Opd 1833

West Hartlepool Harbour
& Railways
Inc 1852   Opd 1854

Hull & Selby Railway
Inc 1836   Opd 1840

Londonderry Railway
Act 1863   Opd 1855
(retrospective)

Edinburgh & Hawick Railway
Inc 1845   Opd 1847

Edinburgh, Leith &
Newhaven Railway
Inc 1836   Opd 1842
Name changed to:
Edinburgh, Leith &
Granton Railway
Inc 1849

Merged with ENR 1847

Edinburgh & Northern Railway
Inc 1845   Opd 1847
Name changed to:
Edinburgh, Perth & Dundee Railway
Inc 1849

Monkland &
Kirkintilloch Railway
Act 1824   Opd 1826

Ballochney Railway
Act 1826

Slamannan Railway
Act 1835   Opd 1840

Monkland Railways
Inc 1848 to
Edinburgh & Glasgow 31.7.1865

Edinburgh & Glasgow Railway
Inc 1838   Opd 1842

Forth & Clyde Junction Railway
Act 1853   Open 1856

Forth Bridge Railway
Inc 1873   Opd 1890

Newcastle & Carlisle Railway
Inc 1829   Opd 1836

Stockton & Darlington Railway
Inc 1821   Opd 1825

Blyth & Tyne
Act 1852   Opd 1860

Cawood Wiston & Selby
Act 1896   Opd 1897

Hull & Barnsley Railway
Inc 1880   Opd 1885

Edinburgh & Dalkeith Railway
Inc 1826   Opd 1831

Merged with NER 1862

Absorbed into NER 1863

Purchased by NER 1872

Vested in NER 1874

Purchased by NER 1900

Merged with NER 1922

Absorbed by NBR 1846
North British Railway
Inc 1844

Amalgamated with NBR 1860

Merged with NBR 1862

Leased by NBR 1862

North British Railway
New incorporation 1865

Leased by NBR 1866

Operated by NBR from 1878

Operated by NBR from 1890

Amalgamated with NBR 1908

Peebles Railway
Inc 1853 Opd 1855
Leased by NBR 1861

Border Union Railway
Inc 1859   Opd 1862

Border Counties Railway
Inc 1854   Opd 1862

Port Carlisle Dock & Railway
Act 1853   Opd 1854

Carlisle & Silloth Bay Railway & Dock
Inc 1855   Opd 1856

West of Fife Railway
Inc 1856

Tay Bridge Company
Inc 1870   Opd 1878
New bridge Opd 1887

West Highland Railway
Inc 1889   Opd 1894

London & North Eastern Railway
Inc 1921   Operational 1923

Manchester, South Junction
& Altrincham Railway
Inc 1845   Opd 1849
Joint line with LNWR

Peak Forest Tramway
Inc 1794   Opd 1799

Wrexham, Mold &
Connah's Quay Railway
Inc 1862   Opd 1866

Great Western &
Great Central Joint Railway
Inc 1899   Opd 1906

Old Meldrum Junction Railway
Inc 1855   Opd 1857

Strathspey Railway
Inc 1861   Opd 1866

Aberdeen & Turriff Railway

Denburn Valley Railway
Inc 1864   Opd 1866

Banff, Portsoy & Strathisla Railway
Inc 1857   Opd 1859

Banffshire Railway
Inc 1857   Opd 1859

Deeside Railway
Inc 1846   Opd 1853

Aboyne & Braemar Railway
Inc 1857   Opd 1859

Manchester & Lincoln Union Railway
Inc 1846

Absorbed by MSLR 1863

Leased by MSLR 1864

Great Central Railway
Incorporated 1897
Vested in GC
Act 22.7.04
effective date 1.1.05

Transferred to GCR 1905

Purchased by GCR 1906
purchase effective date 1.1.07

Great North of Scotland Railway
Inc 1846   Opd 1855

Leased to GNSR 1858

Great North of Scotland Railway
Re-constituted with consolidation
of north-east Scottish railways
Re-incorporated 1866

Merged with GNSR 1867

Amalgamated with GNSR 1876

Transferred to GNSR 1881

South Yorkshire Railway
Inc 1847   Opd 1849

Cheshire Lines Committee
Joint with MR & GNR
Inc 1865

Lancashire, Derbyshire
& East Coast Railway
Inc 1891   Opd 1896

Formatine & Buchan Railway
Inc 1858   Opd 1861

Alford Valley Railway
Inc 1846   Opd 1859

Banff, Macduff & Turriff Railway
Inc 1855   Opd 1857

Keith & Dufftown Railway
Inc 1857

Banff, Macduff & Turriff
Extension Railway
Inc 1857   Opd 1860

Morayshire Railway
Inc 1846   Opd 1852

Great Central Consolidation. With a tender full of coal and blowing off hard, one of the Robinson 2-8-0s No 6227 (its 1924 number) built in November 1912 heads a long down train of coal empties over the old Great Northern main line past Dukeries Junction in 1946. A large number of this class was built for the ROD of the War Department during World War I. In the background is Dukeries Junction station with the overbridge carrying the old Lancashire, Derbyshire and East Coast Railway (later the GC) over the East Coast tracks.

2
FREIGHT

AT any time, day or night, any day of the year, dozens if not hundreds of long, waddling goods trains were carrying their cargoes up and down the system. Tens of thousands earned their living humping meat carcasses, fruit boxes, grain sacks, milk churns in and out of wagons; mechanical aids almost all had to wait until after nationalisation. And a veritable army of clerks grappled with the vast paperwork.

Though freight was less glamorous and received less publicity than the passenger business, it accounted for two thirds of the railway's revenue, the highest proportion of the grouping-era companies. For the LNER was at once the farmer's railway, a surprisingly high proportion of high-value crops being concentrated in its area, and served much of Britain's heavy industry. It also carried most of the country's fish. (Fish traffic is the subject of a separate story.)

To start with coal. Most of the Scottish coalfields and those in Northumberland and Durham, Yorkshire, Nottinghamshire and Derbyshire were on the LNER. Except for privately-owned lines there was a monopoly in Northumberland and Durham: what had made the North Eastern so powerful and profitable. But in Scotland (except Fife), Yorkshire and the East Midlands, there was fierce competition with the LMS. A high proportion of pits were dual served, and LNER and LMS men glared at each other across the fields and wagons of coal. LNER men in the Sheffield district used to say that when Captain Scott reached the South Pole, the first thing he would have seen would have been a Midland engine and brake waiting to see if he found coal.

In the days when most electricity and gas were made locally, and every house had its own grate or solid-fuel boiler, coal almost all travelled in loose-coupled wagons, except on the North Eastern section nearly all privately owned. Though a few block trains were run, the majority of wagons passed through marshalling yards. Not only had the loaded wagons to be marshalled by destination, but so had the empties.

In its first year the LNER carried 102 million tons of coal out of a total British production of 273 million tons. Over forty million tons of this moved in the North-Eastern area, much of it in block loads to staiths for coastal shipment. Shipment coal was also carried in large quantities to ports in Scotland, and from Yorkshire and the East Midlands to Goole, Hull and Immingham. The working at Immingham was particularly intense, with several thousand loaded wagons often in the area awaiting unloading. Loaded wagons were gravitated to the quayside, raised on large hoists and tipped into the ships' holds, and the empty wagons then gravitated back into the appropriate empty siding.

The new Green Arrow. *No 4771, the first of Gresley's class 'V2' mixed traffic 2-6-2 locomotives heads mid-afternoon Kings Cross to Glasgow express goods near Potters Bar in the summer of 1936, soon after its introduction. Allocated to Kings Cross in July 1936 No 4771 became a regular performer on this service which it worked as far as Peterborough. The name* Green Arrow *reflects the LNER's newly introduced registered goods service. Immediately behind the tender are two of the LNER's steel containers. No 4771 is now preserved in the National Collection.*

29

Fast Freight

Star of the LNER freight services before the war was, without doubt, the '3.35 Scotsman' because of its very high average speed. After nationalisation it had become, to railwaymen, the famous 266 down 1515 Kings Cross to Scotland fast goods. For some time, when he was line traffic manager, Great Northern, Gerry Fiennes had, framed on his wall, a Control express freight record showing that 266 down had been delayed south of Retford waiting for the *Talisman* express to clear.

Because of injector trouble on the Pacific 266 down had left Kings Cross goods 23 minutes late and only 2 minutes ahead of the 1540 Kings Cross to Leeds express. Driver Hoole, with a 47 wagon freight train weighing 450 tons, had left the 1540 behind by Hitchin but, understandably, one of the wagons developed a hot box at Huntingdon. The train had to go into Westwood Yard at Peterborough to detach. While it was there the *Talisman* 1600 Kings Cross to Scotland express timed at high speed, went past and 266 left behind it. Before Retford, however, the freight was checked by signals, the *Talisman* still being in the section ahead.

The large marshalling yard at Wath collected wagons from the many pits in the Barnsley and Mexborough area. It was built in 1907, one of the earliest hump yards; it had power-operated points but no mechanical braking of wagons. Throughout its life braking was effected manually by 'chasers' applying wagon hand-brakes, a most arduous and dangerous occupation. One very heavy flow of coal traffic from Wath was that to Lancashire via the Worsborough branch, Penistone and the Woodhead route across the Pennines. The Worsborough branch included the 2½ mile Wentworth bank, at 1 in 40, which required four GC 'ROD' 2-8-0s to move an 1100 ton train. In 1925 H. N. Gresley and Beyer-Peacock produced No 2395, a 2-8-0 + 0-8-2 Garratt, to replace two of the 2-8-0s, and it banked the trains until the line was electrified in 1952. One of the Garratt's firemen once commented that he only had to fire her once each trip – he picked the shovel up at the bottom of the bank and put it down at the top.

The 'RODs' had a long climb from Penistone to Dunford, at the east end of Woodhead Tunnel, but, in many ways, the return journey with empties through the tunnel was the most exacting. The summit was near the east end of the more than three-mile bore, and it was almost constantly full of smoke from the procession of trains.

Other LNER marshalling yards dealing with coal were Annesley (GC) and Colwick (GN) at Nottingham. Many fast coal trains ran from Annesley up the GC main line to Woodford for Neasden and for transfer to the Great Western. In its last years the LNER introduced block workings enabling crews to perform a daily round trip, Annesley–Woodford, obviating lodging allowances and overtime, the accelerated trains being dubbed 'Windcutters' and carrying a daily 1500 wagons south. Crews back before the end of their eight hours could sign off without loss of pay.

From Colwick trains ran to New England yard at Peterborough, and thence into East Anglia or up the East Coast main line to Ferme Park yard at Hornsey. There was also a heavy flow of coal trains up the GN/GE Joint Line from Doncaster Decoy yard to Whitemoor (March) and New England. To relieve the Joint Line some coal trains were routed up the original GN main line via Boston and Spalding.

About twenty-three million tons of 'other minerals' were moved by the constituents of the LNER in 1922. The majority of this consisted of raw materials for the steel industry. The North Eastern moved iron ore from Cleveland to Tees-side, and from Tyne Dock to Consett. Heavy tonnages of ore originated in the Stathern area of the East Midlands and in the Stainby and Sproxton area of South Lincolnshire. The latter flow in LNER days passed from High Dyke siding (south of Grantham) to Scunthorpe via Honington, Lincoln and Barnetby. The trains had to reverse at both Lincoln and Barnetby, crossing two level crossings twice at the former place, both over busy main roads. To avoid this the trains were diverted after the war to run via Boston and the East Lincolnshire line.

Most complications were involved in the movement of general merchandise, because of the wide variety of the traffic and the different

Class 'B' freight. An ex GER 0-6-0 (LNER class 'J15') No 7934 heads a heavy down fast goods near Brentwood about 1925. The engine carrying white discs for its headcode is numbered in the early livery of the LNER and still carries its stovepipe chimney.

types of wagons required. Small consignments were handled by the LNER in goods depots of often vintage character. In some of them making up a large number of outwards wagons the barrow runs were of considerable length. Productivity was low and costs were high. In the larger depots wagons of 'smalls' were loaded in train order. Once the full wagon loads and containers had been attached the trains left direct to destination. Kings Cross despatched numerous trains in quick succession in the afternoon and early evening, fully fitted with the vacuum brake and running at high speed. An 'A4' was frequently booked on the Glasgow goods, which had to average over 40mph. To some people one of these trains, with a long string of ten-foot wheelbase wagons snaking through an intermediate station at 60mph was more exciting to see than the *Silver Jubilee*.

The largest goods depots were Kings Cross, Farringdon Street, Marylebone, Royal Mint Street and Bishopsgate in London; Ardwick (GC) and Deansgate (GN) in Manchester; Brunswick and Huskisson (CLC) in Liverpool; Leeds Wellington Street; Newcastle Forth; Edinburgh Leith Walk and Glasgow (High Street) in Scotland. Many of the wagon loads made up in goods depots, and the inwards wagons bound for them, were handled in nearby marshalling yards. For example Ferme Park yard at Hornsey dealt with traffic for Kings Cross, London Docks, Farringdon Street, and the Southern Railway. Up to 600 'South

Short Flight

A clerk, temporarily relieving at Huntingdon on a Sunday, had a hamper of pigeons for a training flight presented for despatch to, and release at, Retford. Looking up the timetable he found that there was only one suitable train. But after seeing that one off, he realised he had forgotten the pigeons.

His LNER training in the use of initiative came into play. He looked up the time the train would arrive at Retford, allowed ten minutes for release and endorsed the label, worked out flying time at a speed of which he thought a pigeon was capable, and duly arrived at an 'ETA Huntingdon'. As that time approached he released the pigeons, which did one lap of Huntingdon station – and went straight into the nearby loft.

He left a note for the Monday staff asking them to let consignee know his empty hamper had arrived, and also to make a note of what he said when he collected it. Worries dispersed when he was told that the man had remarked that it was the fastest his birds had ever flown. He did, however, add that 'something must have come over the LNER, because it took three days for the empty hamper to come back last time'. Another satisfied customer. – Frank Harrison

Lines' wagons were despatched each day to Herne Hill, Hither Green, Norwood and Feltham, via the Metropolitan Widened Lines to Farringdon, where a banker was stationed to help the trains up Snow Hill bank to Blackfriars.

The LNER ran two types of braked freight trains. Class 1 were fully braked, with an average speed, excluding booked stops, of 45 mph. The wagons had to have screw couplings, oil axle-boxes and a minimum wheelbase of nine feet. Class 2 were partially braked, the speed depending on the proportion of braked vehicles next to the engine.

The company was anxious to retain the higher class freight traffic (often the new branded goods accounting for a higher proportion of the nation's trade) against the competition of road haulage. A booklet was issued to traders giving the timings of the principal Class 1 trains, from which the following selection is taken.

'3.35 Scotsman'	Kings X dep 15.35	Glasgow arr 05.18
'3.55 Southerner'	Glasgow dep 15.55	Serving the West Riding, Midlands and Marylebone (arr 07.08)
'4.05 North Eastern'	Kings X dep 16.05	Newcastle arr 03.28
'6 o'clock West Riding'	Kings X dep 18.00	Leeds arr 04.33
'5.25 Newcastle'	Liverpool Huskisson dep 17.25	Newcastle arr 03.28
'The Lancastrian'	Newcastle dep 18.15	Manchester Ardwick arr 02.17 Liverpool Huskisson arr 04.45
'8.20 Midlander'	Grimsby dep 20.20	Leicester arr 05.37
'New London'	Gateshead dep 20.20	Kings Cross arr 09.30
'9.3 Manchester'	Spitalfields dep 21.03	Manchester Ardwick arr 07.45
'9.38 London'	Leeds Ardsley dep 21.38	Spitalfields arr 06.36
'Newcastle–London'	Newcastle dep 21.00	Marylebone arr 07.08

Though the image was of grimy industry, a large part of the LNER's territory was deeply rural and throughout its lifetime it provided an essential link between farm producers and industrial consumer, carrying over half of the nation's agricultural traffic. The Aberdeen–Kings Cross meat train was one of the most important, leaving Aberdeen around ten or eleven in the morning in time to get the meat into Smithfield Market soon after midnight. From the 1930s this traffic was totally containerised. In Scotland as well as in England, nearly all the grain and many other arable crops were concentrated to the east – as before the more recent agricultural revolution every school boy and girl was taught.

Many of the traffics involved long hauls. Seed potatoes, for example, originated from stations between Edinburgh and Aberdeen and were taken to Lincolnshire and East Anglia. Later in the season, some small stations in South Lincolnshire started their own through trains of potatoes for Kings Cross potato market. The Fenlands produced huge quantities of bulbs and cut flowers in the spring and summer: Spalding, Sutton Bridge and nearby stations despatched them all over the system. Other seasonal business included forced rhubarb from Ardsley, near

Leeds, in late winter, when rhubarb was an essential working class 'afters'. Salad specials made their way northward from the Lea Valley greenhouses in Essex and Hertfordshire. Cleaned cattle wagons, most in demand for their original purpose in the autumn, were used for perishable traffic as their slatted sides gave a flow of cool air which helped keep the produce fresh, though ultimately a few specialist fruit-carrying vehicles were built, especially useful for despatching Scottish raspberries to the Home Counties.

Though in the season the GN/GE Joint was very busy with northbound fruit and vegetable trains, much of the fresh vegetable traffic was concentrated in Bedfordshire. Several fast goods trains heading north from Kings Cross picked up wagons at Biggleswade for Midlands and Northern destinations. Cabbages from Biggleswade, peas from Maldon, rabbits from Thetford . . . baskets, boxes and sacks of whatever was in season were rushed to Stratford, Kings Cross, Covent Garden and Spitalfields. A large corps of clerks and porters was based in Fenland stations for the three harvest months. They loaded special trains to whisk the perishable fruit to markets as far away as Liverpool and Glasgow. The migrant pickers were, of course, brought in cheaply by trains of old stock, often with wooden seats, as their sanitary habits were suspect.

Three major developments happened in LNER days. First, the growth of food preservation between the wars led to the widespread construction of canning and bottling factories which brought their raw materials in by rail and despatched the finished product likewise. The North Walsham factory of Norfolk Canning, opened in 1931 deliberately alongside the station and equipped with its own siding, is an example of the innovation. It exercised a new kind of discipline over growers and transporters alike. Similar factories were rail served at Lowestoft,

Cross London freight. An ex GER 0-6-0 built in December 1922 (the last month of the company's independent existence) and now classified 'J20' takes a transfer goods from the Eastern Region to the Southern on 8 September 1951. The prefix '6' to the old LNER number 4690 indicates that this was an ex LNER locomotive. The train is seen passing Kensington (Olympia).

Railway interchange yard. A World War II Riddles-designed 2-8-0 (which had been on loan to the LNER) moves a heavy freight into the yard north of Banbury in the summer of 1948. The train has come off the old GC section at Woodford and is just about to enter Great Western territory – the photograph is taken from the junction signal box. Note the 'calling on' arm allowing this passage on the signal to the right of the picture.

An unwanted twin. Gresley 'P1' class 2-8-2 No 2394 approaches Hadley North tunnel with an up coal train in April 1938. The only two engines of this class to be built in 1925 were with booster equipment to the trailing pony truck designed to assist starting with heavy loads and on climbing banks. The locomotives were fitted with standard Pacific type boilers. The class proved to be of limited use mainly due to operational factors in obtaining loads to their 100 wagon capacity on the congested main line between New England and Ferme Park. The boosters were only effective when hauling maximum loads and under these circumstances proved expensive luxuries; they were removed during the 1930s and the load limit for the twins was reduced, thus complying more easily with the new signalling arrangements and shorter block sections. Both Nos 2393 and 2394 were withdrawn as early as July 1945 being the first Gresley class to become extinct.

Long Sutton, Wadsley Bridge (near Sheffield) and Bardney.

Secondly, the large dairies became dominant, changing the pattern of the enormous milk traffic. At the beginning of the LNER, the 10 and 12 gallon metal churn was universal – and a hazard on most rural country stations. Beccles was specially equipped with a swinging platform to accommodate transfer of churns from down to up, while at Halesworth such a swinging platform was attached to the level crossing gates in the station's middle. In the North the largest concentration of dairying activity was in Wensleydale and Northallerton where fresh milk was the main trainload but cheese also assumed great importance. A railway trolley was pressed into service to provide an additional run not covered by the regular timetable. Milk was the main traffic on the isolated Derby–Stafford line from the depot at Ingestre.

Gradually from 1928 onwards there was a swing from churns to tank wagons as the large dairies improved their collecting and bottling methods, though some churns were still in use in BR days. The LNER's relationships with United Dairies, Express Dairies and the Co-op was always given high priority. Eventually large depots were set up throughout the system, with large processing plants at Ilford, Finsbury Park and Marylebone.

But the third development was the largest: the widespread introduction of sugar beet. The British Sugar Corporation was set up as a result of the Beet Sugar (Subsidy) Act of 1925 and almost immediately was operating nineteen factories, all but two on the Welsh borders being on the LNER, from Cupar in Scotland and Poppleton in Yorkshire down through Lincolnshire to East Anglia. And the vast majority of the new crop was grown on the LNER – in such quantities that Britain became self-sufficient in sugar during the war. But before the war, at a time of slump in grain prices and production, the new traffic was a particular godsend, and balanced the inward movement of coal and fertilisers. Not only was the raw beet moved to the factories, but bulk sugar, molasses in tanks and pulp nuts travelled long distances, the total traffic adding one and a half million badly-needed tons a year.

Sugar production was concentrated in the 'campaign' during the winter when many small stations, normally fairly quiet, became hives of activity for about five months. Several hundred wagons could be on hand at a factory station awaiting unloading. Once the factory opened it kept in full production through weekends and holiday periods, including Christmas, so a reservoir of wagons had to be on hand. Although the sugar beet traffic brought in very desirable revenue to the country branches, there were many problems. It was carried in standard coal wagons and the peaks at the pits, including the pre-Christmas 'bull-week', coincided with the sugar beet 'campaign'. Traffic was accepted at the factories on a dated permit system. A farmer with a permit in his hand and no wagon into which his beet could be loaded was never very happy.

Despite these important developments, most freight continued to ply its traditional way. Serving the many small stations on branch lines involved the running of 'pick-ups' down each line. The trains would

34

start out each morning, shunt each station yard and arrive back at night. They carried a 'road van', a wagon containing the small parcels for the various stations, and also took in empties required for loading, bringing away the loaded wagons of agricultural produce, empty coal wagons etc. This method of working was unproductive so far as crews, locomotives and wagons were concerned.

For collection and delivery the LNER employed a large number of horses, which were replaced by articulated mechanical horses, the last horse-drawn dray disappearing soon after World War 2.

One of the complexities of freight involved the distribution of the many different types of wagon to ensure that no traffic was lost, a task made difficult by the inherent low productivity of many of the operating methods. The LNER set up a central wagon control at York. Stations reported to districts, and districts to central control, who then issued movement instructions. The system was the best available, but too much time was lost between a situation arising and the necessary instructions being issued, received and acted upon. Moreover, too many staff used too much imagination thinking up ways to beat the system!

Even when its resources were seriously under-used from the point of view of providing enough revenue, the LNER always *seemed* a busy freight system. In part this was due to the inadequate provision of facilities at virtually all levels. The priority given the large new hump

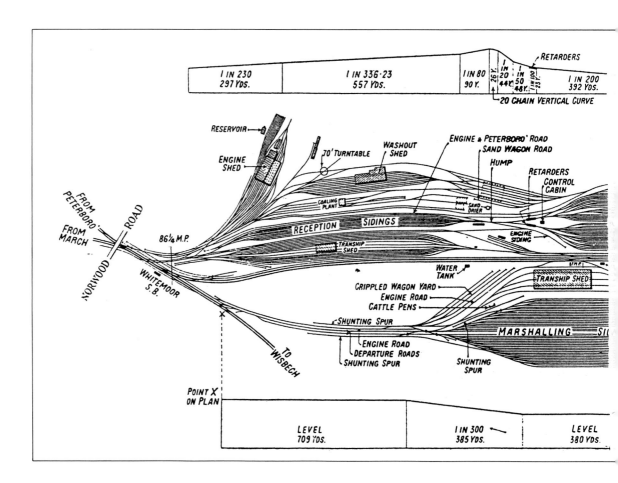

marshalling yard at Whitemoor (March) – the up yard was completed in 1929, the down in 1933, retarders being used for the first time – gave a much-needed boost to morale and helped speed up the increasing East Anglian and Harwich train ferry business. Hull New Inward Yard of 1935 was another welcome development, as was the new Mottram yard on the Woodhead route, also opened in 1935. The burden of freight on this vital trans-Pennine link already mentioned had caused congestion at yards in Manchester and at exchange points with the Cheshire Lines Committee. Mottram yard was on the falling gradient westward from Woodhead Tunnel, and made up trains for a variety of destinations without need for further marshalling. This gravity yard, and its opposite number at Dunford, east of the tunnel, were economical to run as no shunting engines were needed.

But the majority of freight installations remained almost unaltered through the LNER's history. Many were cramped, involving constant shunting especially in and out of inadequate goods sheds, cattle pens and loading bays. Though there were sharp peaks and troughs, the general tendency for freight was downward – and it was of course this that caused the company most of its financial problem, which in turn prevented much modernisation and increased productivity. Most of the freight had to be worked the hard way, over long hours with little comfort even in reasonable weather conditions, let alone in winter when

sampled. 'A4' 60028 *Walter K. Whigham* was like a Pullman Car compared with the 'K2', even when the former was going at twice the speed of the latter. Many impressions remain of this period. For example looking out of the side of 'A1' 60125 *Scottish Union* at high speed, on a winter evening between Kings Cross and Grantham, with the rain and smoke beating down, trying to see the oil lamp in a semaphore. The hard graft of firing Austerity 2-8-0 90270 on a train of coal from Doncaster to New England via Boston and stopping for water at Bardney, and going through the three-mile long Woodhead Tunnel, full of smoke, on 'B1' 61365. – Frank Harrison from *A Passion For Steam.*

Whitemoor (March) Marshalling Yards, L.N.E.R.

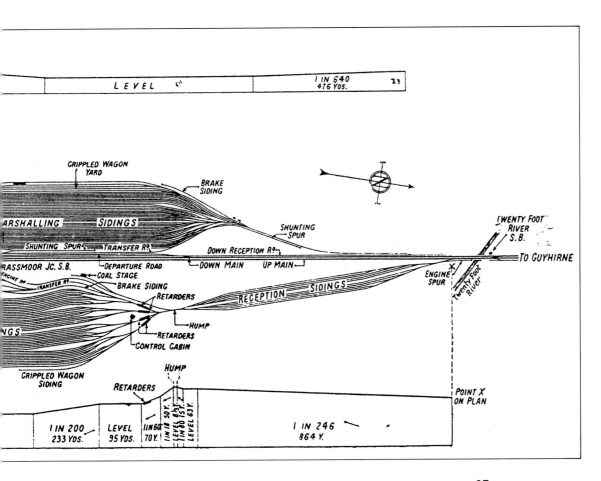

Always Busy

The large urban goods station was linked to its customers by a huge fleet of carts and motors. Right up to nationalisation the forecourt at Marylebone was lined with blue-painted horse carts backed on to the pavement. Larger drays issued from the goods station up the road taking crates, bales and bundles to customers and collecting later for despatch on the night fast goods services. Mechanical horses made their appearance in the 1930s but did not supersede their hoofed ancestors entirely until the 1950s.

In more rural areas there was usually a station with goods facilities within five miles throughout the system. Farmers' and carriers' carts, blue railway delivery trucks and other vehicles gave many stations a busy air for much of the working day. The stationmaster presided over their differing requirements, ordering suitable wagons, answering queries, drumming up business, checking, chasing up missing consignments and generally making sure that the railway served the customer.

tales of delay and hardship in snow and flood are legendary.

The first years of the new company produced a see-saw pattern of traffic receipts, but generally depression hit hard in the twenties. The General Strike was not so serious in itself as the bitter, prolonged aftermath in the mining industry. The normal pattern of coal transport ceased for many months, much exporting indeed ending for ever. Much coal, including that used by the railway itself, had to be imported expensively and carried equally expensively to an unfamiliar pattern. In 1923 coal receipts were £14.7 million; in 1926 only £7.9. The steel industry remained substantially at a standstill, and other heavy engineering suffered a decline from which parts of it never totally recovered, though things were brighter (helped by rearmament) by the mid-1930s. Coal never fully recovered, the 88 million tons carried in 1930 seeming a reasonable achievement against the changing circumstances. It declined again in the LNER's last years, to 63 million tons in 1947.

As already mentioned, the East Anglian traffic – mainly agricultural and horticultural and increasingly varied though including substantial grain and the new sugar beet – burgeoned. But in East Anglia as throughout the system, by the outbreak of war in 1939 much of the more valuable, higher tariffed traffic – and especially the regular flows – had transferred to road. The railway was left with the bulky items and a more volatile pattern of seasonable produce. The company still employed well over a quarter of a million freight wagons (excluding guard's vans of which sometimes there was a shortage just to add a further complication to freight operation), and at quiet times up to a quarter might be out of revenue service mainly waiting their next cargo.

The war was of course another story. What had been heavy flows of trunk routes became uncontrollable floods, till even the most generous of marshalling yards and reception sidings failed to cope and those manning control centres around the system pleaded with each other to prevent total chaos. Not only did most long-distance lorries disappear, but industry boomed in the war, armies and their equipment had to be moved, and by attacking the convoys of small ships carrying coal from the North East to the Thames, Germany succeeded in adding further pressure: the extra coal trains, nicknamed 'convoys', were routed via Doncaster and the GN/GE Joint Line. This had few loops, and up passenger trains were delayed because there was a loaded 'convoy' at every station ahead, needing to be crossed from the up to the down to allow passage. Another special factor was the building of the numerous airfields in East Anglia, and then supplying them, a raid of 1,000 bombers requiring eight trains for the bombs and twenty eight for the fuel. Neither East Anglia nor its railways had seen anything like it. And most of it was carried by locomotives built well before the previous World War, still for the most part proving thoroughly reliable.

Working the Fish

It was still dark on a very cold morning at Grimsby Fish Dock and the trawlers had off-loaded their catches onto the 'pontoon'. The hubbub and, to an outsider, the chaos of the fish auction began, and the 'lumpers' started their task of barrowing the boxes to the various merchants' premises. The rest of the day was taken up with despatches to customers in all parts of the country. The LNER was responsible for most of it. Empty fish vans were placed in three rows right round the land side of the dock, joined together by bridging boards. Each van bore a number, and each merchant was given a gazetteer showing the appropriate van number alongside the name of each town and village in the country.

For several hours the constant noise of barrows continued as the 'lumpers' moved the boxes to the vans. Everyone worked to strict time limits. Early traffic for the south-west left at about 1.0pm for Banbury, and a little before that the bridging boards were dropped, doors slammed to and the engine backed on. It might be a 'K3' 2-6-0 or an ex-GC 4-6-0. The same applied to the

Fast fish. North Eastern Railway class 'C7' Atlantic No 2203 in foreign territory near Cockburnspath in 1928 with an Aberdeen – Kings Cross fish train.

trains leaving in the evening for Kings Cross, Ashton Moss, Whitland, York and so on. Late starts were no more acceptable than they would have been with the *Flying Scotsman*. In some cases the trains from Grimsby and Hull were integrated. The Grimsby–Whitland and the Hull–Plymouth exchanged portions at Marston Sidings, Oxford, for Devon/Cornwall and for South Wales. If this traffic was not in the hands of consignees early next morning there was the devil to pay.

Fish was big business for the LNER served more fishing ports than any other line. Some of them operated on a large scale; Lowestoft and Yarmouth in the south, Grimsby and Hull on the Humber, North Shields on the Tyne, Granton on the Forth, Aberdeen, Peterhead and Fraserburgh in Buchan, Buckie on the Moray Firth, and away in the west, Mallaig. In addition there was a myriad of smaller ports, mainly working the inshore trade. The principal catches were cod, haddock, whiting and the humble herring.

Several ports were able to despatch in trainload quantities to the conurbations, notably the London area. The others, and the big ports sending to lesser destinations, might fill several vans which went as tail traffic on passenger trains, often making smart connections at intermediate junctions. Then there was always a traffic in odd boxes, often specialised stuff like shellfish, which accompanied the passenger guard in his van – to his dismay!

This was the steady traffic. But the migratory herring was more of a problem. As the shoals moved southwards in the North Sea, reaching the Yarmouth area in September/October, catches at a score of ports on the way rose sharply, peaked and fell away again; rail despatches also soared. It was not unknown for the picturesque little ports in the East Neuk of Fife, Crail, Anstruther, Pittenweem, St Monance and Largo to fill six trains a day and send them off down the single line to Thornton and the south, instead of the usual vans on the passenger service. The Midland & Great Northern Joint also felt the surge, fortunately when the hectic summer holiday traffic had waned.

The LNER took over a very mixed wagon fleet for the fish, varying from low-sided opens, via four and six-wheeled vans up to big bogie vehicles. Gradually they settled on a four-wheel long wheelbase insulated van; in the fifties, with recurrent delays and tranships due to hot boxes, BR built similar vehicles with roller bearings, the 'Blue Spot' vans. Haulage was invariably by express passenger or modern mixed traffic locomotives.

Stand in Aberdeen Deeside yard, almost opposite the fish market, at lunchtime: two or (some days) three lines of vans, alongside broad roadways, await their loads. The main London train is the 13.43, but on heavy days, Thursdays and some Mondays, there is a 12.30 also. Then for West Coast destinations there's a 14.15, largely made up of ex-LMS six-wheeled vans. There are two more trains in the early evening for nearer stations. The market begins at 07.00, and there is an agent there to assess the tonnage, contact the principal merchants and decide how many vans will be needed on each train. After the auctioneering chaos the merchants whisk their purchases to their own premises to be filleted, iced and boxed, mostly in one or two-stone sizes. About 11.30 it

starts to arrive on a procession of flat-bed lorries which jockey for position against the appropriate van doors. Most on the London train are for Billingsgate, but there are one or two for cross-London towns, while individual vans on the 14.15 cover several destinations – the East Lancs line, for instance. Aproned loaders and drivers work furiously to stack the boxes. If the consignments are charged by weight, there may be no more than 3 tons in a van; if charging is by the van, then they will stack it high, 8 tons or more, until the bottom boxes risk being crushed.

Twenty minutes before departing time, a shunter sets the Peterhead and Fraserburgh vans on to the 10–15 Aberdeens, followed by the 'A3' that will work the train as far as Edinburgh. Loading continues right up to the last moment; then at 13.42 the foreman calls time and whistles the loaders out. Doors are slid shut and pinned, a wave to the guard on the verandah of his Queen Mary, his green flag flutters and the train is away. *Nothing* is allowed to interfere with its punctual departure – not even more fish. It is a priority run up the main line at speeds up to 75mph; the train will be on the up through at the Waverley by about 16.40, changing engines and picking up a couple of vans from Leith Citadel (the Granton fish), then off again to be in Kings Cross goods about 01.00. Lorries are waiting to get the fish into Billingsgate by about 04.00, where the merchants will set out sample boxes on their stalls. The bulk remains on the lorries until sold.

Rail movement of fish held up well into the fifties, when road hauliers began to eat selectively into the short and middle distance traffic. First, from Aberdeen, the main Glasgow and Edinburgh loads, then the big flow to Manchester Market – not the small tonnages to Blackburn, Burnley, Blackpool and the like, thank you. Wet fish movement began an insidious decline in favour of frozen packs and prepared meals. Finally, in the Beeching era, the fish traffic was adjudged uneconomic; excessive handling costs, too many vans in use, poor wagon loadability, empty return haulage. It was not left to flounder like a cod on a trawler deck, but killed off at a stroke, and along with it went a colourful way of life and many sections of line such as the sprawling former Great North of Scotland system to Fraserburgh and Peterhead on which well into dmu days under the Scottish Region still sported daily steam-hauled fish trains.

The Golden Years of the LNER high speed streamliners. In the second half of the 1930s the LNER was running from Kings Cross to Newcastle in 4hr and to Edinburgh in 6hr. Here the 5.30pm Kings Cross to Newcastle Silver Jubilee train headed by 'A4' Pacific No 2509 Silver Link *in its unique silver and grey livery leaves Welwyn South Tunnel with just over a mile of climbing through the Chilterns to do before dropping down to Fen country.*

English pre-grouping colours. Reproductions of coloured postcards showing LNER constituent trains in their old liveries. These are typical examples of cards which were sold in their tens of thousands during the Edwardian and 1920/30 period showing trains of their day. Some (including the GNR) were produced by the companies themselves others by such well known firms as The Locomotive Publishing Co, Raphael Tuck, Valentine and Salmon: others are examples by Knight or Pouteau. Today these are very much collectors' items but then they always have been. Certainly they give a very real and fascinating insight into the colourful days of Britain's railways.

Top. The illustration shows an unmarked but probable LPC card (it has the pseudonym F Moore) of Kings Cross station with a GNR class 'D1' or 'D2' 4-4-0 and a large boilered GNR Atlantic. The heading on the top of the card is in gold blocked lettering. Note the clean glass in the overall roof.

Centre. One of the Locomotive Magazine Series No 3 cards produced by LPC showing Liverpool Street station with a Claud Hamilton 4-4-0 in glorious blue in the foreground. Note the gas lit six wheeled stock and the disc headcode.

Bottom. Marylebone as depicted on an LPC card with a Robinson class '11B' 4-4-0 No 1038 at the head of a Sheffield and Manchester express. This scene is little changed today though the station is now only the terminus for suburban services and, in recent years, a number of steam hauled special trains.

Top. An LPC card entitled NE Railway East Coast Dining Car Express leaving Edinburgh. The locomotive No 1794 is a Wilson Worsdell V class Atlantic and the train almost certainly an East Coast Joint Stock set in GNR teak. The North Eastern operated the East Coast companies' expresses north of York including the NBR section to Edinburgh Waverley.

Centre. An 'Alpha' series card postmarked Glasgow on 5 January 1921 with a heading NB Railway – Express leaving Edinburgh. The locomotive is one of the massive North British Atlantics No 872 Auld Reekie and again the train appears to be ECJCS stock based (as are all the preceding cards) on an F. Moore painting done in oils on top of a photograph. This card was almost certainly purchased at the bookstall of the hated rival the Caledonian at their Central station as its message states 'A very large 4-4-0 pulled us from Carlisle and a large tank engine pushed for several miles from Beattock to the summit. It was dark and I could not make out its wheel arrangement'.

Bottom. A Valentine 'Artotype' series of a Royal Train (with LNWR stock presumably to or from Balmoral) headed by GNSR 'T' class 4-4-0 (which became LNER D41) garlanded and bedecked with one would think some artistic licence.

N.B. Railway.—Express leaving Edinburgh.

Great North of Scotland Railway—Royal Train

*A number of ex Great Eastern
LNER class 'B12' 4-6-0s were
transferred to the Great North of
Scotland section. No 1543 in
postwar green livery is seen at
Kittybrewster, Aberdeen in 1948.*

3
AN OBSERVER REMEMBERS

IN the early years there continued to be fairly intense rivalry between LNER drivers who had commenced their railway service with different companies. This showed itself in their comments about the various types of locomotives. 'Puggy' (GC) men thought little of GN engines, particularly those used on the branch lines, whilst GN men were sure that J. G. Robinson of the GC had shares in a coal mine. The best the 'Sweedie' (GE) could produce was the 1500 class 4-6-0 which needed a strong fireman to reach the front end of the firebox, whilst the rest of its stock appeared to consist mainly of 4-4-0s and small engines with large chimneys. However, it all settled down far more quickly than on the LMS – and it was to the LMS that most LNER men's rivalry was addressed.

Though average speeds of the Scottish trains were very low until the accelerations of 1932, the East Coast main line never lacked interest. At 10.00 each morning at Kings Cross there was the daily ceremony of seeing away the *Flying Scotsman* from number 10 Platform, usually attended by LNER officers. There was an air of excitement about this departure, with the gleaming green Pacific at the head of a long train of bow-ended coaches equipped with name boards, which no HST could hope to achieve in spite of its much higher speeds. Some of the Top Link drivers built up reputations for speed. Their starts on the gradient into Gas Works Tunnel were sometimes not according to the best standards of driving; a Pacific doing eight mph with its driving wheels doing forty was quite a sight to behold. In the reverse direction, after ex-NE men started working through to Kings Cross, an ex-GN man was heard to say that 'one of those b----- Geordies will finish up in Piccadilly'.

In the first thirty miles from Kings Cross could be seen the suburban trains, usually quad-art sets hauled by 'N2s', labouring up the gradient to Potters Bar and on to Hitchin and the Cambridge branch. In those days Stevenage was merely a small village with its station about a mile north of the present day one. Few main line services stopped at Hitchin in either direction, so suburban passengers to and from the north found it quicker to travel to and from Kings Cross.

Track consisted of 100lb per yard bull-head rails in 60-foot lengths, although some 90-foot lengths were being laid. In 1937 the LNER installed, in the down main line at Holme, south of Peterborough, the first rails in the world to be rolled in 120-foot lengths. Regular passengers for Peterborough could fall asleep at Kings Cross and be awoken at Holme by the change in rhythm. LNER track always had a high reputation.

Day Out from York

Thursday morning 29 January 1953, and the York district officers' inspection special steaming sedately out of York's No 9 on to the Scarborough line to say goodbye to the York to Pickering via Gilling and Helmsley line.

The 'train' consisted of the York six-wheeled inspection saloon (comfortable with open verandah) built in 1896, as NER 41, hauled as customary by a 'Hunt' class 'D49', No 62745 *The Hurworth*. The Hurworth always had the same driver, a kindly and placid man with a strong personal loyalty to the district officers.

Out via Malton to Pickering, and from Pickering after reversal back via Mill Lane Junction on to the day's primary task, calling at every wayside station and saying goodbye to all the staff. At Kirbymoorside the stationmaster quietly presented the writer with a set of mint North Eastern Railway tickets all pre-1900 from the doomed booking office. At another station the lady porter, overcome, burst into tears and had to be comforted before the saloon could proceed. All the stationmasters at these small North Eastern country stations were also the coal merchants, adding to their somewhat poor railway salaries.

The Pilmoor area was of great interest; in addition to the York–Pickering service, the triangular layout provided for through summer trains from Glasgow to reach Scarborough without the need to go south to York, by the expedient of using the north curve to Sunbeck, across to Gilling and to Malton (where a double reversal was required) and so to Scarborough. Also at Pilmoor was the branch to Boroughbridge and Knaresborough, the remains of an embankment over the main line hopefully built to carry a direct line from Leeds to the East Coast via Malton – and some signals used for eyesight tests. –
R. A. Savill.

Outer London suburban train. Very much an LNER scene, an 'N2' class 0-6-2 tank (carrying condenser pipes for working over London's Underground lines) No 4760 heads two 'quad-art' sets as it hurries down the main line to Potters Bar, the destination on the board carried at the base of the smokebox door. The co-acting arms on the upper quadrant signal enable their positions behind the bridge to be clear both at a distance and as the train approaches.

Signalling was mainly manual, with many small signalboxes. No signalbox between Kings Cross and New Southgate signalled both up and down trains. A high proportion of the semaphore signals were of the GN somersault type, introduced after the Abbots Ripton accident of 1876. But as told in the section on signalling, the LNER was early in the field with the use of colour-light signals, apart from those at Kings Cross. Searchlight signals were installed between York and Darlington, many between junctions being worked automatically.

To an LNER man of the early 30s his company was the only one with a fleet of Pacifics. The only other Pacific in the country had been the GWR 'Great Bear', but it was said that George Jackson Churchward would have let Gresley have it if he'd asked for it. And what Pacifics there were on the LNER! The GN ones were mainly named after exotic sounding racehorses, although *Spearmint* always looked rather out-of-place. Then there were the NE Pacifics, named after cities and looking a street-and-a-half long. Apart from these the former GN, NE, NB and GC had fleets of very useful Atlantics. If any double-heading occurred it was most likely to avoid an engine running home light, not like their immediate neighbours the Midland, who seemed to plan for it before Stanier arrived.

In contrast to the Great Northern and Great Eastern sections, the

46

Great Central was a very special bit of the LNER, its operations honed to a keen edge to take on the competition from the Midland Division of the LMS. They seemed to have trained all their passengers, not just to be on their feet ready for the station stops, but also to shut the carriage doors behind them. Normal booked stops at stations like Rugby were just one minute; this was cut as a matter of course if the train was running late. The 10am Marylebone – Manchester was observed on one occasion to be away in just 12 seconds.

What other line would have had the temerity to schedule engine changes at Leicester in two minutes? (It was later expanded to four.) The incoming fireman would judge his moment to drop off the engine before it stopped – the driver was already getting it into reverse – so that he could dive straight under the buffers to part the vacuum pipe and throw off the shackle. A spin of the reversing handle, and off would go the driver like a shot from a gun, leaving his fireman to be picked up on the way back to the shed. Meanwhile the new engine would already be drawing forward circumspectly, the driver watching the movements of the bobby in the North box as he reset the road behind the departing engine. A quick set back – no creeping on to the train until the last few yards – with the fireman already in the four-foot waiting to swing the shackle. A quick blow-up (no time for a brake test), the green flag and they were away.

The arrival of the 'Sandringhams' of the Footballer series in large numbers on the GC brought new running standards. The Gorton men actively disliked them, and the Neasden men were less than overjoyed, but the Leicester crews really produced results. The 15.45 from Manchester would romp out of Leicester, with 8 coaches, 273 tons tare, and maintain 51–52mph steadily up the 7 miles of 1 in 176 towards Lutterworth, day-after-day-after-day, seemingly no matter who the driver was, and all done inaudibly. It was a remarkable uniformity of running. But watch them at speed, rolling on the reverse curves round the island platforms, and you wondered how they stayed on the rails and did not come up the platform ramps.

Then there was the continuous procession of Annesley – Woodford freights and the returning trains of empties, each with its '04' 'Tiny' plugging away at the front. No goods loops in the 33 miles from Leicester South Goods to Woodford before the war, so they were encouraged not to hang about. Otherwise it meant setting back a long train into a refuge siding, in some cases against the ruling 1 in 176. Early in the war they converted Rugby's up refuge siding into a loop, with a phone for the guard to report the train arrived complete to the signalbox. With the down empties, unfitted of course, speeds of up to 50mph were not uncommon in clear weather on the long fall towards Leicester, though the sighting of the distant signals was good. How those old wooden private owners wagons snaked along!

The GN cross-country line from Stafford to Grantham might rub shoulders with this GC paragon in Nottingham Victoria, but the two were as alike as chalk and cheese. That line really had atmosphere, not least in the fusty, gas-lit GN articulated compartment sets (made up

West Highland 'Lighthouse'
When the railway was new, trees were planted round the exposed, isolated cottages by the line to act as windbreaks. To the modern traveller, a clump of trees away ahead is the first indication that he is approaching one of the lonely Moorland outposts. The men of the Moor and their families have intrigued visitors ever since.

As late as the LNER period, the authorities tried to make a mystery of Gorton, and permission to leave the train there was not readily obtained. When a writer and photographer entered the forbidden territory uninvited, the published result of their clandestine visit resulted in 'please explain' letters being sent to railway personnel on the spot. At one time a special engine and brake made a Christmas visit to the lonely stations and cottages, and a railway official from Glasgow, disguised in the familiar red cloak and white beard, distributed gifts to the railway children.

During the early thirties a school was established in an old passenger carriage on Gorton platform. The Argyll authorities found a lady teacher for it, but there was no place for her to stay in Gorton, so she had to travel up from Bridge of Orchy every morning. At one time there were eleven pupils.

All Gorton's domestic water has to be imported. It was once the duty of the fireman of the first up train of the day to deliver from his tender twelve bucketfuls. Sudden illness presents another problem for the people on the Moor. They tell tales of an engine dashing in the night with a doctor on the footplate to the succour of a railwayman who was taken suddenly ill. – Extracts from John Thomas's famous account of the isolated crossing loops in *The West Highland Railway*, still a best-seller.

Land Cruising

Land cruising was introduced by the LNER in 1933 with the *Northern Belle*. leaving Kings Cross at 2320 on Fridays for a seven-day tour of two thousand miles. It consisted of fifteen vehicles including sleeping cars with showers, a wardrobe van, a lounge and writing room, ladies' retiring room, a hairdressing salon and a shop selling newspapers, cigarettes and stamps. The route from Kings Cross was via Darlington, Penrith, Carlisle, the Waverley route to Edinburgh and on to Aberdeen. From Aberdeen the train ran back via Glasgow and Loch Lomond to Fort William and Mallaig. On the return it took in the Border Counties line and the coast to Whitby. Most meals were served on the train, but some were taken in LNER hotels. There were bus tours from Penrith round the Lake District, round Edinburgh, from Aberdeen to Braemar and (if desired) from Fort William to Fort Augustus to look for the Loch Ness Monster. A steamer trip along Loch Lomond from Balloch to Ardlui was included and the paddle steamer *Waverley* took the passengers from Craigendoran Pier round the Kyles of Bute. This was the original *Waverley*, sunk at Dunkirk, not its replacement which has been preserved. At £20 per head the *Northern Belle* was quite a bargain.

A variation was the *Eastern Belle Pullman Limited*. Two trains of first and third class Pullman cars, kept at Stratford for Newmarket race meetings, were also used for high class Sunday excursions to Clacton-on-Sea. The latter was developed into a programme of day excursions to Cromer, Sheringham, Aldeburgh, Hunstanton, Yarmouth, Lowestoft or Skegness. Speeds were high, fares were low and cheap meals were served, if required, at passengers' own seats.

from old low-roofed six-wheeler bodies on new underframes). An elderly GN 4-4-0 would lug one of these 5-sets out of Derby Friargate with asthmatic beat and stagger up Breadsall bank; after making all the stops to Basford & Bulwell, it would dive under the GC main and join it at Bagthorpe Junction, then burrow underground to Nottingham. Halfway through the pungent murk of Mansfield Road Tunnel, enginemen would be alerted to their position and passengers rudely awakened by the ghostly clangour of a treadle-operated gong. In the smoky gloom, barely penetrated by the yellowish carriage lights, it was like approaching the gates of hell itself.

It was on the branch lines that the most variety could be found, with engines and rolling stock going back well into the last century. Throughout the country there could be found towns where several pre-grouping companies met, and they had always been, and continued to be for several years after grouping, places where many classes of locomotives could be seen. Such a place was Lincoln where the GN and GC met, and the GN & GE Joint Line ran through. The former LD & EC arrived at Pyewipe Junction, and the GC even made an end-on connection with the Midland line from Nottingham. Working the passenger trains over the ex-GC lines could be seen D9-11 4-4-0s and 'Jersey Lily' Atlantics, the fish trains usually being hauled by an ex-GC 4-6-0 or a K3 2-6-0. The ex-GN branches were usually worked by D1-3 4-4-0s, 'Klondyke' and large Atlantics, K2 2-6-0s or small 4-4-2 tank engines (C12). Down the Joint Line came the 'Claud Hamilton' 4-4-0s and B12 4-6-0s, and later the 'Sandringham' 4-6-0s. Freights were worked by a great variety of GN and GC 2-8-0s and 0-6-0s, GN 2-6-0s and GE 0-6-0s. In the late 30s the LNER 'Standard' J39 0-6-0s worked many freights and were also used on excursions.

In the early years of the LNER the branch passenger trains were slow and frequently consisted of four-and six-wheeled vehicles, and bogie coaches which had spent their earlier life on the East Coast main line, including some nineteenth-century ECJS clerestory-roofed stock. In those days there were many village stations, and they all got their daily 'Parly' train stopping at all stations. Cars and foreign holidays were for the rich and, when they could afford it, the ordinary people took their holidays in this country. When paid holidays became normal town factories all tended to close during the same week, as they did at Lincoln. 'Trip Week' specials were run to Yarmouth, Scarborough, Blackpool and the Lincolnshire resorts.

The crack train through Lincoln was the 'Boat Train' from Parkeston Quay to Liverpool and York, which split at Lincoln in the down direction and rejoined in the up, a twice-daily important ritual. It was worked by GE 4-4-0s and 4-6-0s, but later by LNER 'Sandringham' 4-6-0s.

The Great Northern and Great Central Railways had been instrumental in popularising the Lincolnshire resorts of Skegness, Mablethorpe and Cleethorpes. The first two were favoured by Nottingham and Leicester people and the last by Sheffielders, principally because of the number of booked services and excursions run from Leicester Belgrave

Modern 0-6-0. One of Sir Nigel Gresley's 'J39' class 0-6-0s No 1543 (introduced in 1926 but built up to 1941) on an up express freight at Low Fell Gateshead. It is one of a later batch built in November 1936 and remained in service until 1961. The 'J39' was a popular class which was used over most of the system including Scotland.

Cross-country local. The LNER worked a number of fascinating services in the north and east Midlands, all of them ex Great Northern Railway sections, Stafford-Uttoxeter, Egginton Junction–Derby (Friargate)– Nottingham and Nottingham– Grantham being some examples. Here ex GNR class 'J5' Ivatt 0-6-0 No 5483 heads a Nottingham to Derby train through Breadsall cutting on 26 June 1947.

Opposite top.
Cross-country main line. Woodhead station in the Pennines and at the exit of the notorious Woodhead tunnel. This was the old main line of Sheffield, Ashton-under-Lyne and Manchester Railway, later the Manchester, Sheffield and Lincolnshire and later still (on the building of the southern extension to London at the turn of the century) the Great Central. The climb up to Woodhead was hard and the single bore tunnels suffocating. An ex GC class 'B3/2' 4-6-0 is about to plunge into the murky depths at the head of an east-bound passenger train probably in the mid 1930s.

A Holden beauty. Ex Great Eastern Railway 4-6-0 as LNER class 'B12' No 8552 at Liverpool Street station around 1935, when the class was still in service on the main-line trains and indeed the engines were handling the principal express trains over the Great Eastern routes. Note the short tender to enable the locomotive to fit on to the small GER turntables and the ACFI feed water heater which scarcely adds to the engine's aesthetic appearance.

Road, Nottingham Victoria and Sheffield Victoria stations, all of which have now passed into history.

During the summer numerous weekend excursions were run to Skegness, a maximum of thirty trains being operated in any one day. The station had seven platforms and twenty-four carriage sidings. As soon as a train arrived a small army of carriage cleaners descended on it, because it had to be cleared in three or four minutes to make way for the next arrival. With all the sidings full the last six trains were taken out to wayside stations to be stabled until the evening.

The problem was different at Mablethorpe, which was on the single-line loop connecting Louth and Willoughby on the East Lincolnshire main line. Mablethorpe itself had only a passing loop. As trains arrived from the south and were emptied the engines ran round and propelled onto the single line towards Louth, closed to traffic on Sundays. Last in was first out.

At Cleethorpes up to thirty trains would be received on one day. After emptying the trains the engines propelled them into the sidings, took water and had their fires cleaned, ran round and then ran the stock to New Clee Sidings for stabling. At the appropriate times, it was propelled back into Cleethorpes platforms prior to departure.

Before the war a fairly large number of old vehicles was stabled for use on excursions. In early LNER days many were four-and six-wheeled, which gave a very lively ride over third class bull-head track. Many trains were operated by using GN suburban quad-art sets. This involved empty stock trains north from the Kings Cross District after Friday evening's peak, returning in time for Monday morning's peak.

The LNER also operated numerous evening excursions. For example many were run from Lincoln to Skegness, giving ninety miles return for 1s 6d (7½p). On any night several trains would be needed. They almost worked on the modern MGR principle – as the Lincoln pubs emptied the Skegness pubs filled up. On the return journey in non-corridor stock, with full tanks and no pit stop, even forty-five miles was a long

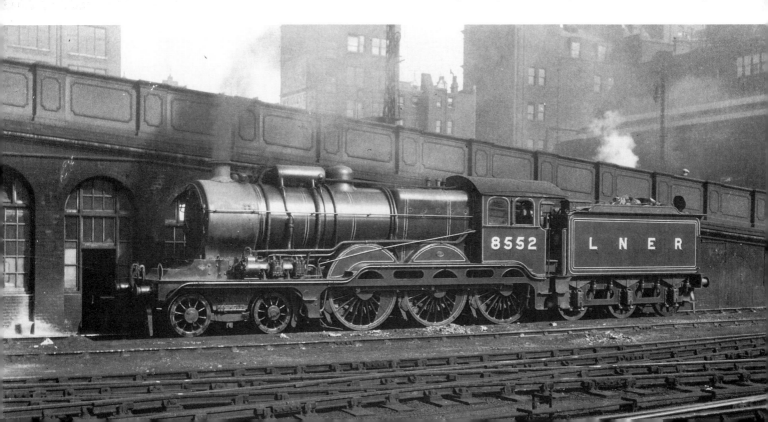

Last main line out of London. An early 1930s photograph of an ex GCR Atlantic as 'C4' No 5266 passing Wendover with an up express. Sadly by this time the smart green livery has gone and No 5266 (a Leicester-based engine) is now in black lined out in red; smart enough but an indication that the class is now considered to be of secondary importance to the newly introduced Sandringham or Football class 4-6-0s which Leicester crews used as well.

distance. Often the trains could be seen in transit with several doors open an inch or two.

At weekends, if there was engineering work on the East Coast main line between Peterborough and Doncaster, the Lincoln area got a rush of main line trains worked by Pacifics, diverted either via Spalding and the Joint Line or via Honington and the Grantham to Lincoln branch. This required a large number of pilotmen. When Kings Cross to Edinburgh non-stop running commenced in 1928 corridor tenders were built which had high sides. This caused consternation at Lincoln because the water cranes were not high enough to go over the tender sides. An extra swan neck had to be inserted, making the cranes unique.

Until long after World War 2 the original GN main line between Lincoln and Spalding via Boston, the East Lincolnshire main line from Grimsby to Boston, and the GN & GE Joint Line from March to Doncaster were very busy. The Joint Line was, in particular, very heavily used by freight trains between the Eastern Counties and the north. For long periods in the fruit season there would be a train in every section. The avoiding line at Lincoln between Greetwell Junction and Boultham Junction was worked on permissive block, and trains often queued up nose to tail. On alternate Saturday afternoons the queue tended to be slow to move forward. The crews of trains overlooking Lincoln City Football Ground were loath to move.

Perhaps the greatest changes have occurred in the duties of station staff. In LNER days clerks at country stations had to know and do everything from the issue of a passenger ticket right through to the station's monthly passenger balance sheet, and on the freight side from the acceptance of a consignment note to the freight balance sheet. There was such a wide variety of traffic to be dealt with. Porters at small stations had to know how to load, sheet and rope bales of hay and straw in such a way that they would not move in transit, and that the sheets would not come loose. Some of them had to deal with cattle and other livestock. They had to perform much heavy labour. In between they would have to trim all the oil signal lamps. They were the lowest paid porters, there being three grades – agricultural, industrial and London. However there was great competition for the jobs as, in those days, anything was better than being an agricultural labourer.

Most of the staff of the LNER were very proud of their company. When No 10000 was built in 1929 in conditions of absolute secrecy rumours were already being passed around by the staff. It ran one trial trip up the GN & GE Joint Line and those who saw it from a distance wondered what Gresley had produced. From that moment, however, they knew they were working for a company that was a bit different. From then until 1938, with the high speed runs of *Flying Scotsman*, *Papyrus*, *Silver Link* and, finally, *Mallard* it was a constant procession of exciting occurrences. Morale was high. Among other things the LNER proved what a fallacy it is that very tight timings result in unpunctuality.

North Sea special. An ex Great Central Robinson-designed 4-6-0 as LNER class 'B4' No 6095 runs over the Metropolitan and GC Joint Line at Northolt Park at the head of a Norway Cruise boat train around 1938. The special will have originated at Marylebone and probably ran via Gainsborough to Immingham.

Cheap day to London. An up half-day excursion from Leicester to Marylebone passes Denham on the GW/GC Joint Line (note the GWR signals) behind Sandringham/ Football Club 'B17' class 4-6-0 No 2854 Sunderland around 1938. By this time these modern Gresley engines were making themselves felt on services until then regularly worked by ex GC Jersey Lily Atlantics and Director class 'D11/1' 4-4-0s.

Soldier Enthusiast in Wartime East Anglia

Twice within a quarter of a century, the East Anglian railways of the Great Eastern and its successor the LNER were exposed to the threat of invasion, and in World War 2 to considerable air attacks; after Dunkirk in 1940 there was a gradual turn towards the region becoming part of the great springboard for offensive operations. In all this the railways played an enormous part, as has been recorded elsewhere. But much of interest about the working of the East Anglian railways could not be told at the time, especially from the viewpoint of the railway enthusiast. Such an enthusiast, D. S. M. Barrie, recalls the six months he spent amid the East Anglian scene in 1941:

When at the end of May 1941 I received orders to report to HQ Movement Control, Cambridge, in the rank of Acting Lieutenant, I was delighted at the expectation of seeing something of the former Great Eastern lines in East Anglia, previous experience of which had been confined to various trips to Cambridge, and one or two day-off excursions to March, Kings Lynn and Harwich.

The initial journey to report at Cambridge HQ was scarcely propitious, however; the 09.10 train from Liverpool Street comprised nine non-corridor coaches hauled throughout by 2-6-2T 472 of Class 'V1', non-stop to Tottenham and thence all stations. Hence when 472 stopped for water at Bishops Stortford, there was a rush along the platform by soldiery and citizenry alike!

After interview at Cambridge HQ, I was detailed to a temporary post (which was to last six months) as assistant railway traffic officer based on Thorpe Station, Norwich, where I was made welcome by my two seniors – both of whom were to move on before the end of August, leaving myself as the sole RTO. Much was to happen before then. To a keen railway enthusiast the Norwich RTO Area was fascinating, embracing as it did part of the main line towards Ipswich, the Ely–Cambridge line to Thetford inclusive, the Yarmouth and Lowestoft lines and the Waveney Valley branch from Tivetshall to Beccles, the whole of the Midland & Great Northern from Norwich and Yarmouth to Melton Constable, Cromer and Kings Lynn, the quaint Norfolk and Suffolk Joint, and indeed the whole coast (much of it under the Royal Navy or protected by minefields) between Lowestoft to Kings Lynn.

Norwich itself was a hive of railway activity, very largely and directly devoted to the war effort, the headquarters of its district superintendent and of a major motive power depot; our immediate responsibilities also covered a supply depot at Trowse, and the outlying goods stations at Victoria (an erstwhile circus), and the M&GN freight terminal at Norwich City. The RTO general office on one of the main platforms at Thorpe was staffed throughout the 24 hours, dealing with service visitors and phone enquirers on matters of train services, 'Lost, Stolen & Strayed', and so on; movements of parties were attended on arrival or departure, while in view of the huge increase in RAF movement, we accommodated a Flight-Sgt and a Corporal of RAF Movement Control. The officers shared a nearby smallish office, the closeness of the internal ventilation accentuated by a sort of oriental aroma deriving from its former use as a railway lamp room.

As almost every station in the district had warlike traffic to deal with – and some of the small ex-GE wayside stations in what was largely branch-line country dealt with some astonishing tonnages – there were numerous occasions when regular or special visits had to be made. There were also the important anti-aircraft practice camps at Weybourne (M&GN) and Wells-next-the-Sea, where the arrival and departure of special trains had to be attended. From time to time strange orders were received from higher authority: 'Report forthwith on present condition of the Southwold Railway'. This could have been answered in one word, but I thought it dutiful and discreet to make a physical check. So I nipped over to Halesworth, where in the narrow-gauge sidings were a number of mostly burned-out coach frames and other debris together at the former engine shed with the skeleton and boiler of 2-4-0T No 3, minus all fittings.

Outside the ordinary public services, most of what one was involved in or knew about at that time was officially secret. Notably there were two lines patrolled by armoured trains; one manned by Poles and working when required between Kings Lynn and Wells-next-the-Sea, and another which from time to time came up from Felixstowe and practised over the Joint M&GN and GE line along the clifftops between Yarmouth and Lowestoft via Gorleston. The star turns of purely military movement, however, were the warflat trains which in the summer of 1941 brought units of the Armoured Brigades into Norfolk and out again on large-scale exercises.

Warflat trains normally comprised nine bogie warflat wagons (FVF) each capable of carrying two of the cruiser tanks or one Churchill, which latter, apart from weighing some 40 tons, were so wide that the treads of their tracks slightly overlapped each side of the warflat. RTOs and railway supervisors therefore used a special gauge on entrainment to ensure that the overlap was within the limits allowed. The rest of the long train comprised passenger coach(es) for the tank crews, a converted train ferry wagon ('the Ferry Van') used to store WD equipment such as spare shackling chains, ramps and sleepers, and the ramp wagon (FVR).

This was not a load-carrying flat but a short-wheelbase runner wagon, one end of which could be lowered to form a ramp, subject to its being secured on the best available piece of concrete, sleeper or ballast which would safely support the jack. We did not normally use this contraption if a sound loading dock (preferably an end dock) was available, but there were few of these at wayside stations in East Anglia which had already unloaded volumes of traffic for road or airfield construction far in excess of the modest tonnages of beet, spuds or turnips, plus the odd road vehicle for repair, which had passed over them in peacetime. (The first time we did tank moves at Kings Lynn, we could not find a dock strong enough, and had to split the train and stow part of it through the engine shed while unloading went on.) Movement of tanks along a train of warflats was normally guided by troopers walking on top of the warflats ahead of the moving tank, or at night by the waving of shielded cigarettes. I only recall one case of a tank going too far and going off the end of the rake of flats; then there was a roar of engines and the tank came charging back along the adjacent siding to repeat its run, this time successfully; we all got out of the way very sharply.

The railheads at which we detrained or re-entrained squadrons of cavalry or yeomanry armoured regiments during the hectic summer of 1941 were mainly Thetford, Watton, Swaffham, Kings Lynn and Wells-next-the-Sea. At all these places and with the heavy train scaling 550–700 tons loaded, the co-operation of the LNER staff of all grades was tremendous.

At both Watton and Wells there occurred lively and exciting incidents. At the former, we had just got rid of three loaded warflat trains from the northern end (the third in 28min, something of a record) when Norwich LNER phoned an urgent order to return one of the two engines on this train to Swaffham in order to assist a train stuck there or beyond; but we had the train staff for the section which was due to be returned to Swaffham by the local passenger, which was stuck at Thetford. So the district inspector and the RTO cooked up a plot whereby the Swaffham cartage driver, off-duty, would bring the train staff to Watton, handing it over en route to my driver Butterworth in my PU. (Butterworth said afterwards that the marvellous sight was that of the Swaffham 'mechanical horse' jumping high over a hump-backed bridge as it raced towards him.) Later, somebody higher-up in the LNER kindly wrote to my district command HQ expressing thanks for the RTO's ready appreciation of the situation and in rendering 'assistance in conveying the railway (sic) staff from Swaffham to Watton'. This was eventually passed on to me somewhat tempered by a reminder to the RTO, Norwich to refer to the instructions governing the conveyance of civilian personnel in WD transport!

Two LNER handbills.

4
STATIONS

THERE were many LNERs and on the whole the stations well reflected their different natures – always remembering that two thirds of the company's business was largely behind the scenes with freight. The policy of decentralisation encouraged the retention of the individuality of the constituent lines' showpieces: at nearly all of them there was a deep sense of history and continuity. Nowhere was this greater than in London where the termini of the 'three Greats' were as different as different could be, and no efforts at unification were made more than logo deep.

At Liverpool Street, vast with its two 'sides', the famous Hook Continental boat trains departing from the longer main-line platforms between, the memory is of constant activity, purposeful crowds, the panting of the Westinghouse brake, the determination to keep going always in grime, sometimes pea soup. Though Liverpool Street's raison d'etre was to serve tidal waves of commuters, the changing tempo of the daily rhythm was felt more strongly at Kings Cross, where despite substantial suburban business the focus was on express comings and goings – with something of today's atmosphere of an airport about it. Like Paddington, Kings Cross was an easily understandable station, enjoyable, frequently memorable. The expresses tended to go out in batteries, French style, including the much-photographed (from 1937) 4pm departures, with long lulls between. But for real inactivity you had to go to Marylebone, built well after the making of great stations was supposed to have gone out of vogue. It of course also had its moments of business and glory, 'but as quiet as Marylebone on the Sabbath' became a way of describing a great hush.

Liverpool Street, the focus of the world's most intensive steam suburban service, opened in 1874, though not available for long-distance traffic until November of the following year. Replacing the old Shoreditch station, later to become Bishopsgate, it was in two main parts, east and west, with train sheds formed of high glazed canopies supported on cast iron pillars, the whole once separated by sidings leading to coal hoists connecting with cellars underground. In later years these became platforms 9 and 10, the much-photographed haunt of the station pilots. The two concourses were linked by subway and a long meandering footbridge. Towards the end of steam the east-side or 'little pilot' was J69 *Buckjumper* No 68619, always immaculately turned-out, and latterly in full Great Eastern livery. The old company's hotel completed the picture, fronting Liverpool Street itself, and towering over the concourse.

Cheaper by Rail

Belle Vue was one of the most popular destinations for winter evening excursions to big cities, using rolling stock that would otherwise have remained idle and allowing whole families to see new places at an extremely modest cost. In the winter of 1934–5, 781 trains ran to cities such as Manchester, Sheffield, Nottingham and Newcastle carrying 300,000 passengers.

In the early thirties the LNER ran an excursion from Lincoln to Belle Vue, Manchester, and back for 2s 6d (12½p), a distance of almost 200 miles. Its driver, Herbert Harrison, who started on the GCR in 1903, took several of his family on the trip.

On arrival back at 2am, a fleet of Lincoln Corporation buses was awaiting, enhanced fares of 1s (5p) being charged because of the late hour.

The air went blue. Herbert Harrison roared: 'I've just taken this lot over the Pennines to Manchester for 1s 3d and you lot want 1s for a mile-and-a-half down Monks Road.'

Gateway to East Anglia. City commuters arriving at Liverpool Street station in the 1930s. Note the preponderance of both men and hats. To the right of the crowd is a line of taxis and beyond them the booking offices for both suburban and main-line trains. The station was in two main parts with the concourses linked by both subway and footbridge.

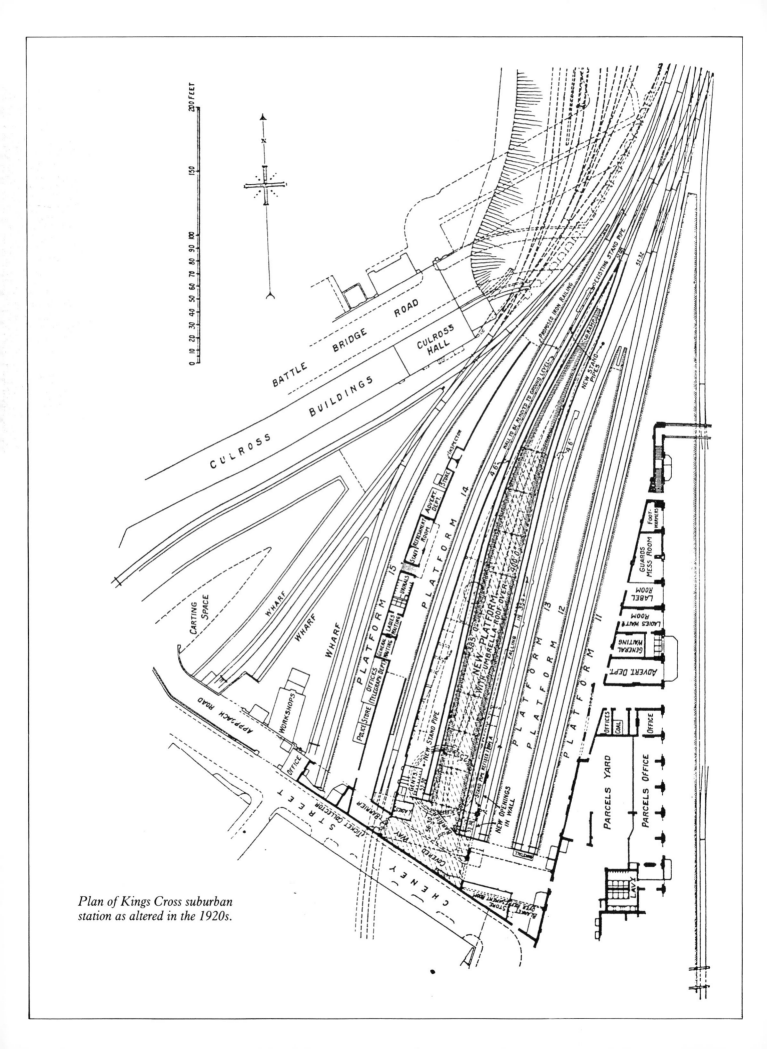

Plan of Kings Cross suburban station as altered in the 1920s.

Atmosphere there certainly was, with the station below street level and suburban trains turning round within five minutes at peak hours in its 18 platforms. Three trains often arrived or departed simultaneously. There was still room to cram in the loco depot – with no allocation of engines – and freight even worked through the station in the dead of night, when transfer trips would go to and from the Great Eastern's depot at New Cross via the East London line and to the Southern yards.

Kings Cross was quite a different affair. The main-line activities were contained within the simple and coherent structure designed by Lewis Cubitt and opened in 1852. The main feature was an elegant double-arched roof, each span being 71ft with a deceptively simple glazed frontage surmounted by a clock tower. Over the years much of this frontage towards Euston Road was allowed to disappear from public gaze behind a jungle eyesore of shops, huts, a show house and other buildings nicknamed the 'African Village'. The present iron roof girders are not the originals; *they* were of laminated timber and gradually spread, threatening the supporting walls. Replacement took place between 1869 and 1887. The pressure from the burgeoning traffic under this roof was such that in 1875 the suburban services were banished to their own adjoining station. Platform numbering was distinctly idiosyncratic. The LNER inherited what became Nos 1–6 and 10 on the main line side and 11–13, 16 and 17 on the suburban. Platforms 14 and 15 were added in 1924 on the site of the old loco yard under a scheme prepared and started by the Great Northern, and 7 and 8 in 1926 in lieu of carriage sidings. There was no No 9. The platform on the up connection to the Metropolitan Widened Lines was always reckoned as a separate station, York Road, and had no link with Kings Cross proper. The down connection (the 'hotel curve' from its path under the Great Northern hotel nearby) used platform 16. The station throat was always very restricted, a permanent way man's nightmare, because of the nearness of the wide-spread platforms to Gasworks Tunnel. It could be taxing in the extreme to get a heavy train out of the platform and up through the tunnel on its 1 in 107 gradient, and after an accident in which a down express slipped and drifted back into the buffers the LNER installed lights on the tunnel walls so that drivers could be sure which way they were moving in the perpetual murk.

Liverpool Street bustled with suburban traffic, and Kings Cross exuded an air of long-distance romance: Marylebone again was a place of quiet gentility. With only four platforms – which were quite enough for the business in hand, though the concourse made provision for eight – it was a very civilised station, beautifully designed for the traffic that never really materialised. The Great Central hotel, the glazed carriage approach, the wood-panelled ticket office all spoke of an unhurried calm, disturbed occasionally by a fast, comfortable and light express. Indeed, this pattern was repeated all along the main line: the stations of the London extension had very much the 'family look', being neat in their red brick, the more important ones with awnings; their very newness and the fact that the staff had plenty of time between trains to keep them smart made them attractive. Most were of the island pattern – even such

Light and shade at Liverpool Street station.

Safety Last
The main entrance to Peterborough station is on the up side. Before the layout was remodelled there was only a footbridge to the down side, with no such luxuries as ramps or lifts. Anything which couldn't walk, such as parcels, mail bags or prams, had to be carried across the two main lines by the porters, who had a very restricted view of down trains approaching round the curve from the Nene bridge.

On the wall on the up platform was a very enlarged block indicator showing 'Line Clear' or 'Train on Line' for down trains. When asked if it was intended as a warning to him not to cross the line with parcels, one of the porters scratched his head, pondered for a while and then said: 'I suppose it must be'.

as Leicester – with platforms reached either by subway or steps down from a roadbridge. It all had the look of having been planned with care and being entirely appropriate to the passenger service, while making provision for the anticipated surge in traffic which never quite came.

Nottingham Victoria was a large station whose central site and extensive acreage were the product of Sir Edward Watkin's ambitions for his expanding Great Central. Essentially it had two large islands, with bays at each end, all contained within an impressive building and located within a cutting; it constituted something of an operational bottleneck by reason of the double-track tunnels at each end. Although built by the Great Central, it was in fact a joint station with the Great Northern, who had previously used their own terminus at London Road, and which had become 'Low Level' when the through platforms were added to take the tracks into Victoria. Even the name was a compromise, since the GN could not possibly have agreed to its being called 'Central'; eventually it took it from the fact that it opened on the Queen's birthday (24 May) in 1900.

In spite of its size and the fast services that it offered to a variety of destinations, many available via the link to the Great Western at Banbury, Nottingham Victoria shared the overprovision of capacity of most of the London extension, and apart from its clock tower has been swept to oblivion. Far less generously built were the original Great Central points inherited from the Manchester, Sheffield & Lincolnshire

Making history at Kings Cross. Crowds line the platforms on 1 May 1928 to watch the departure of the first non-stop Flying Scotsman appropriately hauled by the famous (and now preserved) Gresley class 'A1' Pacific No 4472 Flying Scotsman *driven by Albert Pibworth of Gateshead shed. The load was twelve coaches weighing 386 tons tare. Note that the number is now on the cabside. This was to facilitate the exchange of the new corridor tenders amongst the Pacifics working this service. It was applied generally from 1929.*

Railway forged over the Pennines from Manchester London Road through the notorious Woodhead tunnel, into Sheffield Victoria, and on to Lincoln and the docks at Grimsby. The Pennine stations reflected their surroundings: solid, almost dour, though Woodhead itself had the flourishes of its castellated towers, demolished when the new tunnel was built for electrification. Together with Dunford Bridge at the other end of the tunnel it had been a popular destination for whole and half-day trips for Mancunians, a habit assiduously fostered by the Great Central with excursions and cheap fares. They offered special tickets further afield into Lincolnshire for anglers, since the company had a number of lines in that county. There had also been much rebuilding and improvement to cope with increased traffic generated by the railway docks at Immingham, and stations such as Brocklesby and Barnetby found themselves with four platforms. At the former, the buildings were especially ornate, since Lord Yarborough – first chairman of the MS&L – lived at the nearby hall. The Great Northern had competed with the Great Central for coal traffic, especially in the Derby and Nottingham areas, and they met also at Grimsby, where the passenger station was on the GCR line, though there were separate goods facilities.

The Great Northern had always been planned as a high-speed trunk line, yet its principal stations seem to have been built with maximum economy, above all else, in mind. Even places such as Retford and Newark, on the main line, were spartan affairs with little shelter for

Nottingham Victoria. The southern end of the station looking north with a local train headed by 'B8' class (ex GCR) Glenalmond small wheeled 4-6-0 No 5280 standing in the centre road. The date is the middle 1930s.

A meeting of Atlantics. Sheffield Victoria station in the early 1930s. Three pre-grouping companies are represented here, an ex GNR class 'C1' No 4428 with an ex GCR 'D11' class Director 4-4-0 behind it, stand on the middle road while ex NER 4-4-2 class 'C7' No 2199 is about to leave platform 4 probably with a down Bournemouth to Newcastle express. A station sauntering picture par excellence.

Dilapidation and dirt at York. A less usual photograph of the station, taken from the south end looking north. The date is 1946, just after the end of World War II when the railways were at their most run down with bomb damage often unrepaired (see absence of glass in platform canopy) and engines filthy. In the station are (left to right) No 70 (old No 2569) Gladiateur, one of the NBL batch of 1924, and only just re-numbered (6/46), an unknown 'V2' class 2-6-2 and No 1421, a 'B16/2' class 4-6-0.

passengers. Throughout its twenty-five years existence the LNER had the albatross of Peterborough North station round its corporate neck. It was a cramped, mean-looking edifice, gloomy and chilly under its overall roof. Operationally it was dogged by its 20mph speed restriction over its approach connections. The Great Eastern had its own station (Peterborough East); connections between the two – always important to travellers to East Anglia – were difficult at the best of times.

Doncaster, a major hub of the system, was rebuilt in 1936 to remedy operating bottlenecks, particularly on the up side. The result was a station of two island platforms with new buildings on the up platform in a somewhat 'art deco' style; a tiled subway replaced the original footbridge. At the south end the works footbridge would see quite a stampede at the end of the day's shift.

The North Eastern's main stations reflected a unified approach involving large arched roofs and were monuments to design and elegance. York's present station opened in 1877, and although there have been some alterations, it remains substantially unchanged today. Its magnificent roof, arched and on a curve, covers the main lines and platforms, with other arches over the bays. There were fourteen platforms; two more, Nos 15 and 16, were brought in as through platforms in 1951 with the resignalling, their stark awnings contrasting harshly with the older parts. Closure of some of the platforms took place in 1988–9 as the layout was prepared for electrification. York was a place of great activity, where engines were once changed on the Scottish trains; heavy traffic from the Leeds direction; holidaymakers to Scarborough, trains to Harrogate and branches to Whitby via Pickering and Hull via Market Weighton all contributed. The situation was incomparable: right by the city wall, with the covered portico leading into the booking hall, which had its NER map made from glazed wall tiles (a feature of many of the company's stations). Between York and Northallerton, widening to four tracks between 1933 and 1942 resulted in the attractive rebuilding of four country stations, either totally or on one side only. Beningbrough, Alne, Raskelf and Otterington were built in brick with stone entrances and chalet roofs. Alas, their public life was short.

Newcastle Central was the largest and busiest on the North Eastern. In some respects it closely resembles York. On the north bank of the river Tyne, it was orientated on a curve on an east-west axis, though its major services ran from north to south. It was also the focus for the North Eastern's only real suburban service, most of what remains now being incorporated into the Tyne & Wear Metro. Designed originally by John Dobson, it was opened in 1850, though the colonnade and portico was not provided until 1863. It featured a soaring main arched roof flanked by three smaller arches. Local trains to the coast used bay platforms at the east end on the north side. Trains from the lines over the High Level bridge conflicted with those from the coast via Manors at the much-photographed 'largest railway crossing in the world', with its myriad of cast manganese steel diamonds. Trains to Carlisle used bays at the west end. For a station of its importance, it is perhaps surprising that Newcastle had only three through platforms.

Hull Paragon. A late LNER photograph taken on 14 April 1947 of a local train (probably to Hornsea or Withernsea) headed by ex GNR Ivatt class 'C12' 4-4-2T No 7394.

Too Many

Summer Sundays and Bank Holidays could be exhilarating – and sometimes excessively worrying – to the operating people on the LNER's seaside lines. You never knew how many excursionists were going to turn up, extra trains from industrial centres often having to be put on at short (or no) notice.

The real nightmare, however, was if it suddenly rained and thousands abandoned their day at the sea and made for the station, expecting instant cartage home. At least they normally went to the beach for a while. A problem of an entirely new kind arose at the Cup Final in 1923 when, after 120,000 poured into and overfilled Wembley Stadium, thousands were told it was full and to go home. With nowhere to go they spilled onto the tracks. The return trains were rapidly in action, to the chagrin of their crews enjoying a well-deserved rest.

Marylebone's inadequate traffic was added to by a shuttle service to Wembley. It used a loop line, Merry-Go-Round principle, with a single platform, and proved especially effective for the British Empire Exhibition in 1924 and 1925.

The North Eastern had always had its own architect, of whom the most notable was probably William Bell. Early railway development was often piecemeal, with a line being opened in stages by different companies; enlargements and alterations then took place to further complicate matters. However, later lines often had much more of a uniform appearance, and one such was that between Alnwick and Coldstream, where Bell provided a series of stations of pleasing and uniform basic design. Built of local stone, they had a station house flanked by booking office and other buildings. Half-hipped roofs were characteristic, and a wooden-fronted waiting shelter was incorporated on the platform side. The line was not opened until 1887 and, as with so many relative latecomers, these beautiful stations suffered an early loss of passenger services, in 1930. But many of them survive in private use.

The North British was Scotland's largest before Grouping, owning both the East Coast main line from Berwick and the celebrated Waverley route. Its tentacles reached up the west coast to Fort William and Mallaig, though it needed running powers over the Caledonian to reach Aberdeen from Kinnaber Junction. It was a major railway by any standards and in terms of acreage its showpiece, Edinburgh Waverley, was the LNER's largest. It lay in the bottom of a narrow valley between old and new towns and was approached through tunnels at both ends. The Waverley – it was always 'the' Waverley in the Scottish capital – was opened in June 1846, and later that year the Edinburgh & Glasgow extended its line from Haymarket, through Princes Street Gardens in the shadow of the Castle rock into its west end. It was completely rebuilt, under intense pressure of expanding suburban services, between 1892 and 1900. In this form it became a very broad island platform, its two through faces long enough to handle two expresses with scissors crossovers in the centre.

Set in the ends were series of seven and eight bay platforms, from which departed not only the local services but also the Aberdeen and Waverley route expresses. Access to the station was by two inclined carriage roads from the Waverley Bridge or for pedestrians by the Waverley steps (eighty or so of them!) up which a strong and often icy wind consistently blew. The extensive stone building in the centre housed all the necessary facilities including a fine booking hall with mosaic floor and stained glass ceiling feature. All was enclosed between high stone walls and covered within a transverse ridge and furrow roof, as though the station wished to go about its business out of sight of the vulgar horde. Outside the wall on the south side was a long island platform – the 'suburban' station, clearly an afterthought – providing platforms 20 and 21. High above the whole complex strode the North Bridge, the main access to the suburbs beyond the old town: it was overshadowed by the ornately magnificent bulk of the North British hotel and its clock tower – always three minutes fast to hurry the tardy traveller. Though great had been the opposition to the railway conquering the very centre of the capital and dominating it even from

Newcastle Central. A view from the east c1959 showing an unknown 'A4' class Pacific on the famous crossing with the up Elizabethan; the visible stock is of Thompson design in BR maroon livery. Note the Tyneside electrics in the platform to the right and the class 'J72' 0-6-0 tank as station pilot.

Hurry, Please

The Great Northern suburban services were worked by N1, N2 and N7 0-6-2s, the N2s being the most popular. The trains ran from Hitchin and the Cambridge branch and from the branches serving Hertford North, Edgware, High Barnet and Alexandra Palace. All these services converged on Finsbury Park, from whence the trains ran to Kings Cross, Moorgate via the Widened Lines, or Broad Street via Dalston, giving good services to the City. Most of the trains in LNER days were made up of two quadruple articulated sets, each train holding 648 passengers sitting six-a-side with their knees interlocked. For standing passengers it was probably the most uncomfortable journey possible.

In the down direction in the evening peak at Finsbury Park three trains were periodically platformed side by side, the middle train having a platform each side. One train would be from Moorgate, one from Kings Cross and one from Broad Street, and they would be for three different destinations. Station time was very short. Only today's oldest commuters would believe what a scramble it used to be interchanging passengers through the very restricted compartments of the middle train, already full of passengers, between the two outer trains.

Another experience never to be repeated was to ride in an evening peak train from Moorgate. Before the peak commenced a light engine
continued opposite

its bottom-of-the-valley position (though the great hotel standing aloft almost challenged the castle), the Scots became justifiably proud of 'the Waverley'. Indeed it has been at the very pulse of the nation's life. Mean is not an adjective that could possibly be applied to it – yet mean is exactly what Dundee Tay Bridge was, a bit like Waverley seen through the wrong end of a telescope. Even the modest Dundee East, the original terminus of the line to Arbroath, had more style.

In Glasgow matters were chaotic for many years. The North British's principal passenger station was at Queen Street beneath another high, vaulted overall roof. This had been heavily congested, but in 1886 in conjunction with the new underground railway, Queen Street Low Level, four platforms of Stygian gloom, was opened, and eased matters considerably. Not least of the problems of the High Level station was the fierce Cowlairs Incline, which had originally required cable haulage: only in recent years and with modern traction has this ceased to be the operators' nightmare.

On the Waverley route towns such as Hawick and Galashiels had fine stations of local stone, the first featuring a footbridge that went *under* the line, which emerged on to a viaduct at this point. Riccarton Junction's only raison d'etre was to act as a transfer point with the line to Reedsmouth and Hexham, and to house engines. Railway staff, for whom the company had built cottages, had no other link with the outside world. For sheer charm the West Highland line stations between Craigendoran and Spean Bridge were unequalled. They showed considerable uniformity of style; most were of the island pattern, and had chalet-style buildings with hipped roofs, wide overhangs and central shelters; even the signal boxes were on the platforms. Crianlarich was one of the larger examples, having an engine shed and boasting a refreshment room. The isolation of some West Highland stations was

North Eastern Railway penetrating line. Barnard Castle station – a junction on the single-line railway from Darlington to Kirkby Stephen and Tebay or Penrith linking east coast with west. In the platform on an eastbound train is ex NER 0-6-0 now LNER class 'J21' No 899. It is a wet 4 June 1935.

Peterborough

Although Peterborough North has always been a key junction of the GN and LNER East Coast Main Line, the GE and two constituents of the LMS were the first to arrive in the city. The LNWR branch from Blisworth to Peterborough was opened in 1845, and the Midland arrived from Stamford in 1846. From 1 January 1847 the latter was worked in connection with the Eastern Counties extension to Peterborough from Ely and Cambridge. By 1848 this constituted a through route from the Midland main line at Syston through to the Eastern Counties, across what was to become Great Northern territory. The Great Northern finally arrived from London in August 1850, the original main line to the north being via Spalding, Boston, Lincoln and Retford. The route via Grantham and Newark to Retford was opened two years later.

The last route to arrive was that of the Peterborough, Lynn & Sutton Bridge Railway, which became part of the Midland & Great Northern Joint Railway. It came into Peterborough from the east, crossing the GN and Midland lines by a large overbridge known locally as 'Rhubarb Bridge' and connecting with the Midland at Wisbech Junction and the Great Northern at Westwood Junction. The Midland continued south alongside the GN past the North station and under the GN to the GE's East station, which also accommodated the trains of the LNWR. The GN had access to the GE via the connection with the Midland at Crescent Junction, at the south end of Peterborough North station.

At one time there were four locomotive depots in the Peterborough area, and several marshalling yards. The Midland and LNW freight trains were handled at the marshalling yard at Peterborough East. GN fast freights were handled at Westwood Yard, where sections were attached and detached, an operation carried out very quickly. The main marshalling yard was New England. From Werrington Junction there were three up freight lines to New England North, independent of the up Main, and there was a heavy flow of freight and coal trains arriving from the north via the East Coast main line or the loop line via Spalding. New England was also the location of the GN locomotive depot, which was always one of the most important on the whole system. Sorted trains were despatched south from New England either via the GE line to the Eastern Counties or up the GN Main Line to Ferme Park Yard. There was also a heavy flow of brick traffic from Fletton, south of Peterborough.

The layout at Peterborough caused many problems. There is no wonder that when lines were chock-a-block with traffic tension mounted as time approached for one of the LNER's famous expresses to pass through – having to reduce speed considerably but treating Peterborough with the disdain of an aircraft overhead.

The North station was on a very sharp curve, restricting through trains to 20mph. An up relief line passed on the west side of the station, but trains using it to by-pass one standing in the up platform had to cross the down main line twice. Down freights calling at Westwood or New England had to cross the up main. In LNER and LMS days most of the trains from Stamford ran straight past North station to the East, very annoying to any passengers wanting to go forward on the GN side of the LNER. Although a shuttle service operated between the two stations many passengers had to walk between them. After nationalisation the LNE and LMS lines all became part of the Eastern Region. In the course of time East station and yard were closed, as were the LNW lines and the M&GN. Midland trains were diverted into North station, and trains to and from the Eastern Counties ran from there.

Signalling had always been controlled by numerous manual signalboxes. One curiosity was that down Midland trains crossing to the GN at Westwood Junction became up GN trains. In BR days a major NX power signalbox was constructed on the west side of the Midland lines controlling many route miles of track. The GN Down Slow was removed to a point beyond Helpston. The old up Midland line to Stamford is now also used as the Down Slow of the GN, northbound trains crossing back beyond Helpston. The greatest improvement has been the rebuilding of North station and the straightening of the main lines to remove the speed restriction. As at so many places the operating problems have disappeared – along with most of the traffic which caused them.

Peterborough North station (serving the GN main line and MR stations to Leicester plus the M & GN to Wisbech and Sutton Bridge) looking north from the roadbridge. On the left are the MR lines which come from the East station (former Great Eastern Railway) under the GN main line, then curving sharply round and rising to run parallel.

5
EAST ANGLIA

Stripping

After the war we had a spate of people pulling communication cords; suburban trains mostly to Enfield or Chingford; boy also meets girl. The procedure was for the operating department which was understandably indignant at the damage to its punctuality and the duty to the people in the three or four following trains to apply to the Chief of Police for a prosecution. We got nowhere with this. Magistrates thought Norman Jesper's men were of full and merry habit who thought a turn-up with a girl in a train no more than anyone could expect and did not care a fig for our punctuality. The six hundred people in the trains behind could get on with it too if they had a mind.

Eventually came a case which I thought even wall-eyed old Norman could not ignore. Between Bethnal Green and Cambridge Heath there descended from a window a scarf, a pullover, a bra and a roll-on. Then she rose like a rocket and pulled the cord. The guard's report was in highly puritanical tone. I wrote in a state of high moral indignation to Norman once again, who once again said No and added that we must leave him to judge where to draw the line. I wrote back: 'In order to save further useless correspondence would he lay down as a principle whether he was going to draw the line above or below the belt.' Norman took this with the utmost gravity and reported me to my boss for the exercise of a Wiccanical sense of humour on serious subjects. And I suppose it was a serious subject. Certainly the punctuality was. – Gerry Fiennes.

IT is perhaps ironic that while BR started by having a North Eastern Region, at the time of writing it is instead East Anglia that has a form of autonomy. The need for some self government and improved pride of course results from poor morale, and part of that can be traced back to LNER days. For in 1923 it was obvious that the Great Eastern section would be the odd one out, the hardest sensibly to absorb into any kind of unity, and so it proved. Not that the LNER, at first particularly tolerant of local practices, ever sought standardisation in the LMS manner, but there were many unique and difficult features about East Anglia.

The chief of these was that while the Great Eastern easily excelled any of the other constituents in passenger traffic, it was almost entirely due to the enormous volumes of what we today call commuters emanating from the eastern and north-eastern suburbs of London – carried on the celebrated 'Jazz' service it had inaugurated in 1920; the most intensive steam service in the world. The sheer number of passengers alas did not translate into attractive economics, for the overwhelming majority were third class and conveyed at extremely cheap fares.

To cope with this, electrification had been proposed and one joint GER line, the East London Railway, was actually electrified in 1913 but worked by Metropolitan trains. However Holden's (the locomotive engineer) demonstration of the 'Decapod' and the remarkable acceleration of his little 0-6-0Ts and later the 0-6-2Ts of Hill enabled trains carrying 1000 passengers to be hauled up the 1 in 70 of Bethnal Green bank very speedily, operating on close headways and with very tight timetables. From this base Sir Henry Thornton was able to introduce the Jazz service in 1920.

He used existing locomotives and carriages many of them four-wheelers. A short bay was installed at the end of each suburban platform to make quick turnrounds possible. The compartment stock could empty and fill very quickly, so that a four minute interval between arrival and departure was practicable. As the incoming train drew into Liverpool Street, the outward locomotive followed it in. The crews at both ends uncoupled and coupled at furious speed while the passengers boarded and the train could then plough through the murk to Walthamstow or Enfield alternately. The GER spent about £80,000 on track and signalling improvements rather than the millions that electrification would have cost. It was the passengers who continued to endure six a side seating in sooty surroundings to the accompaniment of the Westinghouse pump.

70

Murk at Liverpool Street. The city atmosphere is further polluted by two ex Great Eastern Railway classes during the late 1930s. On the left is a class 'F4' or 'F5' tank fitted with condensing pipes for use over the Underground lines, whilst about to leave for East Anglia is reboilered 'B12' class 4-6-0 as 'B12/3' No 8578, a Gresley modification.

Up from the flatlands. A Gresley-designed 'B17' class three-cylinder 4-6-0 No 2814 Castle Hedingham takes an Ipswich to Liverpool Street train up Belstead bank in 1937. Built in 1930 No 2814 was reconstructed by Thompson as a two-cylinder 'B2' in 1946.

Beyond the suburbs, the Great Eastern served an almost entirely rural area, with no major centres of industry. To be sure, it enjoyed almost as much a monopoly as did the North Eastern in its region, but the nature of the territory and traffics could scarcely have been more different. In East Anglia the potential was at best modest, the volume of coal and mineral business very small. All-the-year-round long-distance passenger business on the main lines via Colchester and Cambridge was also surprisingly modest, the Great Eastern having to rely heavily on its peak summer seaside traffic to the coastal resorts (again much of it at cheap fares yet because of its sharp seasonal nature expensive to operate) and on its Continental service via Harwich (Parkeston Quay). The latter assumed an importance beyond its actual scale through lack of more substantial regular flows elsewhere.

The main line from Liverpool Street through Colchester to Norwich was difficult enough, with its bottleneck immediately on starting from London, heavy gradients and severe restrictions especially over the bridges with their curved approaches at the heads of navigable water, but most places in East Anglia were served by branches of which there were many of varying quality. Some, such as the Clacton and Harwich branches and the East Suffolk line, the lines between Norwich and Lowestoft and Yarmouth, and the line from Haughley via Bury St Edmunds to Cambridge and Ely, were subsidiary main lines, whose trains were generally fewer not to mention slower than visitors from

Essex junction. An unknown 'B12/3' class 4-6-0 enters Marks Tey with an up empty stock train in the summer of 1949. Marks Tey was the junction for a straggling cross-country line to Cambridge which ran a through train from Birmingham to Clacton on summer Saturdays (up to 1958).

more progressive parts of Britain imagined possible. Most others were of course single line, generally even less well served. They varied from the long branches, such as that from Marks Tey to Shelford via Sudbury (Suffolk), some 43 miles, to the Kelvedon & Tollesbury and the Elsenham & Thaxted Light Railways which, however important a role they played in the economy of their districts, seemed simply light years away from the world of twentieth-century progress. Oddities also included the Wisbech & Upwell Tramway, with its little tramway engines, looking rather like goods brake vans with their chimneys protruding through the roof. These little engines, of which there were 0-4-0 and 0-6-0 classes, also worked on some of the dock tramways at Wisbech, Yarmouth, Ipswich and Hythe (Colchester).

In addition to the ex-GER branches, there were two independent railways which became subsidiary companies under the LNER; one was the Colne Valley & Halstead Railway, an efficient and well-managed line, which ran between Chappel and Haverhill via Halstead, joining the ex-GER Marks Tey – Shelford line at each end; the other was the Mid Suffolk Light Railway, running for 19 miles from Haughley to Laxfield through beautiful but sparsely-populated country. It was only a part of the system originally projected, the remainder not having been built because of lack of money. The CV&HR posed no problems for the LNER, which duly absorbed it in 1923, but the Mid Suffolk caused more difficulty, as the company had been in the hands of a receiver since

Sweedie Junction. Thetford in East Anglia, on the main line from Ely to Norwich, was the junction station from Bury St Edmunds and Swaffham. These single lines into the heartlands of East Anglia were regularly worked by ex Great Eastern Railway engines, usually the sturdy 'E4' class Intermediate 2-4-0s (the last of the type to be operable in Great Britain) and 'J15' class 0-6-0s. In the spring of 1952, 'E4' class No 62788 has come in from Swaffham with the morning train. Note the tender cab for tender first running when necessary.

Mid Suffolk Light Railway. Laxfield station, the terminus of the line from Haughley Junction, situated on the main line from Ipswich to Norwich. This was worked by tender cab fitted 'J15' class 0-6-0s using old GER six-wheeled stock on mixed trains. No 5470 is at Laxfield on Easter Tuesday 1952.

1906, and the LNER did not wish to take it over until all its debts had been settled – if at all. Litigation ensued, and it was only under a Court Order that the LNER was induced to take control on 1 July 1924.

At the time of the grouping, increasing road competition was becoming felt, and between 1928 and 1932 the LNER was obliged to withdraw the passenger services from the Wisbech & Upwell Tramway, the Ramsey (East), Stoke Ferry, Eye and Hadleigh branches, as well as the line from Ely to St Ives via Sutton. The freight services, however, were retained, the Wisbech & Upwell Tramway, in particular, carrying an enormous fruit and vegetable traffic.

Throughout the interwar years, the beet season was marked by sidings full of sugar beet wagons at every small station in East Anglia, helping cushion the effects of the loss of other freight. And though there was generally over capacity, the only major competitor to the Great Eastern, the Midland & Great Northern Joint (running on the GE's northern flank from Peterborough to the northern parts of Norfolk) was kept busy in the beet as well as the short tourist season.

The LNER fairly soon began to change some Great Eastern practices. Distant signals were given a yellow instead of red light for their 'caution' aspect, and upper quadrant signals fitted as older ones needed replacement – though several GER signals survived well into BR days. (Electric signalling installed at Cambridge in 1926 had lower quadrant semaphores.) More radical and certainly more welcome by passengers was the immediate start on replacing the GER's still largely four-wheeled suburban stock.

74

The GE did of course boast some excellent trains of its own bogie stock and Pullmans, notably to seaside resorts and Harwich Parkeston Quay. Pullmans continued to operate on the latter along with ordinary restaurant cars until the outbreak of war in 1939, but the others – less successful – were transferred to the GN section. However, in 1928 an all-Pullman *Clacton Pullman* was introduced on Sundays only. Immediately successful, next summer it was renamed the *Eastern Belle* and in addition to running to Clacton on Sundays took a different route to the seaside each day from Mondays to Fridays. Extremely popular, it ran every summer until 1939. Saturday was the day of mass transfers at the beginning and end of the holiday week and there was no room for a luxurious Pullman. Timekeeping on the busiest Saturdays was at best unreliable, though the mood at Liverpool Street more jovial.

The operation of the peak summer Saturday trains, and also Sunday and Bank Holiday excursion traffic, as well as the suburban services, was greatly helped by the quadrupling of the Colchester main line from Romford to Gidea Park in 1931, and thence to Shenfield in 1934. Colour light signalling went along with the widening and was continued to Chelmsford in 1937. Though always well below East Coast main line standards, and always suffering from its weight limitations, the Colchester route saw steady accelerations culminating in 1937 with the introduction of the *East Anglian* between London and Norwich calling

Station peculiar. Halesworth station on the GER main line, well known for its level crossing in the middle of the platforms, with the platform faces forming an integral part of the crossing gates (clearly shown in the photograph) and for its being the junction with the somewhat notorious 3ft 0in gauge Southwold Railway – the first of Britain's public narrow-gauge lines to close to all traffic (1929) in the inter-war years.

Main line to Cambridge. An ex GER 4-6-0 as LNER class 'B12' No 8559 at the head of a twelve-coach train mostly of Great Eastern stock near Whittlesford on 23 June 1932. This was the Indian Summer period for the 'B12s' as the new Gresley 'B17' class, three-cylinder 4-6-0s, had been introduced at the end of 1928.

Class 'J24' 0-6-0 No 1956 heads north out of York on a pick up freight in August 1938. The towers of the Minster can just be seen under the signal gantry which has 100 per cent NER lower quadrant arms.

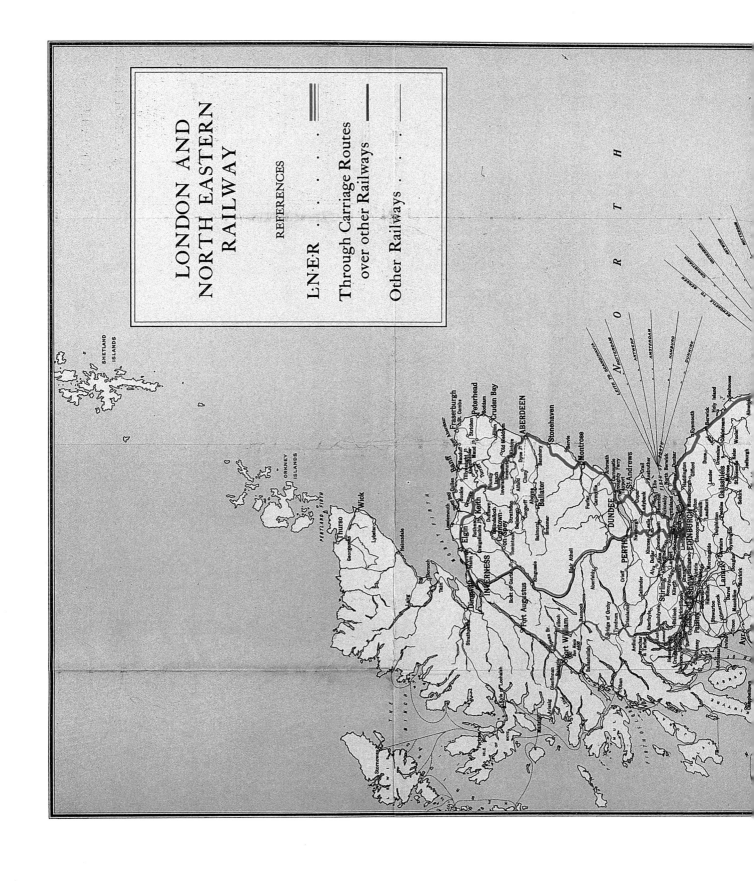

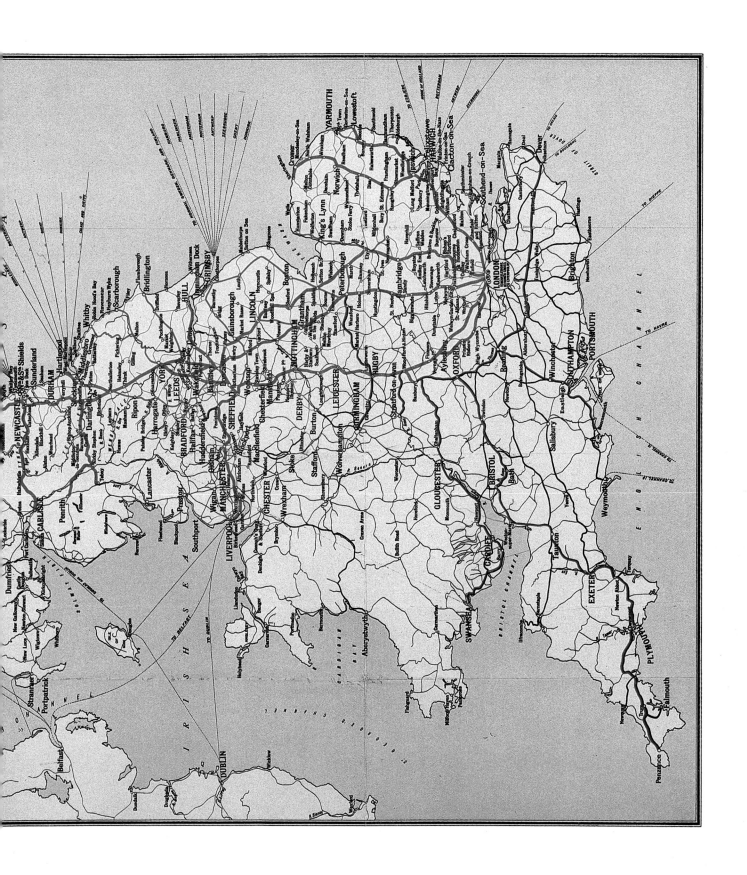

only at Ipswich. This covered the 115 miles in 140 (later 130) minutes. In the same year, two non-stop buffet expresses were started between London and Cambridge in each direction in the unprecedented time of 65 minutes. In 1938 a luxurious new train was built for the *Hook Continental* which, including two Pullmans, totalled thirteen coaches.

So at least East Anglia participated in the general revival and enthusiasm for the new age in the thirties, and its travellers generally regarded the Grouping and the LNER as good things. Clacton and Ely were early station rebuilds. Steam heating at last became the norm on suburban trains. The final abolition of second class on the suburban services at the end of 1937 meant that many paying third-class fares could for the first time enjoy a modicum of comfort on their journey to work; great was the competition for the ex-seconds now marked 3, which is not surprising considering how rudimentary the real thirds were. (First class was abolished in 1941.) Three GE slip carriages survived Grouping, and the LNER added a fourth at Shenfield in the winter of 1929–30. The last was at Marks Tey on 30 June 1939.

The war naturally brought severe reductions in speeds and frequencies of passenger services, but even some of the most rural lines were taxed to capacity with increased agricultural and other freight, and the GE system also carried a massive amount of military traffic, especially when the US Air Force established its numerous air fields through East Anglia. At the end of the war, many of the Great Eastern lines and their rolling stock were in even more run-down condition than most of Britain's railways. The little branch train, hauled by an old Holden engine, remained as much part of the East Anglian scene as the ancient churches and pink-washed cottages of the villages through which it passed for over half a century well into BR days.

Yet the Great Eastern's locomotive stock of 1923 was of excellent quality. It just grew older. Though from 1928 onwards Gresley's 'Sandringham' 4-6-0s, with some other standard LNER and ex-GNR locomotives, were drafted into use on the hardest main-line duties, the great majority of trains continued to be hauled by Great Eastern engines throughout the LNER era and well beyond. What had once been the most modern piece of machinery in the countryside ended almost as an anachronism. The nature of the traffic it carried changed several times, in peace and war, with the agricultural revolution and the coming of buses and lorries, and in many cases it died away until at the end many trains were nearly empty. No region was to suffer more from closures after nationalisation than East Anglia; no terminus has seen a greater reduction in the number of destinations served by through train or coach than Liverpool Street. Yet today's railwaymen have to work much less hard than their GE and LNER forebears in linking London with the regional capital, Norwich. Whatever criticisms might have been levied at LNER East Anglia, they tried hard, with often smart working against harsh obstacles.

Class 'B3/2' 4-6-0 No 6166 Earl Haig *with Caprotti valve gear leaving Aylesbury in December 1938 at the head of a Manchester–Marylebone express. This photograph shows the varnished teak livery well. No 6166 was rebuilt with two cylinders, a larger wheel version of class B1, in 1943.*

Class 'A1' 4-6-2 No 2548 Galtee More *under the coaling plant at York North Shed in 1937. Although impoverished the LNER still managed to keep its main line locomotives reasonably clean.*

LNER Personalities

The LNER was extremely fortunate in its choice of senior management. The company had a goodly array to choose from the amalgamated companies where co-operation had been good in pre-grouping days. They worked together from 1923 until 1938 when William Whitelaw retired, taking the railway through the depression and restoring its pride if not fully its finances before World War 2 took it into uncharted waters.

Whitelaw and Wedgwood

The first chairman was William Whitelaw, a landowner, industrialist, MP, and deeply involved with the General Assembly of the Church of Scotland. A former chairman of the Highland Railway, he was chairman of the North British Railway at grouping and his appointment helped give Scottish pride in the new LNER. In competition with him were Lord Faringdon of the Great Central, Viscount Grey of Falloden of the North Eastern, and possibly Sir Eric Geddes, formerly of the NER but latterly a minister in Lloyd George's government with special transport flair. The chairmen of the other major constituents were in their seventies, less eligible for the mammoth task ahead.

The work of first assembling an able management team and then of assigning duties, creating a new structure on a scale three times that ever attempted before, was led by Ralph Lewis Wedgwood who came from the NER as Chief General Manager. He had graduated in classics at Cambridge, been the first traffic apprentice on the NER scheme that the LNER unsurprisingly adopted and had risen to be general manager. As with Whitelaw, Wedgwood faced little competition for the post as Sir Sam Fay of the GCR was near retiring age and Sir Henry Thornton of the GER had been lured back to his native North America by the offer of a top post with the new Canadian National Railways. Wedgwood's assistant was Robert Bell, a Scot who had likewise assisted his chief on the NER. He became mainly involved in personnel management, appointing the young 'high flyers' whom he moved around in a large range of jobs with great rapidity so that they could prove themselves at an early stage. There were of course casualties of this system, but it did produce many who went on to become major figures both on the LNER and later BR.

The organisation decided for the new company by this formidable trio was federal in nature. Four areas, Southern, North Eastern, Southern Scottish and Northern Scottish represented the GER, GNR and GCR in the south, NER and Hull & Barnsley in north east England and the NBR and GNSR in Scotland. The two Scottish areas were later amalgamated so that the balance of traffic in the areas was roughly 50 per cent for the Southern, 30 per cent for the North Eastern and 20 per cent for the Scottish. Each area had its hierarchy locally, often composed of stalwarts of the original companies, such as Sidney Parnwell of the GER who became Divisional General Manager Southern Area, based at Liverpool Street. This resulted in fewer noticeable changes on the LNER than on any other company except the GWR. Given the wide geographical spread of the LNER and its endemic poverty, this was probably the best possible scheme.

For the next fifteen years the general manager (who was knighted shortly after the grouping), was apprised of system-wide problems by his area staff and took decisions which with hindsight appear generally of a high standard. William Whitelaw presided genially, travelled extensively and was famed for getting to know staff of all grades. He particularly liked the tours in the inspection coach and checking over stations and staff. The more scholarly Wedgwood appeared somewhat more aloof, but there was no doubt about his firm grip on detail amid the looser federal structure of the LNER.

Whitelaw's retirement in July 1938 was quickly followed by Wedgwood's in March 1939, marked by the renaming of an 'A4' Pacific at Marylebone as a farewell tribute. The LNER not only lost the services of Wedgwood but also the 'A4' named after him – which was destroyed in an air raid on York in April 1942.

It was the end of an era in more ways than one. Their successors, Sir Ronald Matthews replacing Whitelaw and C. H. Newton succeeding Wedgwood, although ably steering the LNER through the war years, never had the same aura as the company's founders; the men who had modernised on a shoestring, supported the advances of the 1930s, brought in a host of able youngsters, often from university backgrounds, were indeed a hard act to follow.

Nigel Gresley

Herbert Nigel Gresley (Sir Nigel as he became in 1936), first as locomotive superintendent of the Great Northern Railway from 1911 and then chief mechanical engineer of the LNER from 1923, held the reins for thirty years. He was an enduring feature of the railway scene; his long experience ensured that his work provoked interest and his opinions were sought and respected even if sometimes challenged. In the 1930s he was a mellowed figure who exuded confidence. His unexpected death in harness in 1941, at the age of 64, thus seemed doubly tragic.

In his early days Gresley was highly ambitious and shrewd. Trained at Crewe and thereafter starting up the promotional ladder on the Lancashire & Yorkshire, he could see himself waiting for dead men's shoes if he did not break away. So he transferred to the Great Northern, whose locomotive superintendent, H. A. Ivatt, was within six years of retirement. Gresley slipped behind Ivatt's desk, at the early age of 35, as naturally as a hen on its nest.

Come the LNER in 1923, and Gresley found himself facing two other notable possibles for the CME's chair; Sir Vincent Raven (NER) and John G. Robinson (GCR), were senior to him. The LNER Board seriously considered appointing Robinson, then 64, but it was

A mark of respect. Marylebone station on 3 September 1939 when 'A4' Pacific No 4469 (originally Gadwall) was re-named *Sir Ralph Wedgwood.*

H. N. Gresley Chief Mechanical Engineer LNER.

Robinson who recommended Gresley. The appointment was without doubt right, for Gresley had already shown, with his first two Pacifics completed by the GNR in 1922, the better grasp of locomotive needs for the new company. But he had the virtue of being able to recognise the good features of other people's products and use them to advantage.

Astutely, Gresley promptly moved his personal office away from the Doncaster Works atmosphere to Kings Cross. Here he was at the seat of power, adjacent to the chief general manager and the Board. He was a master of the diplomatic but persuasive approach, which usually got him what he wanted. despite the severe financial stringency. He managed to get money to build a fleet of locomotives which were total masters of their work with something in reserve for the future (which was not always the case elsewhere). The footplate staff were generally delighted with what he gave them. Those responsible for their maintenance were expected to contend with their mechanical weaknesses as best they could.

And there *were* weaknesses, some of which reached quite serious proportions as speeds were pushed upwards and workings became harder. Some were speedily put right. Others – mainly of works relevance – were seemingly not recognised or else ignored. Perhaps liaison between the CME and the people at the sharp end needed to be closer, or perhaps there was a stubborn streak of self-satisfaction.

But by their deeds ye shall know them, and Gresley could overlay the blemishes with a great deal of solid achievement. In the forefront must be his work to produce the streamlined trains of 1935–7, not just in the locomotive field but also with the coaches; they set new standards of design and comfort, be it noted by engineers rather than interior designers. The result was to revolutionise the LNER's passenger image, and thereby that of the whole railway. With the achievement must go the convincing capture of the world speed record with steam traction of 126mph, established by his 'A4' *Mallard*, which was never surpassed. The engine's preservation is a constant reminder of Gresley's eminence.

L. P. Parker

Though not so high up the management tree as the others in this selection, Leslie Preston Parker is included as an outstanding and 'running' man of his generation. He had been a Great Eastern premium apprentice, obtaining the coveted Whitworth Scholarship. At an early age he moved into the running department and in 1925, when no more than 37, he was appointed district locomotive superintendent at Stratford, ruling that vast and volatile empire with a rod of iron, until he became locomotive running superintendent of the Eastern Section of the LNER in 1940. Retiring in 1953, he died a year later.

He will never be forgotten by those who served him. He drove them very hard indeed but he was intensely interested in their performance and prospects – provided that they measured up to his demands. Bespectacled, smartly dressed with bow tie, he would start the day by analysing the morning peak running. 'Tell me, why was the 6.58 from Clacton five minutes late arriving this morning?' 'I don't know, sir, but I'll find out.' 'You don't know? You really are an amateur!'

While he delegated, he knew exactly what was happening, and when he paid a visit to a shed, the man in charge would expect to be systematically dismembered, especially by the familiar 'Tell me why?' But he was capable of great kindness and generosity and a humour all the more enjoyable for its unexpectedness. 'LP' had the great strength of character and purpose to impose on the enginemen of the Eastern Section his dictum of the 'Open Regulator'. Through his subordinates, he persuaded that marvellously independent breed to work their engines expansively with a well-opened regulator, and there is no doubt that the success of the 'Britannias' and others on the GE Line was due to him.

Having maintained the GE practice of crews keeping to their own engines, with its great advantages of pride, interest and reliability, he was appalled to find that standards on the GN main line had barely recovered from wartime levels due to the operating superintendent's reliance on common-usage. The last great years of steam on the East Coast main line would never have been possible without Parker's implacable insistence that engine changes and long-distance lodging turns should be so arranged that men kept their own engines.

Parker's young men emerged sometimes as discerning managers and administrators, as managers of men, as able engineers: all had the 'seeing eye' of their chief. Men respected but feared him. He rarely if ever raised his voice, he used no strong language, he was precise and economical of speech, and he feared no one. Soon after 1948, when the steam suburban service out of Liverpool Street was at its worst, he was called upon to be present at a large meeting chaired by Barrington Ward attended by senior officers. 'Now, Parker, what have you got to say?' LP, at his smartest, said nothing. Then, with formidably twinkling eyes, he drew quietly on his pipe, expelled a single and delicate puff of smoke and replied: 'Nothing to report'. He never made excuses.

It could not be said that he had the common touch, but then he was not expected to have it. He rarely went into the vast Stratford shed, but on one pre-war occasion he was crossing the front of the Jubilee shed, bowler, furled umbrella and spats. A tank engine was taking water nearby. Suddenly the water overflowed on to axle-boxes, valve gear and track; the fireman, who had been making the tea, dashed across to turn the water off and found himself confronted by Parker. 'Tell me, fireman, when you are at home, do you allow your bath to overflow?' 'Barf, guv, barf, I ain't got a bleedin' barf!'

When he died, many who had suffered under his rule went to his funeral saddened, for they knew they had lost their champion.

6
LOCOMOTIVES

THE often-told story has already been hinted at in earlier pages but remains one of the fascinations of locomotive history, a paradox that grows more interesting as you study the detail.

The LNER inherited an old and rapidly ageing locomotive stock and had no alternative but to let it grow steadily older. Cases were cited of enginemen spending a whole long career (cleaner, fireman, driver) on a single class. Many classes were confined to small districts and remained unknown even to those taking a keen interest in 'their' LNER, while the general lack of glamour resulted in the company's machines being poorly represented on model railways.

Yet this was the company that developed what are generally accepted as the finest express locomotives Britain ever saw – possibly the best in Europe. They included what was undoubtedly the world's single most famous locomotive and that whose steam speed record will probably never be beaten. Gresley's Pacifics were however not just show pieces but fine everyday working machines which forged new levels of high-speed service and especially paved the way for InterCity's achievement on the East Coast main line in our own time.

Now, the Great Central line from Marylebone to Manchester was not *the* LNER by a long chalk, but in the early 1930s it vividly illustrated facets of locomotive policy typical of the whole system. Unlike the LMS, which it crossed at Rugby (on which new standard engines seemed to appear almost daily), it was worked almost entirely by pre-grouping types, still doing the job they were designed for well before World War I. They hammered over the Great Central bridge with predictable regularity. On the 10.00 and 12.15 one saw 'Directors'. The 15.20 down was either a 'Director' or 'Lord Faringdon' job. The prestige 16.55 to Sheffield and the 18.20 Bradford were invariably Robinson Atlantic preserves. The freights between Annesley and Woodford saw nothing but Robinson's 'O4' 2-8-0s. They were all running substantial, tightly-timed trains over a road abounding in long 1 in 176 gradients and worse. Gresley was little more than a name; standardisation meant an occasional 'J39' on a local and a fairly regular 'K3' 2-6-0 or 'B17' 'Sandringham' working the Swindon–York out of Banbury (though it could as easily be a GC Atlantic).

Within a couple of years of the outbreak of World War 2, the scene was much the same. By then the keen engine spotter was beginning to have to look hard for LNWR originals to make their appearance, and LMS expresses were all about Pacifics. 'Directors' remained in charge of many Marylebone trains. The general take-over of the passenger

Classification

The LNER system of classification of locomotives was simple. The letter denoted the wheel arrangement. 'A' denoted 4-6-2, 'B' 4-6-0, 'C' 4-4-2, 'D' 4-4-0. But drivers tended to prefer nicknames.

The small-boilered GN Atlantics were referred to as 'Klondykes', having been introduced at the time of the Gold Rush. One of them, which became LNER 3990, was the only GN engine, until the first two Pacifics, to bear a name (*Henry Oakley*). At one time it and another of the same class were stationed at Lincoln. The unnamed one was referred to by drivers as 'Annie Oakley'. The K2 2-6-0s were known as 'Ragtimers', and the K3s 'Jazzers'. The ex-GC J11 0-6-0s were 'Pom-Poms', because the exhaust sounded like the naval cannon of the same name. The ex-GC ROD O4 2-8-0s were known as 'Tinies'. In some parts of the LNER the ex-GE B12 4-6-0s were named 'Hikers', some said because of the pack (the feed-water heater) it carried on its back in LNER days, though firemen thought it was because of the distance between the tender coal-hole and the firebox door.

Some classes were named after the first loco produced, such as the 'Clauds', the 'Sandringhams' and the 'Green Arrows'. The 'Hunts', 'Shires' and 'Directors' were self explanatory, but the name 'Antelopes' for the B1 4-6-0s did not last long.

The ex-GC Atlantic (C4) was known as the 'Jersey Lily', attributed by most authors to Lily Langtry and the fact that the class was said to be one of the most beautiful designs ever produced. But, another version: the large fat-boilered engine was named after a lady of the same proportions who looked for business outside the gates of Gorton GC works ('the Tank') on pay nights. She was also known as 'Jersey Lily'.

What's in a name? Class 'A1' Pacific No 2561 Minoru *rouses the echoes as it climbs up to Stoke Tunnel with an up East Coast express in August 1932. But except to the racing community, did that short name mean anything?*

service by the 4-6-0 'Sandringhams' was not until 1937, and graduation to Pacifics and 'Green Arrows' happened only just before the war.

It was an extreme example of what was happening more or less everywhere. When the LMS ordered new locomotives in fifties, because of its financial plight the LNER could only think of ten or twenty. As long as the pre-grouping types could do the necessary work – and a high proportion proved both suitable and competent – they were maintained, cherished, if necessary reboilered, and where suitable rebuilt in more modern form. Anything but use capital on starting afresh.

The five principal companies in the newly-formed LNER were in fair agreement on what locomotives were needed for the traffic. In the freight field, except on the Great Eastern and North British (where special circumstances governed) the eight-coupled engine, either 0-8-0 or 2-8-0 was the standard power. For express passenger work only the Great Eastern, with its restricted axleloads, shunned the 4-4-2 and opted for 4-6-0s, though the Great Central and North Eastern also used the 4-6-0 in some measure. The mixed-traffic locomotive, a comparatively new

86

concept before 1923, had been accepted by three companies, either as a 2-6-0 (Great Northern) or 4-6-0 (Great Central and North Eastern). For heavy suburban passenger work six-coupled wheels were de rigueur, though the 0-6-2 tank fought it out with other arrangements.

Nigel Gresley had had over eleven years as locomotive engineer at Doncaster when he was appointed chief mechanical engineer of the new railway. He had established an engineering style which was to last throughout the remaining eighteen years of his life and, albeit in modified form, to the end of steam. He had introduced two-cylinder 2-6-0s and 2-8-0s in 1912 and 1913 which were modern for the time. In this second decade in Britain three-cylinder locomotives – apart from a handful of compounds and specialised shunting and mineral engines – were confined to two new North Eastern Railway classes, the stately Raven Atlantics on express duties and 4-4-4 tanks for secondary work. Just how Gresley came under the three-cylinder spell is not clear, though in later years he was able to carry out comparative tests of two- and three-cylinder designs, the results of which were held to confirm his inclination. He was certainly not happy with Raven's use of three sets of Stephenson valve gear, though he agreed that all cylinders should drive on one axle.

He dipped a toe into the water in 1918 with a single 2-8-0 (GNR No 461); its two outside cylinders used Walschaerts gear, the inside valve being driven by a conjugated gear using oscillating shafts from the outside valve spindles. It was not a happy arrangement, although the three-cylinder engine *per se* was adjudged better at starting heavy mineral trains. It took H. Holcroft of the South Eastern & Chatham to show Gresley, at the beginning of 1919, how a simpler version of the conjugated gear, involving two horizontal levers and fewer joint pins, would give a better cylinder layout. Gresley seized on this avidly and

Passenger mover, whisky hauler. The Great North of Scotland Railway handed over 100 tender engines to the LNER in 1923, and remarkably every one was a 4-4-0. No 6899 of class 'D41', here in wartime unlined black livery, was typical of the later builds, which were used indiscriminately on passenger and freight work.

Atlantic elegance. Maintaining the pre-amalgamation tradition into the 1920s of North Eastern Railway running powers over the North British into Edinburgh, Raven three-cylinder 4-4-2 No 719 recovers from a signal check. The train is a motley collection of stock including five Great Eastern corridor coaches headed by a vintage gangwayed full brake.

told Holcroft that as a result 'it was his intention to build nothing but three-cylinder engines'. It was a momentous, perhaps hasty decision on the basis of experience with a single locomotive, and Gresley himself did not strictly abide by it.

The first venture along the Holcroft road, emerging in 1920, was the 'K3' mixed traffic 2-6-0. It was notable for its 6ft diameter boiler – and for its rough riding – but it proved the conjugated valve gear in fast freight and some express passenger service. Construction of more three-cylinder 2-8-0s (later class 'O2') followed in 1921 with the revised front end layout.

With experience with the 'K3s' under his belt, Gresley could now put the Doncaster design team to work on his new express locomotive; the concept of a 4-6-2 with very large wide-firebox boiler was far-sighted in the British climate of the time, for with the exception of the North Eastern Railway the other principal railways were satisfied with 4-6-0s for comparable duty. The result, No 1470 *Great Northern*, appeared just in time to carry the letters 'GNR' on its tender.

Gresley's appointment as chief mechanical engineer of the LNER clearly presaged a greater field for three-cylinder engines of existing and new designs throughout the system. But one aspect of his work is not always appreciated. He is usually thought of as a 'horses for courses' engineer, and in large measure rightly, but running through all his locomotives was a strong vein of standardisation. He used only five

88

Short-lived City. The five Raven Pacifics, named after cities on the North Eastern Railway, were completely outshone by Gresley's Pacifics of basically Great Northern design. No 2402 City of York was built by the LNER in 1924 but was scrapped after only twelve years' service. Even here (believed to be approaching Grantshouse on the East Coast main line around 1932–3) it is clearly working an inferior express.

Ivatt Atlantics. This stopping train of six coaches, seen near Knebworth in June 1933, certainly does not need two engines. Large Atlantic No 3301 is the train engine, with Klondyke small Atlantic No 3252, acting as assistant and marshalled inside in line with LNER practice. The second and third coaches are an articulated twin using bodies of ex Great Northern six-wheeled coaches.

coupled wheel diameters, in 6in steps from 4ft 8in to 6ft 8in, to cover all duties (and the 6ft 2in size was not adopted until 1934). Leaving aside the solitary Garratt, only three classes departed from boiler barrel diameters of 5ft 6in (parallel, and initiated with the 2-8-0 of 1913) or the tapered 5ft 9in – 6ft 5in of the wide-firebox engines, though different lengths were used. Until 1927 the standard boiler pressure was 180lb/sq in. Cylinder stroke was 26in except for the original three-cylinder 2-8-0s. Thus his design staff could settle the salient dimensions of a new locomotive from a very limited catalogue.

There were three 'odd men out' in this overall process. The need for a simple engine for second-line freight and colliery trip work brought in two classes of inside-cylinder 0-6-0s with 5ft 2in and 4ft 8in wheels but otherwise identical (classes 'J39' and 'J38'). The third was the 'B17' 4-6-0 'Sandringham', where the design work was largely done by the North British Locomotive Co and the stringent weight and hammer-blow limitations of the Great Eastern section could only be met by dividing the drive. These latter engines, together with the 'D49' 4-4-0s, were unique in having the conjugated valve gear behind the cylinders, where it was better protected from the abrasive effect of smokebox char than in the more usual forward position.

The first upset to Gresley's ideas arose from the Wembley Exhibition of 1924/5, where one of his Pacifics was exhibited with a GWR 'Castle'.

Early Gresley. In the middle road No 9 between platforms 8 and 10 at Kings Cross, two-cylinder 2-6-0 No 4668 of class 'K2' waits to draw its empty stock out into a platform for a late-afternoon stopping train – probably to Cambridge. It is summer, because the carriage heating steam pipe has been removed from the engine buffer beam.

Exchange trials between the two showed the 'Castle' to be the more economical machine. This focused attention on the valve gear deficiencies of the Pacific, and also awakened interest in the benefits of higher boiler pressure. Modifications to give longer valve travel produced economies in coal consumption of the order of 20 per cent. The stepping up of boiler pressure from 180 to 220lb/sq in in itself had only a marginal effect but resulted in a more powerful engine, which commended itself; a simultaneous increase in superheater size promoted economy. So emerged the 'Super-Pacific' of class 'A3'. There was a marked reluctance to push pressures still higher, however, and not until 1935 was it increased to 250lb/sq in on the 'A4' streamlined Pacifics for the new high speed trains. Significantly, in this case the piston valves were also increased from Gresley's normal 8in diameter to 9in to give more 'punch' and a freer exhaust. The form of the streamlining resulted from contact with Bugatti, of French racing car fame.

Besides his 'A4s', Gresley will be particularly remembered for his brave attempt to solve the problems of the difficult Edinburgh–Aberdeen route, with its curvature, heavy gradients and severe speed restrictions which led to much double-heading. His answer was a large three-cylinder 2-8-2 with 6ft 2in wheels; the first, No 2001 *Cock o' the North*, was given poppet valves which were not entirely suitable, but the remaining five were given traditional piston valves. They were magnifi-

Fife coal hauler. Class 'J38' 0-6-0 No 1400 poses for her portrait in 1926. New from Darlington in works photographic grey she exhibits such distinguishing features as smokebox door hinges and cab shape to show that she was designed there before drawing work was centralised at Doncaster. She was the first of a class of thirty-five engines; almost identical, but with coupled wheel size increased from 4ft 8in to 5ft 2in, was the more numerous class 'J39'.

Super Pacific. Such was the semi-official title bestowed on the first engines of Gresley's class 'A3', thanks to the redesign of the original Pacifics in class 'A1' to incorporate higher boiler pressure, bigger superheater and long lap valve gear. No 2743 Felstead *was the first such engine, appearing new from Doncaster in 1928.*

Silver Jubilee beauty. The first steamlined class 'A4' Pacific No 2509 Silver Link, *appeared from Doncaster in September 1935. For the first two weeks of the high-speed Silver Jubilee service between Kings Cross and Newcastle, this engine worked the train without relief until a second engine became available.*

Right *Magnum opus. Gresley's 'P2' 2-8-2 No 2001* Cock o' the North, *as originally built with Lentz rotary cam poppet valves, takes water on haymarket shed before working an Edinburgh–Aberdeen express. Within four years the engine was modified with Walschaerts valve gear and an 'A4'-style streamlined front end to improve the lifting of the exhaust steam. At ten years of age it was completely rebuilt as a Pacific by Edward Thompson.*

Mixed traffic muscle. Class 'V2' 2-6-2 No 4845, new and resplendent in passenger green livery, stands outside Doncaster works in June 1939.

Tally ho! The three-cylinder class 'D49' 4-4-0s were built to handle secondary express passenger trains in the north-east and Scotland, emerging in 1927 and named after shires served by the LNER. Later engines built from 1932 at Darlington were fitted with Lentz rotary cam poppet valve gear and named after hunts. No 201 The Bramham Moor *was the first of this group: note the fox above the nameplate.*

cent machines, though when opened out they were beyond the capability of one fireman to sustain. But their chassis did not take kindly to the curves and they were costly to maintain; they were rebuilt after a life of only ten years.

Gresley's most significant design in his later years was probably the 'V2' mixed traffic 'Green Arrow', built to handle the growing numbers of fast fitted freight trains. The LNER regarded it as the engine that won the war. The boiler was a shortened version of that on the 'A3' Pacifics in order to suit the unusual (for a tender engine) 2-6-2 wheel arrangement, but they soon proved able to hold their own against the Pacifics in heavy haulage. On a smaller scale and for a very specialised usage, the six 'K4' 2-6-0s for the West Highland line, with 5ft 2in wheels, were outstanding examples of *multum in parvo*. But Gresley's judgment failed him when a lighter mixed traffic engine was needed; the two 'V4' 2-6-2 prototypes were an extremely expensive way of catering for run-of-the-mill traffic, with their three cylinders and wide-firebox boiler, yet being no more capable than a cheap two-cylinder 4-6-0.

It is interesting to look at the Gresley engines which were *not* built. 2-6-4 tanks with both two and three cylinders were schemed out for London suburban passenger work; they used a 5ft 6in boiler. There was also a three-cylinder 2-8-2 tank for Nottinghamshire colliery trip work. They were not proceeded with for a variety of reasons. A *magnum opus*, a 4-8-2 with a modification of the 'P2' 2-8-2 boiler to give a deeper combustion chamber was planned for the heaviest passenger trains, with the idea of using the greater boiler power for faster uphill running to give faster timings; it *might* have been built but for the war, though its ability to turn on existing 70ft turntables would have been in some doubt.

There was considerable innovation during the Gresley reign. From 1923 experiments were conducted with booster engines to increase the low-speed power of passenger, freight and shunting engines. 1927 saw

The Not-So-Stainless Master Cutler

In 1950–51, the twelve-crew top link maintained Leicester Great Central shed's reputation for fine enginemanship. After forty years, two drivers stand out in the memory – Henson and Walls.

Henson was a hard runner but he used his head and got results; he was probably the best of the twelve. Having got to know him well there came a time for fun. It was on the down *Master Cutler*, 18.15 Marylebone–Sheffield, a heavy train (for the GC) of 11 coaches, 373 tons tare, and he had an A3 Pacific. The train went out by the Joint line via High Wycombe and rejoined the GC main at Grendon Underwood Junction with a speed limit of 60. From there to Culworth Junction, 20½ miles, some timetable genius had laid down a timing of 20 minutes to pass. It was a counsel of perfection because nearly 11 of those 20½ miles were uphill at 1 in 176, so drivers habitually dropped 1–2 minutes on this stretch and recouped it later.

So before we set off, we ridiculed this timing . . . quite impossible. Henson rose to the bait, he would show whether it was impossible or not! Once past Grendon, he started his demonstration, dropping her down to 25–30 per cent, for the climbing. It was obvious that the 'A3' wasn't going to stand for *that*; with single chimneys they regarded themselves as racehorses and did not like too much use of the spurs. The pressure gauge began to wilt and the water sank down in the gauge glasses.

By about Brackley the fireman decided that he had had enough of this nonsense. He put down his shovel and shouted to Henson: 'If you want to drive the effing engine this way, you'd better fire the effing thing as well'.

We didn't make it in 20 minutes!

continued on page 95

Football favourite. The three-cylinder class 'B17' Sandringhams were first built in 1928 to provide enhanced power on the Great Eastern section, but it was the later batch from 2848, named after major football teams, which made the class reputation by their sparkling performance on the Great Central line. No 2856 Leeds United *shows off its green lined livery in the sun on Neasden shed in 1937. Note the brass football below the nameplate, flanked by panels on the splasher in the club's colours.*

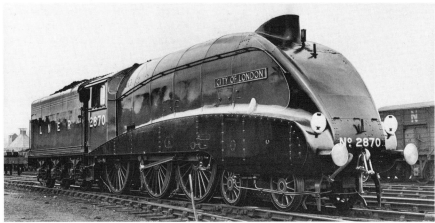

East Anglian streamliner. For working a new fast East Anglian service inaugurated in 1937 between Liverpool Street and Norwich, Gresley applied streamlining in the 'A4' style to two of the later 'B17s', though the speed of the service hardly warranted it. Class 'B17/5' No 2870 City of London *was finished in LNER green.*

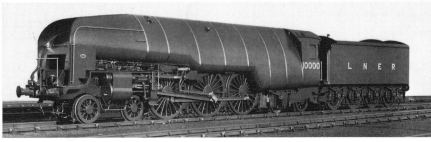

Maid of all work. The 'J39s' were versatile engines with a good front end, quite at home on stopping passenger trains as well as freight. Alas, their frames and axleboxes were hardly up to the work they did, and caused heavy works repairs. This is No 1813, built by Beyer Peacock in 1936.

Hush Hush. Gresley's brave experiment No 10000 stands in all her pristine newness at Darlington works, where she was built in 1929. The experiment was not successful in the medium term, and No 10000 was rebuilt with three cylinders and conventional boiler in 1938.

Battling banker. Getting 1,200-ton trains of Yorkshire coal over the Pennines from Wath yard to Manchester was a brutal business. Each train needed two 2-8-0s on the front and two assisting in the rear to get the trains up Worsboro' bank, which included 2½ miles of 1 in 40. Beyer Peacock built this six-cylinder Garratt in 1925 for banking, the biggest steam locomotive to work in Britain.

the start of trials of four different designs of poppet valve gear, some of which continued well into the 1940s. The same year saw extensive fitting of the ACFI feed water heater on ex-GE 'B12' 4-6-0s (and one or two other engines) in the quest for economy, though this fitting did not survive rebuilding in the 1930s. There was some dabbling with articulation of engine and tender, which was short-lived. Draughting came under review in 1934 with the first installation of the Kylchap double blastpipe; it was applied in penny numbers until adopted as standard for most of the Pacifics after nationalisation. But the most remarkable move in the search for improved thermal efficiency was the building in 1929 of a large 4-6-4 express locomotive, No 10000, fitted with Yarrow water-tube boiler working at 450lb/sq in, the steam being used compound in two high-pressure and two low-pressure cylinders. The early promise shown by this remarkable machine, however, was not sustained, and its reliability in traffic suffered; it was scrapped in 1937, some parts being used in the three-cylinder streamlined 4-6-4 which took its number.

In engineering terms, what can be said of Gresley's work? He was a firm believer in building engines big enough to be masters of their work with something in reserve. One must question whether he was given adequate feedback on the mechanical behaviour of his engines in service, or some sacred cows would surely have been slaughtered. It was known for many years that at speed the conjugated gear had sufficient 'whip' to cause serious overtravel of the middle valve, causing that cylinder to perform more work than the other two. This in turn caused extra stress on the inside marine-type big end, which was prone to overheat; it was not redesigned until BR days. His solid bronze coupled axleboxes were more susceptible to heating than those on other railways, despite generous bearing sizes, and caused plenty of work at sheds, but they lived on. Frame fractures were very prevalent on most classes, and complete replacement of frame plates was not uncommon. The use of a maximum cut-off of 65 per cent made his engines prone to going 'blind' when starting; it must have been responsible for a lot of aggregate delay. But he always considered very carefully the comfort of the enginemen.

In retrospect, was Gresley right to go so single-mindedly down the three-cylinder road? With the Pacifics and 'V2s', undoubtedly yes, in order to get sufficient drawbar pull. With the 'K3s' and 'B17s', perhaps – at least while reluctant to increase boiler pressure. With the remainder, probably not.

Certainly Edward Thompson, when thrust into the CME's chair on Gresley's untimely death in 1941, agreed with that assessment. The Gresley/Holcroft conjugated gear was anathema to him, and the retention of three cylinders was to be avoided where this was feasible. So came his most successful engine, the simple two-cylinder mixed traffic 'B1' 4-6-0 of 1943, built to a total of over 400 engines over the next eight years. Its 225lb/sq in boiler formed the basis for rebuilding certain pre-grouping classes, notably the ex-GCR 'O4' 2-8-0s, which then became the new standard class 'O1' heavy freight engine. His new 2-6-4 tanks of class 'L1', however, were something of a mechanical

---

continued

Then there was Walls. He was basically a good engineman, but before he got on to this train, a real worrier; the sort of chap who would give a good home to a duodenal ulcer. Never able to leave well alone. One afternoon he had brought up a 'B1' to return on the *Cutler*. It was a quick turn-round job, so the men would take the engine on to the loco siding at Marylebone, turn, run the rake through the fire, top up with coal, and set back on to their train in good time for a brew. But on this occasion Walls looked at the fire and decided that it needed cleaning properly, using the drop grate.

All was fine until they tried to get the drop section up again; they got it up part way, and then it jammed. Nothing would shift it. This left a gap of about 2 inches at the front. There was no replacement engine readily available at Neasden. They looked in the little ashpit to see if there were any arch firebricks to plug the gap; none. There was a pile of ordinary house-bricks that the engineer was going to use for a tidying-up job, so they heaved about two dozen of these in to block the hole, followed by turves which they dug from the bank, and then started to rebuild the fire.

By the time they got the train moving, they were 5 late and with only 160 pounds of steam. However, they got up to Kilburn not too badly, and when they shut off for the Northolt Junction slack she blew off. So far, so good. Things went normally through High Wycombe, but as they started to shift down from Saunderton it was clear all was far from well. Red hot coals started to shower from the ashpan in increasing quantities and the pace got slower. Walls had no option but to stop at Finmere.

Ubiquitous Antelope. Thompson's class 'B1' 4-6-0 was built to a total of 410 engines between 1943 and 1952 for general mixed traffic work; earlier engines bore the names of antelopes, often obscure and difficult to get the tongue round. Here No 61016 Inyala leaves Leeds City assisting a 'V2' on a through Liverpool-Newcastle express.

disaster. The 5ft 2in wheels were too small for fast outer suburban work, and they quickly knocked themselves to pieces. Axleboxes suffered, water tanks split, oil pipes broke off, crossheads wore rapidly. They were bad news.

His Pacifics, too, left a great deal to be desired. They retained three cylinders, but with divided drive and three independent valve gears; Thompson attached great importance to all the connecting rods being of equal length, which was not warranted. The result was the placing of the outside cylinders behind the trailing bogie wheels, with the inside cylinder well forward, rather like the fashion of pre-war Hornby 4-4-2 models. It was a hideous arrangement, encouraging flexing and fracture of the frame plates and the lengthy exhaust channels. Three classes of Pacific with 6ft 2in wheels were produced in this mould (including the 2-8-2 rebuilds), but their maintenance problems were such that they preceded many of their older counterparts to the scrapheap. Also rebuilt in this form was Gresley's pioneer Pacific *Great Northern*; this was regarded by some as a piece of sheer vindictiveness on Thompson's part towards his old chief.

The LNER came very late into the diesel field, getting just four 350hp diesel-electric shunters for Whitemoor yard in 1944. Then in July 1947 a submission was made for the building of 25 1600hp main line diesel-electric locomotives to work in pairs on the principal Kings Cross–Edinburgh passenger services with a few other turns to give intensive utilisation. It would have displaced 32 Pacifics. Maintenance facilities at Leith Central, with a subsidiary depot in the London area were included, but rather naively the excellent experience with the shunters was quoted as applicable to the main line engines. Impending nationalisation killed the proposal.

The last CME, Arthur Peppercorn, had little time to make his mark before the LNER was submerged in the new nationalised organisation. However it was a fruitful period in putting design of the large engines back on the rails. His new 6ft 2in Pacific appeared in 1947, and betrayed some 'foreign' influence in a front end layout of divided drive with three sets of Walschaerts gear reminiscent of the rebuilt 'Royal Scots' of the LMS. The corresponding 6ft 8in 'A1' Pacifics, built to the same general pattern, proved to be some of the finest engines ever produced in terms of capacity, reliability and mechanical excellence.

Locomotive practice on the LNER was for long dominated by Gresley, with generally good effect. With Thompson the good news was quickly followed by a whole lot of bad. Peppercorn, had nationalisation not intervened, could well have taken it to new heights.

Royal Train engine. Immaculate two-cylinder class 'B2' No 1671 Royal Sovereign, *the Cambridge engine earmarked for Royal workings to and from Sandringham, drifts into Kings Cross station from Gasworks Tunnel with a Cambridge train. By the date of nationalisation, nine of these conversions from three-cylinder class 'B17' Sandringhams were in service.*

Mauled Mikado. Thompson's rebuilding of Gresley's class 'P2' 2-8-2s as Pacifics produced ungainly looking engines which could not emulate the success of earlier Pacifics. Here rebuilt engine No 60502 Earl Marischal, *now classed 'A2/2', sits among the clinker on York shed in the early to mid 1950s. The small smoke deflectors alongside the chimney were not effective, but were never replaced. These were the first Pacifics to be withdrawn, the first being 60503 and 60505 in 1959.*

Locomotive Stock 31 December 1947

4-6-2 (139). A1 : 113 (1). A2 : 525 (1). A2/1 : 507-10 (4). A2/2 : 501-6 (6). A2/3 : 500/11-24 (15). A3 : 35-67/9-112 (77). A4 : 1-34 (34). A10 : 68 (1).

4-6-2T (117). A5 : 9800-42 (43). A6 : 9791-9 (9). A7 : 9770-89 (20). A8 : 9850-94 (45).

4-6-0 (547). B1 : 1000-1273 (274). B2 : 1603/7/14-7/32/9/71 (9). B3/3 : 1497 (1). B4 : 1482/3/5/8 (4). B5 : 1680/1/5/6/8-90 (7). B7 : 1360-97 (38). B8 : 1353-5/7/8 (5). B9 : 1469/70/5/6 (4). B12/1 : 1500-5/7/8/11/3/21/4/6/8/9/32/6/9/43/52/60/3 (22). B12/3 : 1509/10/2/4-7/9/20/3/5/30/3/5/7/8/40-2/5-7/9/50/3-9/61/2/4-80 (50). B16 : 1400-68 (69). (Nos. 1406/21/35/7/8/55/7 are rebuilt to class B16/2 and Nos. 1403/7/17/8/20/39/44/8/9/53/4/64/7/8 are rebuilt to class B16/3.) B17 : 1600-2/4-6/8-13/8-31/3-8/40-70/2 (64). (Nos. 1659/70 are B17/5 streamlined.)

4-4-2 (53). C1 : 2808/10/7/21/2/8/9/39/49/54/70/1/5-7/81/5 (17). C4 : 2900-3/8-10/2/4-25 (20). C6 : 2933/7 (2). C7 : 2954/70/2/3/5/8/81-3/8/9/92/3/5 (14).

4-4-2T (152). C12 : 7350-95/7-9 (49). C13 : 7400-39 (40). C14 : 7440-51 (12). C15 : 7452-81 (30). C16 : 7482-7502 (21).

4-4-0 (507). D1 : 2203/5/7-9/14/5 (7). D2 : 2150-7/60/1/3/5/7/9/72/3/5/7/9-81/7-90/3-5/7-9 (31). D3 : 2000, 2116/22-6/8/31-3/5/7/9/40/3-5/8 (19). D9 : 2300-9/11-5/7-9/21/2/4/5/9/30/2/3 (26). D10 : 2650-9 (10). D11 : 2660-94 (35). D15 : 2501-9/12/20/8/38 (13). D16/2 "Super Clauds" : 2543/7/52/3/8/64/9/70/7/80/90/1, 2603/12/3/20 (16). D16/3 "Rebuilt Clauds" : 2510/1/3-9/21-7/9-36/9-42/4-6/8/9/51/4-7/9-63/5-8/71-6/8/9/81-9/92-4/6-9, 2600-2/4-11/4-9 (88). D17/2 : 2111/2 (2). D20 : 2340-5/7-9/51-5/7-63/5-7/9-84/6-92/5-7 (50). (Nos. 2349/60/71 are rebuilt to class D20/2). D29 : 2400-6/9-13 (12). D30 : 2417-32/4-42 (25). D31 : 2059/60/2/4-6/72 (7). D32 : 2443-6/8-51/3/4 (10). D33 : 2455/7-64/6 (10). D34 : 2467-85/7-90/2-8 (30). D40 : 2260-2/4/5/7-79 (18). D41 : 2225/7-32/4/5/8/40-3/6-9/51/2/5/6 (22). D49/1 "Shire" : 2700-25/8-35 (34). D49/2 "Hunt" : 2726/7/36-67/9-75 (41). D49/4 "Rebuilt Hunt" (2-cyl.) : 2768 (1).

2-4-0 (18). E4 : 2780-97 (18).

2-4-2T (118). F1 : 7097/9, 7100 (3). F2 : 7104-9/11-3 (9). F3 : 7114/5/7/9/24/6-8/34/9-41/3/9/50 (15). F4 : 7151-87 (37). F5 : 7188-7217 (30). F6 : 7218-39 (22). F7 : 7093/4 (2).

0-4-4T (110). G5 : 7240-7349 (110).

0-6-0 (1698). J1 : 5002-10/3/4 (11). J2 : 5015-23 (9). J3 : 4105-7/14-9/22-5/7-9/31-3/5-7/40-2/5/8/50-3/8/63 (33). J4 : 4109/10/2/20/1/60/2/7 (8). J5 : 5480-99 (20). J6 : 4170-4279 (110). J10 : 5126-8/30-49/51/3-73/5-99, 5200-5/8/9 (78). J11 : 4280-4453 (174). J15 : 5350-7/9/61-99, 5400-2/4-79 (127). J17 : 5500-49/51-89 (89). J19/2 : 4640-74 (35). J20 : 4675-99 (25). J21 : 5025-33/5-44/7/9/51/2/6-64/6-70/2/3/5-84/6/8-95/7-9, 5100-5/7-12/4-23 (83). J24 : 5600-4/6-9/11/2/4/5/7/9/21-9/31-4/9-42/4 (34). J25 : 5645-51/3-77/9-81/3-99, 5700/2-8/10/2-8/20/1/3-8 (76). J26 : 5730-79 (50). J27 : 5780-5894 (115). J35 : 4460-4/6/8/70-80/2-99, 4500-2/4-7/9-35 (70). J36 : 5210/1/3-8/20-2/4-61/4-8/70/1/3-83/5-98, 5300/3-25/7-31/3-5/7-46 (123). J37 : 4536-4639)104). J38 : 5900-34 (35). J39 : 4700-4988 (289).

0-6-0T (818). J50 : 8890-8991 (102). J52 : 8757-81/3-99, 8800-89 (132). J55 : 8317 (1). J60 : 8366/8 (2). J62 : 8200/1/3 (3). J63 : 8204-10 (7). J65 : 8211/3-5 (4). J66 : 8371-88 (18). J67 : 8490/2/3/6/8, 8509-23/9/31/6/40/7/72/83/4/6/8-95/7, 8606/8-11/6/28 (45). J68 : 8638-66 (29). J69 : 8491/4/5/7/9, 8500-5/7/8/24-8/30/2-5/7/8/41-6/8-63/5-71/3-9/81/5/7/96/8/9, 8600-3/5/7/12/3/7-9/21/3/5/6/9-33/5/6 (89). J70 (Tram): 8216-26 (11). J71 : 8230-6/8-40/2-56/8-60/2-73/5-99, 8300-14/6 (81). J72 : 8670-8754 (85). J73 : 8355-64 (10). J75 : 8365 (1). J77 : 8390-3/5-9. 8400-2/4-10/2-7/20-38/40/1 (46). J83 : 8442-61/3-81 (39). J88 : 8320-54 (35). J93 : 8484/8/9 (3). J94 : 8006-80 (75).

2-6-0 (274). K1 : 1997 (1). K2 : 1720-94 (75). K3 : 1800-62/4-99, 1900-92 (192). K4 : 1993-6/8 (5). K5 : 1863 (1).

2-6-4T (22). L1 : 9000 (1). L2 : 9070/1 (2). L3 : 9050-62/4-9 (19).

0-6-4T (2). M2 : 9076/7 (2).

0-6-2T (619). N1 : 9430-7/9-85 (55). N2 : 9490-9596 (107). N4 : 9225-37/9-47 (22). N5 : 9250-9370 (121). N7 : 9600-9733 (134). N8 : 9371-87/9-99, 9400/1 (30). N9 : 9410/1/3-5/8-29 (17). N10 : 9090-9109 (20). N12 : 9089 (1). N13 : 9110-9 (10). N14 : 9120/4/5 (3). N15 : 9126-9224 (99).

2-8-0 (681). O1 : 3578/90-2/4, 3610/9/30/46/50/2/63/70/6/8/87/9, 3711/2/25/40/52/5/60/8/73/7/80/4/6/9/92/5/6, 3803/6/8/17/54/63/5/7-9/72/4/9/86/7/90, 3901 (51). O2 : 3921-87 (67). O3 : 3475-86/8/9/91/3/4 (17). O4 (parts 1, 2, 3 and 6, small G.C. Belpaire boiler) : 3571-4/6/7/80/1/3-7/93/7-9, 3601/2/4-9/11/2/4/7/8/20-7/9/31/2/5-42/4/5/7-9/54/6-60/4-8/71/2/4/7/9-86/8/90-8, 3700-4/7/9/10/3-24/7-37/9/41-4/6/50/1/3/4/6/7/9/62-7/9/71/4/6/8/9/81-3/7/90/1/3/7-9, 3800/1/4/5/7/9/12/3/21-3/9/32/3/5/7/8/40-2/5-7/9/50/2/5/6/8/9/61/2/4/70/3/7/8/81/3/5/8/9/95/7-9, 3900/2/4-8/11-5/7/20 (213). O4/5 (round-topped firebox, smokebox on saddle) : 3579/89, 3628, 3726/45/88, 3816/51 (8). O4/7 (round-topped firebox, G.C. pattern smokebox) : 3570/82/8/95/6, 3600/3/15/6/34/43/55/61/2/9/73/5/99, 3705/6/8/47-9/58/61/70/2/5/94, 3824/39/43/8/57/60/76/80/4/91/4 (41). O4/8 (O1 type boiler, original cylinders and motion) : 3575, 3613/33/51/3, 3738/85, 3802/18/9/27/8/36/53/82/93 (16). O6 : 3500-67* (68). O7 : 3000-3199 (200). (No. 3152 is oil-burning.)

* See Locomotives on Loan, (LMS 8F)

0-8-0 (246). Q4 : 3200-7/10/2-4/6/7/9-21/3-9/31-6/8/40/1/3 (34). Q5 : 3250-7/9-64/7/8/70-87/9-99, 3300/1/3/5-8/10-9/21-3/6-8/30-6/8/9 (77). (Nos. 3253/63, 3301/5/6/16/22 are Q5/2 with large boilers off extinct Q10 class engines.) Q6 : 3340-3459 (120). Q7 : 3460-74 (15).

0-8-0T (13). Q1 : 9925-37 (13).

0-8-4T (6). S1 : 9900-5 (6).

4-8-0T (13). T1 : 9910-22 (13).

2-8-0+0-8-2 (Garratt) (1). U1 : 9999 (1).

2-6-2 (186). V2 : 800 83 (184). V4 : 1700/1 (2).

2-6-2T (92). V1 : 7600-33/5-68/70/1/3/4/6-81 (78). V3 : 7634/69/72/5/82-91 (14).

4-6-4 (1). W1 : 10000 (1).

0-4-0T (88). Y1 (Sentinel): 8137-51 (15). Y3 (Sentinel): 8154-65/7-9/71-6/9-85 (28). Y4 : 8125-8 (4). Y6 (Tram) : 8082/3 (2). Y7 : 8088/9 (2). Y8 : 8090/1 (2). Y9 : 8092-8124 (33). Y10 (Sentinel Tram) : 8186/7 (2).

0-4-2T (4). Z4 : 8190/1 (2). Z5 : 8192/3 (2).

Total Steam Locomotives – 6,525

Electric Locomotives (14). 600 volt **0-4-4-0** ES1 : 6480/1 (2). 1500 volt **0-4-4-0** EM1 : 6000 (1). 1500 volt **0-4-4-0** EB1 : 6490-9 (10). 1500 volt **4-6-4** EE1 : 6999 (1).

Diesel Electric Locomotives (4). **0-6-0** DES1 : 8000-3.

Petrol Shunters (2). **0-4-0** Y11 : 8188/9.

Total Locomotives – 6,545

RAIL MOTOR VEHICLES (305).

Steam (1). Sentinel Rail Car, 100 H.P. (6-cyl gear drive) : 2136.

Electric (304). London and Newcastle suburban services.

SERVICE LOCOMOTIVES (21).

B13 : 1699. J52 : 8782. J55 : 8319. J66 : 8370. J92 (Crane Tanks) : 8667-9. Y1 : 8130-6//52/3. Y3 : 8166/77/8. Y4 : 8129. Y5 : 8081.

MISCELLANEOUS LOCOMOTIVE (not included in stock).

Y11 : NE Area Engineers Dept. L4.

Locomotives on Loan 31 December 1947

2-8-0 (270). From Ministry of Supply. Austerity : W.D. 70802/7/17/34/9/50/71/7, 77003/4/6/8/10/3/6-20/2/3/31/2/4-7/9/41/2/4/7/50/1/5/7/61/3/6-8/70/1/3/5/6/8/81/5/7-9/95/6, 77104/7/11/8-21/4/7-9/35/8/44/7/9/52/5/7/63/4/6/7/9/70/3-6/8/81/2/5-7/95/8/9, 77201/4/6-9/15/8/21/2/7/8/30-2/5/48/9/52/8/60/1/3/71/4/8/83/92, 77302/3/5/7/9/12-5/7/9/20/3/4/7-9/34/8/42/50-3/6/8/62/4/71/2/5/81/6/90/2/4/5, 77401/2/4/6/11/3-6/8/9/24-6/8/31-4/6/9-42/5/9/52-5/7-9/61/2/4/5/7-70/6/80/4/8/92/4/7/9, 77503, 78514/25/6/32/7/8/53/9/61/4/8/72/5/8/85/7/8/92/4/8/9, 78600/1/9/10/4/6/37/43/50/82-4, 78700/15, 79178/81/2/4/6/94/8, 79202/4/6/8/9/20/7/9/39/42/3/59/63-5/71/6/80, 79306/10/2 (270).

Total Locomotives Held on Loan – 270

2-8-0 (67). To L.M.S. O6 : 3500-53/5-67 (running as LMS 8705-58/60-72). (67).

0-4-4-0 Electric (1). To Netherlands Railways : EM1 : 6000 (1).

Total Locomotives Away on Loan – 68

Locomotive Allocation 11 January 1947

SOUTHERN AREA (Western Section)

ANN Annesley: 1349-59, 1801/8/95, 1974-7/9/80, 2901/24, 3517/56/66/8/75, 3605/14/8/81/94, 3735/48/67, 3851/3/9/62/94, 4292/4, 4300/18/24/54/61/4/5/70/5/86, 4409/31, 4716/9/20/39/47/50/7/62, 4805, 4955/80, 7105/10, 8927/9/35/72/5/6/82. **(74).**

ARD Ardsley: 1346/7/8, 1484-7, 3154-8, 3205/13/21/3/6/2/6/41, 4115/9/27/9/42/8/50/73/4/82, 4208/14/50/60/7/72/7, 4751/4/60/96, 4801/6/11/25/36/96, 4911/79/85, 7440-6/9/51, 8766/90, 8848/71/2/96, 8900/1/3/4/7/9/10/4-7/9/21/5/30/1/8/9/47/8/9/51/60/6, 9452/61/73. **(93).**

BRN Barnsley: 3202/12/4/9, 4290, 4343/66/91/8/9, 4436/48/52, 4718/32/5, 4810/79, 4903/72/4, 7409/11/34, 9268/77/8/85/91, 9303/20/5/34/45/8/55/7/65/7/8. **(40).**

BID Bidston: 8205/7, 8588, 8671, 8701/14/27, 9289. **(8)**

BOS Boston: 1725/31/44/55/60/2, 2136/54/9/60/3/71/2/3/80/1/3/5/90, 4113/32/7/9/49/80/1/90/6/8, 4201/4/10/29/42/4/7/8/76, 5016/7/20, 7387, 8527/8/43/60, 8655/7/8/9. **(50).**

BFD Bradford (Bowling Jct.): 3217, 4108/30/43/6/70, 4226/68, 4749, 8892/5/7/8, 8902/6/8/12/22/3/32/3/4/40-4/59/61/9, 9253/61/80, 9437/8/43/7/8/9/54/7/8/9/64/74/8/9/82/3/5. **(50)**

CHR Chester: 5167/9, 7366, 7405/7/13/4/30/6, 9274/81/90. **(12).**

CLK Colwick: 1650/1/2/67, 1720/2/3/4/6/7/8/32/3/5/9/41/9/50/1/6/8/63/8-71/3, 1802/16/21/6/65, 1905, 2133/50/1/62/6/8/9/77/87/8/94/8/9, 2201, 2903/12/4/8/20, 3502/3/46/53/7/65/9/71/3/4/89/96/9, 3609/13/31/6/8/9/41/62/85/95/9, 3713/6/21/9/39/42/6/9/50/6/81/7/94/8, 3801/4/27/41/8/58/76/93/5, 3965/8/79/82, 4194/7/9, 4200/2/12/3/5/22/3/4/30/1/3/53/69, 4317, 4763, 4831/2/7, 4981/3/8, 5000-6/8/10-4, 5480-5/90-9, 7511/2, 8382, 8762/7/8/79/92, 8807/10/2/4/39/58/9/63/7/75/82/7, 8981, 9263/86, 9312/24, 9550/2/5, 70818/21/7/48, 77236, 77322, 78515, 78628/30/45/8/79, 78707, 79191. **(198).**

DON Doncaster: 48/9, 58, 63, 103, 815/30/1/2/46/52/7/61/7/70/2/5/7/80/90/6, 902/6/30/56, 1805/12/7/31/56/61, 1907/10/8/73/8, 2832/50/1/3/4/66/77/85/6, 3500/5-11/9/21/4/7/37/8/45/52/4/5/93, 3616/21/3/7/47/68/82/97, 3728/31/41/58/65, 3800/32/47/64/83/91, 3900/11/5/22/44/63/75, 4179/83/5/93/5, 4209/18/9/32/6/41/3/55/8/9/61-4/70/9, 4713/21/37/58/9, 4835/85/91/3/8, 4902/8/9/10/51/2/61/7/76/7/84, 8317/8, 8763/9/75/86, 8800/4/6/13/35/6/7/41-7/9/57/60/5/9/70/85/6/90/3/9, 8918/26/36/74/9/80/5/6/7/9/91. **(174)**

FRO Frodingham: 2178, 3475-94, 3518/26/35/62/84/95, 3602/6/26/42/5/9/55/96, 3726/44/88/93, 3802/18/24, 3920, 4280, 4308/9/39/62/93/5, 4407/22/9/51, 8962/4/8/70/1/3, 9930/2/4-7. **(66).**

GOR Gorton: 826, 917/28/48, 1070/3/5/7/8/9/82/3/5/6, 1366/7/8/70/1/3-6/81/2/8-96, 3529/42/60/1/3/7/78/90/1/2, 3619/30/46/50/2/63/70/87/9, 3725/52/68/80/4/6/95/6, 3808/17/54/63/5/8/9/72/9/86/7/90, 3901, 4298, 4311/6/22/6/32/8/46/57/63/7/8/81/2/3, 4401/15/34/5/7/40/53, 4712/4/7/40-3/5/55, 4807, 4918/54/62/6, 5133, 7097, 7101, 7400-3/8/10/2/5/6/7/9/21-7/31/7/9, 8063-7, 8531/98, 9256/60/70/96/9, 9307/8/46/7/53, 70813/22/8, 77131, 77318/36/43, 78584, 78665, 78712. **(161).**

GRA Grantham: 7, 8, 14/5, 22/8, 30/2/3/4/9, 102, 2000, 2161/7/79/96, 2810/2/22/35, 3201/6/7/25/8/40, 3929-41, 4106/18/24/31/3/6/72/5/8, 4203/6/27/37/65, 4746, 4965, 7380/2, 8801/16/77. **(61).**

HAT Hatfield: 8565/72, 9455, 9501/2/34/7/51/4/8/9/80/2/6/7/94, 9689-92/4/5/6/8. **(24).**

HIT Hitchin: 1089-99, 1105/6/7, 2126/48, 2849, 4105/14/7/22/38/40/5/53, 4240, 8512/41, 8605, 9515/57/93. **(32).**

HSY Hornsey: 4188, 4234/9/51/6, 7376, 8757-61/73/4/6/7/8/81/3/4/5/7/8/91/3-6, 8808/11/5/25/6/7/9/33/4/51/3/6/83, 9431/2/3/5/9/41/2/5/50/1/3/6/60/3/5/70/5/7, 9505/13/30-3/47/56. **(66).**

IMM Immingham: 1490-4/6, 1800/3/6/36/7/8/42/5/91, 1912/63, 2132/8/9/42/7, 2662/3/70, 2896/7/8, 2904/7/13/7/21, 3679, 3878, 4284, 4305/7/12/4/23/55/72, 4411/39/46, 4734, 4827/8, 4937/71, 8006/9/12/3/8/20/2/6/8/30/3/4/68-76/8/9/80, 8162/71/9, 8203/4/6/8/9/10, 9305/9/22, LMS 8511/7/32/49/50/3. **(94).**

KX Kings Cross: 3, 6, 10/3/7, 21/5/6/9, 46/7, 50/1/5/6/9, 62, 89, 96/7/8, 104/5/7-10/2/3, 500/7/8/13/4, 800/13/4/7/8/20/1/3/9/73/92, 900/3/9/14/5/22/83, 1112/3/4, 2800/1/2/11/7/21/3/5/34/40/1/2/5/59/68/70/1/2/6/9/81/8,

Pom-Pom. This was the universal nickname bestowed on Robinson's class 'J11' 0-6-0s from the Great Central, on account of their staccato exhaust. No 5226, its lines not enhanced by the very straight chimney, is here getting some shunting done at a steelworks in the Sheffield area.

Military choice. The ex GCR Robinson 2-8-0, later class '04' was selected for production for use in France during World War I on War Office (Railway Operating Division) account, and afterwards the LNER bought many of these cheaply to supplement their own stock. No 5404, always a Great Central engine and pictured at Neasden shed in the 1930s, still carries the disfiguring 'flower-pot' chimney used in the 1920s. Remarkably, some of these engines were called up again in World War II, finishing up in the Lebanon, Egypt and elsewhere.

Gorton's star turn. The GCR works at Gorton built the first Director 4-4-0s in 1913, and they were an immediate success on the nippy Great Central expresses. Further batches were built in 1920 (including No 5506 Butler Henderson) and 1923 with various improvements. Gresley was sufficiently impressed with the design to order a further 24 in 1924 for use in Scotland. In LNER days they were classed 'D11'.

Black Pig. These massive four-cylinder mixed traffic engines, built for the Great Central in 1921–3 for working express goods trains (and some heavy passenger workings) displayed a very healthy appetite for coal and earned themselves this unofficial nickname. No 5479 was one of ten further locos built by the LNER in 1923–4 and classified 'B7/2'.

Through freight. Having fired a round of coal the fireman of ex GNR class '01' two-cylinder 2-8-0 No 3473 looks back to see that all is well with his train, bowling along on the down fast line at Sandy. This was a 1913 design, very modern for its time and still so in this 1920's view apart from the spartan cab.

7106/7/8/11/3, 8764/70/1/2/80/97/9, 8802/3/5/9/18/22/8/ 30/1/2/8/54/5/61/2/4/73/4/8/81/4/8/9, 9434/62/6-9/76/80/ 1/4-90-9, 9504/6/12/7/20/1/3-9/35/8-44/6/8/9/60/1/6-79/ 81/3/5/8-92, 10,000. (181).
LNG Langwith Jct.: 2120/1/8, 3203/4/16/20/7/33/5/8, 3528/87, 3651/65, 3921/3-8/42/3/5/6/64/6/7/9-74/6/7/8/ 80/1/3-7, 4281/9/97, 4321/33/5/40/58/78/9/89, 4414/8/ 26/7/50, 7351/7/84, 9284, 9319/23/7, 9928/9. (70).
COP Leeds (Copley Hill): 853, 1483/8, 2828/9/75, 4107/11/6, 7104, 7353/6/77/83/6, 8911/3/37/45/6/78/84/ 8, 9266/71, 9430/6/40/4/6/71/2. (32).
LEI Leicester (GC&GN): 1664/9, 2910/5, 5007/91/1, 15/8/9/21/2/3, 8491. (13).
LIN Lincoln: 1481/2/9, 1681/3/4/5/9, 1807/22/52/9, 1966/82, 2123/5/35, 2815/30, 3691, 3819, 4285/6, 4301/ 3/15/59/96, 4430, 4702/15/22/8/36, 4881/3, 4904, 7350/ 64, 8376/85, 8529/37/53/8/87/99, 8610/8, 9311. (50).
LIV Liverpool (Brunswick): 1470/8, 2300/2/3/4/6/8/9/ 11/2/5/8/9/21/4/32/3, 4376, 4405/6/17/20, 5126/7/36/44/ 63/72/82, 5207, 7099, 7100, 8547/59, 9250/8/88, 9337/ 9/42. (41).
LTH Louth: 2143, 4320/8, 7352/5/9/74/9/81/9/98, 9306. (12).
MEX Mexborough: 1678/82/7/8/90, 2665/6/7, 3100/2/ 5/6/9/13-7/9-22/7/8/32/3/46/50/1/60-4, 3229/34/43, 3501/4/13-6/31/3/4/6/40/1/8/76/88/97, 3611/2/5/22/4/44/ 8/56/7/9/66/72, 3703/9/15/7/37/47/76/91, 3807/13/33/7/ 40/2/70/84/8, 3902/6/17, 4283/8/96, 4302/19/34/52/6/ 74/7, 4400/3/4/32/42/9, 9225/31/9/46/64/82/97, 9314/6, 9900/1/4/5/99. (115).
NEA Neasden: 1479/80/95/7/8, 2660/1/4/8/9, 4313/29/ 94, 7418/20/38, 8172/5, 9050/3-6/9/60/1/4-71/6/7, 9257/ 9/73/83, 9300/2/13/5/8/41/50/4/8/69, 9516/9/22/36/45/ 84, 9800-29. (86).
NTH Northwich: 2101/6, 2305/22, 5131/4/8/9/40/2/6/ 7/9/52/5/6/8/65/6/71/4/90/1, 5202/5/6, 9052/62, 9262/ 93, 9335/49. (32).
NWE Peterborough (New England): 44, 52/3/4, 61, 90, 106/11, 803/28/41/2/50/4/5/8/9/62/3/5/6/9/71/4/6/8/ 9/93/7/9, 905/8/11/2/3/6/21/4/35/6/8/43/5/50, 1736/47, 1804/9/11/25/7/8/32-5/40/1/3/4/8/50/3/60/2/4/7/9/73/7/ 80/90/6, 1915/29/38/9/46/50/1/4/61/7/72/81, 2131/65/ 86, 2808/33/9, 4109/10/2/20/1/3/8/35/51/7-60/2/4/71/6/ 7/84/6/7/9/91/2, 4207/11/6/7/20/1/5/8/35/8/45/6/9/52/4/ 7/66/73/5/8, 4729/38/48, 4969, 5058/70/95, 5117, 7361/ 2/3/5/8/73/90, 8185, 8380/7, 8546, 8632, 8765/89/98, 8817/9/20/1/3/4/40/50/2/66/8/76/9/80, 70826/31/2/42, 77009/21, 77220/33/43/65/72, 77373/85, 77410/20/96, 78565/82, 78635/42/70/3, 78703/9/10, 79180, 79236/47, 79305. (201).

RET Retford: 2116/40, 2900/6/19/23, 3200/10/24, 3550, 3637/88, 3763/74/5/82/5, 3877, 3905/7/8/14, 4125/52/5, 4205/71/4/82/7/95, 4306/41/7/8/9/80/5, 4402/10/3/6/21/3/5, 4830/86/7, 4906/56/70/87, 8165, 9294, 9321. (55).
SHF Sheffield (Darnall): 845/9/81/9, 1063/6/87/8, 1108-11, 1360-5/9/72/7-80/3-7/97, 1647/53/7/62, 2650/ 1/2/4-9, 3579/81/3, 3629/61/86, 3714/33/66/71/83/90, 3821/2/46/60/82, 4134/41/4, 4291, 4360/87, 4412/9/41/ 3/5/7, 4753, 4808/9/78/90, 4960/73, 7404/6, 8163/84, 8202, 8928/83/90, 9051/7/8/63, 9226-30/2-8/40-5/7. (110).
STV Staveley: 2153, 3539, 3633/75, 3702/20/34/59, 3838/50/73/89/99, 3912, 4331/6/42/5/50/1/71/3/84, 4428/33/44, 8371/9, 9279/92/5, 9301/51/60/3. (35).
STP Stockport (Heaton Mersey): 1469/71/5, 1680, 2314, 5132/5/7/45/50/4/7/60/4/78/9/81/5/6/8/93/4/7/8, 5200/9, 9251/76, 9317/28/31/2/59. (33).
TFD Trafford Park: 1472/3/4/6/7, 1679/86, 2301/7/13/ 7/25/9/30, 4723/5/44, 4823/4, 4901, 5141/61/8/83/4, 5201/4, 7358/69/70/2/8/88, 8540/84/5, 9252/5, 9304/36/ 43/61/4/70. (44).
TUX Tuxford: 3570, 3604, 3852/61/85, 4293/9, 4310/ 37/44/53/92, 4424, 9082, 9275/87. (16).
WAL Walton-on-the-Hill: 2328, 2653, 4304/97, 5130/ 77/80/92/5, 8365, 8581, 9265/98, 9338/44/56. (16).
WIG Wigan: 5128/51/9/62/70/3/5/6/89/96/9, 5203/8. (13).
WFD Woodford: 1810/24/9/39/68/70/94, 1908/13/25/ 43/4/56/60/4, 2902/8/9/16/22/5, 3547, 3674, 3706, 3829, 4327/30/69/88/90, 4408/38, 5486-9, 8891/4, 8920, 9269, 9310, 70810/44/45, 77091, 77284, 77339/ 82/97, 77427/30/48/91, 78550/91, 78627/61/92/7, 78706, 79187, 79200/16/14/5/53, 79308. (67).
WRX Wrexham: 5143/8/53/87, 7428/9/32/3/5, 8164/7/ 76, 8200/1, 8366-9, 9254/67/72, 9326/9/30/3/40/52/62/ 6. (29).
Doncaster Loco Works (Stored): 6000, 6498, 8132.
Doncaster Wagon Works (Departmental Stock): 8134.
Boston (Departmental Stock): 8133/66.

SOUTHERN AREA (Eastern Section)
BSE Bury St. Edmunds: 2503/8/66/9, 2615, 2785, 5362, 5442, 7115/33/4/6, 8497, 8597. (14).
CAM Cambridge: 1003/4. 1608/10/1/7/9/21-4/7/8/31/3/ 8/41/2/3/54/63/5/6/71/2, 2124/30/7, 2516/25/7/31/6/51/ 7/67/71/2/4/82, 2601/6/7/18, 2780/1/3/4/6/8/90/1/4/5/6, 4675-81/3/4/7, 5350/6/64/6/9/71/9/83/91/9, 5405/6/12/3/ 20/38/48/51/7/61/8/74/7, 5501/2/3/6/17/20/5/35/7/8/46/

7/63/75/85, 7121/2/4/38, 7360/7/75/85, 8173, 8214, 8372, 8516/7/30/6/66/83/97, 8609/45, 9926. (124).
COL Colchester: 1512/23/44/9/53/6/7/8/76, 1757/9/61/ 5/6, 2510/9/65/98, 2608/17, 5357/84/5, 5414/24/32/40/ 3/5/54/6/63/6/75, 5522/31/9/64, 7141/52/62/88/90/1/4/5, 7206/7, 8226, 8378, 8616/29/36. (53).
IPS Ipswich: 1053-9, 1562/4/6/70/7, 1600/1/2/4/18/25/ 9/34/45/9/59/68, 2526/52/3/6/70/90/4, 2611/2, 2782, 4724/52, 4800/3/26/9/34/72/80/92/4/5, 4900/5/53/7/8/ 64, 5377/86, 5407/9/15/21/3/9/30/47/59/65/7, 5510/60, 7143/4/8, 7447/8/50, 8211/2/6/9/21/4/5, 8373/4/5/7/86, 8498, 8510/8, 8651. (89).
KL King's Lynn: 2501/2/4-7/12/3/4/8/75, 2614, 4642/ 68/70, 5359/68/78/82/96, 5416/25/37, 5527/9/30/44/8/9/ 72/80, 7114/7/47/9, 8082/3, 8217/8/20/2/3, 8490/3/4, 8502/14/5, 8600/56. (50).
LOW Lowestoft: 4726, 4889, 4912/59/68, 5351/3/5, 5400/35/62/71, 7118/9/20/5/9/35/7/42. 8602/11/40. (23).
MAR March: 1630/5/6/46/8/56/60/1, 1721/30/4/7/8/40/ 2/3, 1820/30/46/77/9/66/86/7/93, 1914/9/21/6/40/2/7/8/9/ 70/1/89, 2539/42/7/8/79/84/9, 2603/5, 3101/8/10/25/47, 3522, 3653, 3701/4/5/8/18/24/30/79/92, 3836/9/67/80/ 97/8, 3904/13/47-62, 4640/1/3/4/6/7/50-7/9-67/9/71-4/ 88-94/7/8/9, 5372, 5419/33/9, 5500/7/8/11/2/3/5/8/24/ 54/5/6/68/71/3/6/7/83/4/7, 8000-3, 8383, 8654/64, 9902/ 3, 70823/40/58/70, 77083, 77100/13/36, 77213/50/1/79/ 81, 77300/54/63/9/70, 77412/37/73, 77502/4/7, 78513/ 6/62, 78603/34/9/51/67/76/7/86, 78716, 79192, 79211, LMS 8507/21/34-8/54/5/9. (209).
MC Melton Constable: 2155/6/7/77/89/95/7, 2515/20/ 8/33/62/78, 2610, 5472, 5514/52/7/66/7/78/86, 7131/40/ 50/6, 7354, 8489, 8570. (29).
NOR Norwich: 1040-52, 1509, 1626/44/70, 1745/6/8/ 52/3/4, 1997, 2203/10, 2511/22/9/35/41/5/6/55/63/4/76/ 7/81/3/5/8/93/9, 2613/9, 2787/9/92/3/7, 4730/1/61/97/9, 4802/33/82/4, 4913, 5352/8/60/7/73/89/94/8, 5401/3/8/ 11/7/22/60/70/3/8/9, 5516/51/3/69/70, 7123/7/45/6/54, 7663/4/5, 8384, 8495, 8501/86/95, 8603/41/3. (100).
PKS Parkeston: 1000/1, 1603/15/6/32, 1767/77/8/80, 2523, 4804/88, 5365, 5431/76, 7199, 7213/9, 8519/21/ 6/63/96, 8642. (25).
SL South Lynn: 2115/22/7/44/5, 2534/43/58/9/73, 4156/61/3/7, 4645/8/9/58, 5504/5/21/6/32/3/45/61/2/5/ 79/82/ 8/9, 8482/4/5/8, 8542, (37).
STR Stratford: 1005/6/8/9, 1104, 1510/4/5/7-20/2/5/7/ 30/3/5/7/8/40/1/2/5/6/7/50/4/5/9/65/7/8/71-5/8/9/80, 1605/6/7/9/12/3/4/20/37/9/40/55/8, 2500/9/30/2/8/49/60/ 87, 2600/2/9/16, 4682/5/6/95/6, 4708/27/33/64-77/9-83, 4873-7/99, 4907/63, 5354/61/3/70/4/5/6/80/1/7/8/92/3/5/

Ex North Eastern Railway 4-4-0 No 2106 rebuilt with superheater was looking somewhat woebegone when photographed in the 1930s on secondary duties. But before World War I these machines yielded pride of place only to the bigger Atlantics on express work. The class dated from 1908 and became 'D20' under the LNER.

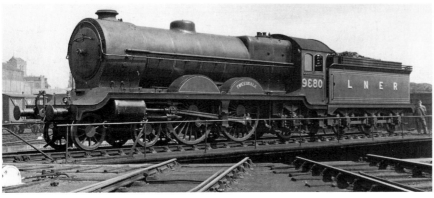

The class that got away. But for World War II, the LNER would have preserved a Reid Atlantic of the NBR, but the last one went for scrap in November 1939. No 9880 Tweeddale rests on the turntable at Dundee Tay Bridge shed in 1934. She only lasted another two years.

7, 5402/4/10/8/27/8/34/6/41/4/6/9/50/2/3/5/8/64, 5519/23/8/36/40-3, 7116/26/8/30/9/53/7-61/3/5/6/8/9/70/2/3/4/6/9-83/5/7/9/92/3/6/7/8, 7200-5/8-12/4-8/20-39/69/79, 7322, 7667/8/9/71/2/3/5/6/7/9/80/1, 8125-8/68/9/74/88/9, 8215, 8381/8, 8496, 8500/7/8/9/13/20/2/3/32/4/8/45/8/9/54/6/7/61/9/71/3-8/89-94, 8601/6/7/8/12/3/7/9/21/6/30/1/3/8/9/44/6-50/2/3/60-3/5/6, 8905/24/50/63/5/7/77, 9600-88/93/7/9, 9700-33. **(434).**
YAR Yarmouth (S.T. & Vaux.): 1516/61/9, 2517/21/4/40/4/54/68/80/6/91/7, 2604, 4798, 5390, 5426/69, 7109/32, 8186/7, 8625. **(24).**
YB Yarmouth Beach: 2152/70/5, 2207, 2561/92/6, 2620, 5509/34/58/9/74/81, 7112/67/77/8/84/6, 8213, 8628. **(22).**
Stratford Works (Stored): 8135.
Stratford Works (Departmental Stock): 8081, 8129, 8370, 8667/8/9.
Lowestoft (Departmental Stock): 8130/1/77/8.

NORTH EASTERN AREA
ALN Alnmouth Jct.: 2347/9/51/2/71/7/96, 5099, 5889/92. **(10).**
ALS Alston: 5100, 7315. **(2).**
BLA Blaydon: 2448/9, 3252/5/9/60/2/72/7/8/85/93/5, 3300/2/6/17/8/31, 4700/1/3/4/5/7/9/11, 4813-7/42/3/4/6/9/52/3/4/71, 4915/7/20/3/4/6/7/34/41/7, 5025/9/62, 5111/2, 7255/9/65/77, 7323/5/39, 7636/58, 8010/4/5/24/9/35-8/58/9, 8257/84, 9095, 9851/3/7/65. **(84).**
BOR Borough Gardens: 3251/4/7/71/83/4/6/7/9/96/8, 3320/1/42/52/62/3/88, 3400/34, 5600/3/4/5/10/1/8/24/7/33/4/40/1/4, 5817/46, 8287/8/99, 8679, 8704/5/6/8/36/7. 9400. **(47).**
BOW Bowes Bridge: 9097, 9100. **(2).**
BRI Bridlington: 2345/53/60/83, 8148/55. **(6).**
CON Consett Jct.: 3351/7/9/61/5/72/7, 3404/18/33/9/55, 9394, 9411/4, 9861. **(16).**
CUD Cudworth: 3311/32, 5667, 5703/14, 9771/89. **(7).**
DAR Darlington: 864, 963, 1415/46, 2978/81, 3304/28/

34/5/7, 4710/56/78/91, 4812/9/21/47/8/50/1/8/62-5/7-70/97, 4919/21/5/8/9/31/3/6/8/9/40/2/5/9/78/82, 5031/3/8/78/88/90/1/8, 5110/9, 5646/8/50/3/64/72/88/91/2/5, 5701/8, 7250, 7342, 8007/8/25/7/47-52/60/1, 8235/6/9/59/61/79/81/95, 8300/8/91, 8417/21/5/32, 8688, 8738, 9410/5/8/9/23/6, 9798, 9830-42. **(121).**
DNS Duns: 2357. **(1).**
DUR Durham: 7258/63/98, 7307. **(4).**
GHD Gateshead: 1, 2, 5, 16/8/9, 20/3, 36/8, 40/2/5, 60, 70/1/4/5/6/8/9. 81/4/6, 518. 801/5/6/7/9/10/1/33/5/60/8/83/4/5/7, 910/23/6/40/2/52/9/64/5/7, 1011-4, 1100, 1875/8/81/97, 1904/28/30/85/6, 2736/8/9/42/5/7/9/50/64/6/71, 2931/4/7/47, 7634/82/3/7-90, 8154/60/80, 8234/47/51/62/5/7/70, 8314, 8674/80/5/94, 8720/42, 9090/1/3/9, 9102/3/5/6/7/9, 9931/3. **(115).**
GUI Guisborough: 7281. **(1).**
HAV Haverton Hill: 3270/88/89, 3301, 5787, 5806/18/30/53/5/9/66. **(12).**
HTN Heaton Jct.: 69, 72/3/7, 80/2/3/5/8, 92, 511/2/5/6/7, 802/8/12/86/91/5, 939/44/7/9/57/66, 1818/84, 1901/3/6/17/52/62/5/9/84/7, 2954/73/4/91/6, 3104/7/11/8/23/30/1/4/6/7/8/40/2/5/8/9/67, 5030/5/40/80/1/6/7, 5102/4/14/22, 5649/97, 5704/20/7/81/94/5, 5824/6/42/62/3/4/86/93, 6480/1, 7241/6/9/66, 7303/33, 7635/7/40/1/2/51/3/4, 8237/41/3/5/56/64/71/3/8, 8363, 8675/82/3/7, 8725/32/43/4, 9092/4/6/8, 9104/8, 70815, 77146, 77298, 78577, 78646/53, LMS 8502/8/9/10/2/4/8/9/47/51. **(144).**
HEX Hexham: 5295, 7245/68, 7313/29, 8141. **(6).**
HLA Hull (Alexandra Dock): 8360/1/90/5, 8402/6/13/29/35, 8670/86, 8724/47/8/51/2/3. **(17).**
HLB Hull (Botanic Gardens): 1010/71/4/80/4, 2184/91/3, 2355/61/2/7/9/82, 2700/1/3/7/10/20/2/3/4/7/37/41/3/4/5/4/7/67, 7242/56/80/2, 7301/5/11/2/7/21/40/71/91-7/9, 8151, 8296, 9854/5/66/7/8/73/90. **(60).**
HLD Hull (Dairycoates): 1693/6, 1819/63/71/4/99, 1902/20/2/3/32/4/5/41, 2933/9/41/58/71/80/6/8, 3353/76/85/91/8/9, 3403/8/12/32/44/8, 3525/58, 3628, 3764/

70, 3812/6/23/43/55, 5041, 5118, 5619/20/1/31/9/47/51/60/3/6/8/71/9/90/8/9, 5705/12/3, 7171/5, 8137/9/40, 8232/42/52/77/88, 8304/11/6, 8673/6, 9371-7/9-83/5/6/7/9-93/6-9, 9401, 9770/2/3/5/7-80/2/3/4/6/8, 9912/5/20/2. **(123).**
HLS Hull (Springhead): 3673, 3732, 3849, 5654, 5707/24/8, 8090, 9089, 9110-3/6/9, 9774/6/85, 70804, 77002, 77110, 77211/54, 77474, 78540. **(25).**
ILK Ilkley: 7337. **(1).**
KBY Kirkby Stephen: 5028/46, 5103/13/5, 5655/69/73/81/4, 5717. **(11).**
NEV Leeds (Neville Hill): 1060/2/5/8/9, 1813/4/5/72/83/8/9/92, 1927/45, 2746/8/52/3/6/8/62/5/8/9/70/2-5, 3410/4/22/9/36/40/9/50/1/6, 5036/7/45/9/77/94/7, 5106/7/9/16, 5861/83/5/8/94, 7240/74/90, 7319/45, 7645/6/7/56/7, 8158, 8416/36, 8672/81, 8746, 9114/5/7/8. **(76).**
LEY Leyburn: 7346. **(1).**
MAL Malton: 5607/15/28/36/42, 7155, 7273/5/6/84, 7330/49, 8147/50. **(14).**
MID Middlesbrough: 3263/6/8/9/92, 3305/8/19/22/33/9, 4943, 5084, 5657/61/76/80/5/6, 5702/10/25/6/33/64/71/5/6/9, 7338, 7684/5/6/91, 8260/83, 8303/7/12, 8490/14/22/3, 8690, 8711/2/3/21/40/54, 9858/9/60/78/80/8. **(56).**
MIT Middleton-in-Teesdale: 7309. **(1).**
NPT Newport: 3265/73/91, 3307/16/23/30/8/41/3/4/5/7/9/50/4/5/8/60/6/71/3/5/84/6/96/7, 3401/5/9/11/5/7/9/20/3/5/30/1/8/42/3/5/6/53/8/9, 5601/2/8/26/32, 5730/1/4/6-46/9-56/8-63/5-70/2/3/4/7/8, 8011/23/41/62, 8407/8/10/31/41, 9910/1/3/6/7/9/21, 70800/24/37/47/72, 77276/90, 77357, 77506, 78520/34/70, 78633/56/62/74/87/90, 78718, 79285. **(127).**
NMN Normanton: 5108, 5782,8238/92/4. **(5).**
NLN Northallerton: 2388/91/7, 5645/58/74/93, 7324/44, 8159, 8301, 9101. **(12).**
NBH North Blyth: 5783/6/9/97/9, 5801/4/11/9/28/51/76/7/9/80, 8396/7/8, 8405/26. **(20).**
PAT Pateley Bridge: 7253. **(1).**

PEL Pelton Level: 9424. (**1**).
PMN Percy Main: 5780/4/91/2/6, 5802/9/12-5/21/2/5/31/7/8/9/52/8. (**20**).
PKG Pickering: 8157. (**1**).
RMH Reedsmouth: 5101, 5331/43. (**3**).
RBY Rothbury: 5083, 7296. (**2**).
SAL Saltburn: 5732, 9872/5/6/82/3/4/9/91/2. (**10**).
SCA Scarborough: 2960/72/5/89/92/3, 8016/7, 9881/5/94. (**11**).
SEL Selby: 2340/1/8/50/72/4/6/8/86, 3276/9/80/90, 3310/2/3/78/82/7, 3406/47, 5042/3/66/72/5/93, 5105/20, 5827/36/44/5/8/9/74/5/81/2/90/1, 8039/40, 8143/56/61, 8285, 8313/56/7/62, 9914. (**52**). RAIL CARS: 2135, 2267.
SBH South Blyth: 5063/9, 5123, 5808/10/29/34, 7244/61/85/95, 7304/20/6/34/41/7, 8415/28. (**19**). RAIL CAR: 2231.
SBK Starbeck: 2342/3/63/4/6/70/3/5/9/80/1/9/92/3/5, 4706, 4818/45/55/7/9/60/1/6, 4914/6/22/35/44, 7278/86/9, 7332, 8392/3, 8404/33/4/8, 9790-7/9. (**48**). RAIL CAR: 2147.
SKN Stockton: 1400/2/13/30/2, 3340/56/70/4/80/9/90/3, 3407/13/6/26/8/37/41, 5052/7/89/92, 5735/57/88, 5800/5/7/57/60/5/7/70/87, 7254/72/88/94, 7318, 8144, 8305, 8412/20/7, 9781/7, 9918. (**49**).
SUN Sunderland: 5785/93/8, 5820/3/33/5/40/3/7/54/6/72/8/84, 7243/7/51/2/7/60/4/7/70/83/97/9, 7300/6/10/28/36/48, 8691/8, 8707/18/30, 9384, 9413/6/21/5/7/8/9, 9850/74/87. (**49**).
TWD Tweedmouth: 932, 2344/54/8, 2970/82/3/95, 5026/39/67/82, 5869/73, 7248, 8400/24/30/7. (**19**).
TDK Tyne Dock: 3261/4/7/74/5/82, 3324/5/6/46/79, 3402/60-74, 3603/20/67/76, 3712/40/51/3/4/5/60/9, 3828/35/45/56/7/74/81, 5606/70/94, 5716/21, 8086/8/9, 8146/81/3, 8266/72, 8728/9/31, 9378/95, 9412/20, LMS 8529/56/8. (**69**).
WHD Wearhead: 5064. (**1**).
AUK West Auckland: 3314/5, 5032/61, 5659/62/5/75/7/8/83/7/9, 5706/15/8, 7638/9/52, 8142/9/82, 8249/54/5/69, 8678/96, 9422, 9856/69/70/7/9/86. (**35**).
WHL West Hartlepool: 2359/65/84/7/90, 3250/3/6/8/81/94/7, 3303/27/36/48/64/7/8/9/81/3/92/4/5, 3421/4/7/35/52/4/7, 5747/8/90, 5803/16/32/41/50/68/71, 7271/91, 7314/63/41/43, 8053-7, 8145, 8233/44/8/58/63/74/6/90/1, 8302/6/55/8/9/64, 8684/9/92/3/7, 8702/3/16/23/34, 9862/3/4/71/93. (**84**).
WBY Whitby: 5609/12/29, 7262/93, 7302/8/35, 9852. (**9**). RAIL CAR: 2136.

YK York: 837/9/43/7/56, 901/4/7/18/25/9/33/4/41/6/54/60/1/2/8/74-9/81/2, 1015, 1115, 1401/3-12/4/6-29/31/3-45/7-68, 2111/2, 2726/40/51/5/9/60/1/3, 5027/44/7/51/3/6/9/60/8/73/6/9/96, 5121, 5656/96, 5700/23, 8019/21/31/2/42-6/91, 8230/1/40/6/50/3/68/75/80/2/6/93/7/8, 8309/10/99, 8401/40, 8677/95/9, 8715/22/6/35/9/41/5, 77316, 77486, 78680/91/6/8/9, 79185, 79240/88. (**169**).
Darlington Works (Stored): 6490-7/9, 6999.
Darlington North Road Works (Departmental Stock): 1699.
Darlington (Faverdale Wagon Works): 8136.
Darlington (Geneva Permanent Way Depot): 8153.
York (Engineers Yard): 8152.

SCOTTISH AREA
ABD Aberdeen (Ferryhill): 501/2, 819/22/51/88/98, 919/70/3, 4794/5, 4839, 9128/9, 77423/35/87, 78608/41. (**20**).
BGT Bathgate: 2072, 2463/5, 4468/91. 4504/10/29/34, 5211/25/9/30/4/5/50/4/61/5/9/71/2/6/7/8/80/2, 5301/3/14/8/27/41/2, 9142/56-9, 9216, 9500. (**41**).
CAR Carlisle (Canal): 68, 91/3/4/5, 1851/4/8/76/82/98, 1936/7/90/1, 2059/65, 2729-32/4/5, 4478, 4511/26, 4785-90/3, 4838/40/1, 4930/2/46/8/75, 5216/7/93, 5304/12/21, 7458/74/81, 8499, 9139/55/74/85/97, 9215/8. (**58**).
DEE Dundee: 804/38/40/4, 920/37/69/71, 1101/2, 2408/9/10/2/8/34/8/85, 2713/8/28, 4482/5/93, 4506/12/3/23/30/7/48/75/6/87/93, 4615/9/20/7/31/4, 4784/92, 4820, 4950, 5319/28/30/3, 5614/22, 7461/71/84/6/9/90/1/8/9, 8100/7/8/10/4/23, 8446/52/5/62/6, 70852, 77277, 77505, 78654, 79251. (**76**).
DFU Dunfermline Upper: 2441/55/9/64, 3124/6/9/35/9/41/3/52/9/65/6, 4475/6/80/1/3/7/96, 4505/45/54/60/1/7/8/74/90, 4604/17/28/30, 5219/39/52/3, 5320/3, 5900/5/9/16/7/22/3/4/6/8/30/3/4, 7453/62/6/9/78/83, 7644/61, 8101, 8465, 8635, 9135/6/54/60/4/92, 9201/2/4/21, LMS 8526/30/9/42. (**79**).
EFD Eastfield: 1700/1/29/64/72/4/5/6/9/81/4/5/6/92/3/4, 1855/7, 1993/4/8, 2068, 2411/39/58/60/2/9/70/2/3/4/71/19-82/9/93/6/7/8, 2671-6/80/1/2/4/6-9, 4540/1/58/78-81/3, 4601/10/1/3/22/3/32/3/8/9, 5221/7/8/31/45/8/64/70/3/96, 5308/15/35/6/9, 7456/60/7/82/5, 7500/1/2, 7600/1/2/74, 8094, 8109/18/24, 8326/7/30/1/3/6/45/7/9, 8447/68/75/6/9/80, 8551/2, 8709/33, 8953-8, 9120-4/6/7/31/8/45/63/5/6/70-6-84/8/9/91, 9203/5/8/22, 9925/7, 77223, 77498, 77501. (**165**).
FW Fort William: 1782/3/7-91, 1995/6, 5215/37, 5300/13/44. (**14**).

Metropolitan takeover. One of the elegant 4-4-4 tanks, of Kerr Stuart origin in 1920, built for the Metropolitan Railway's Aylesbury service. With only half their weight available for adhesion they were far from ideal on this heavily graded route with numerous station stops. They were taken over by the LNER in 1937 as class 'H2' but were no match for the ex Great Central class 'A5' 4-6-2 tanks and only lasted until the end of World War II.

Waverley pilot. After World War II the LNER had the happy idea of painting the station pilots at certain major stations in distinctive livery for the delectation of waiting passengers. Here ex NBR class 'J83' 0-6-0 No 8477 shunts the up side of Edinburgh Waverley in spruce LNER passenger livery in April 1948. At the base of the bunker the letters and figures 'RA4' indicate the route availability scheme introduced in 1947.

Spotless on the table. Gresley three-cylinder 2-6-2 tank No 2909 of class 'V1', well cleaned – and not just above the footplate, either – sits on the turntable at Dunbar being readied for working a stopping train back to Edinburgh. But a black mark shows; the engine should have been put in mid-gear before climbing down to turn it.

HAW Hawick: 2208/16, 2417/22/3/5/8/32/40, 4463/94, 4509, 4986, 5232/42/59/79/, 5317/40, 7457/9/65/72/3/7, 8138. **(26).**
HAY Haymarket: 4, 9, 11/2, 24/7, 31/5/7, 41/3, 57, 64-7, 87, 99, 100/1, 503-6/9/10, 816/34/6/48/82/94, 927/31/51/3/5/8/72/80, 1007/72/6/81, 2212/4, 2403/13/33/7, 2677/8/9/83/5/90-4, 2702/5/6/9/11/2/5/9/21/33, 5240/3, 7610/5/20, 8328/59, 8457/60/73/8/81, 9169, 9220. **(84).**
KEI Keith: 1500-3/31, 2238/9/40/3-56/61/2/4/6, 7287/92. **(28).**
KPS Kipps: 4460/70/2/3/98, 4507, 5210/23/6/36/8/47/9/55/6/60/6/85/7/9/94, 5325, 7455, 7627/60, 8103/6/12/6/7/20/1, 8329/43/4. 8442-5/61, 9141/96, 9206/7, 9503/8/9/11/8/53/63/96. **(52).**
KIT Kittybrewster: 1064/7, 1504/5/7/8/11/3/21/4/6/8/9/32/6/9/43/51/2/60/3, 2060/2/4/6/9/73, 2225/7-32/4/5/6/41/2/60/5/7-80, 7151/64, 7327, 7505, 8190-3, 8700/10/7/9/49/50, 9125. **(70).**
PKD Parkhead: 4559/63/73/84, 4609/26, 5212/4/74/83/98, 5302/24, 7454/70/9/80/7/8, 7603/4/11-4/6/9/21/2/3/5/6/8/31/2/3/43/8/55/62/78, 8503/67, 9143/51/61/71/90/3/4/5/8/9, 9209/10/2/3/4/7, 9507/10/4/62/4/5/95. **(66).**

PTH Perth: 1002/61, 2205/15, 2426/7/56/7/66, 2714/25, 4536/88/91, 5213/97, 5309, 7455, 8469. **(19).**
POL Polmont: 2476, 4484/90, 4502/28/31/51/70/1/89, 4621, 5220/2/33/41/4/6/57/68/75/90, 5306/29/37/8, 7463/4/8, 8104/13, 8324/50/4, 8471,8524/33/44, 9137/62, 9200. **(40).**
StM St. Margarets: 824/5/7, 1823/79/85, 1900/9/11/6/24/31/3/55/68/83/8/92, 2400/2/4/5/7/20/1/4/35/43/4/5/50-4/71/83/4/7/8/90/4/5, 3103/12, 4462/5/79/86/9/92/9, 4503/15/7/8/9/24/7/32/3/5/8/9/43/7/52/5/7/62/72/7/82/6/92/4/5/9, 4603/5-8/14/24/5/36/7, 4822, 5224/51/8/67/84/6/8/92/9, 5305/10/1/6/34, 5617/23/5, 5906/12/4/5/8/9/20/7/9, 7093/4, 7492-7, 7605-9/17/24/9/30/49/59/66/70, 8092/3/5-9, 8102/5/11/5/9/22, 8320/5/34/8/40/8/52, 8448/9/50/4/63/4/70/2/4/7/92, 8505/11/25/62/8, 8623, 8952, 9000, 9130/3/4/40/4/6-9/52/67/8/72/3/5/86/7, 9219, 70841, 78527/8, 78625/63/4, 78708/11, 79177, LMS 8528/43-6. **(208).** RAIL CAR: 38.
STG Stirling: 2209, 2461, 4461/71/97, 4501/20/5/42/4/56/69/85, 5281, 5307/22/46, 7618/50, 8342/6/51. **(22).** RAIL CAR: 31073.
THJ Thornton Jct.: 1103, 2401/6/15/9/29/30/1/6/42/6/

7/67/8/75/8/91/2, 2704/8/16/7, 3144/53, 3610, 3806, 4464/6/7/74/7/88/95, 4500/14/6/21/2/46/9/50/3/64/5/96/7/8, 4600/2/12/6/8/29/35, 5218/91, 5332/45, 5901-4/7/8/10/1/3/21/5/31/2, 7452/76, 8321/2/3/32/5/7/41/53, 8451/3/6/8/9/67, 8504/35/50/5, 9132/50/1, 9211/23/4, 70816/30, 77033, 77360/7, 78655/68, 78702/13, LMS 8504/15/6/24/5/40/57. **(113).**

After 11 January 1947, the 191 class O7 locomotives included in the above allocation were renumbered in the series 3000-3199. The class O6 locomotives Nos 3100-67 were renumbered 3500-67 and the 59 class O1 and O4 locomotives numbered between 3500 and 3569 took the 59 blanks from 3572 to 3809. The numbers shown above are those carried before that renumbering.

104

7
SCOTLAND

STAND on Dundee Tay Bridge station in 1933, and you might have thought that the LNER after ten years was just another set of initials applied to the North British Railway. Little had changed. The next Edinburgh–Aberdeen train *might* come in behind a Gresley Pacific, but it was more likely to be hauled by an ex-NB Reid Atlantic assisted by a 'Scott' 4-4-0 marshalled behind the train engine. The engines would still be changed here, the halfway house on a 131-mile journey; Dundee was a sort of frontier post to keep Aberdonians and those from the capital apart. The coaches had changed from North British crimson to varnished teak, but except on the expresses many were still the same vehicles. The train service itself changed little, and there was a strong air of 'déjà vu'. Or look over the fence at Gunnie yard; it was the same story. 'J36' and 'J37' 0-6-0s came and went with freight, and while the railway owned wagons bore new initials the preponderance of private owners' wagons carried the same colliery and merchants' names. Even the 'Return to . . .' instructions on them still referred to the NB Rly. What had it all been in aid of?

The LNER's essentially decentralised organisational structure accorded well with the national identity of the Scots. It was natural that the general manager of the North British Railway, James Calder, should be retitled 'General Manager (Scotland)', taking over the Great North of Scotland in the process. Below him was a full Scots team, divided for certain functions between Southern and Northern Scottish areas following the lines of the old companies. There was considerable local autonomy. Engineers, be they mechanical, civil or signal, ran things their own way under the lightest of control from London. Operating arrangements, through workings and the like with companies now swept into the LMS net were maintained. Apart from the decision to separate locomotive running from the mechanical engineer and make its superintendent answerable directly to the general manager, responsibilities were little altered. The whole organisation was run from the old North British offices at 23 Waterloo Place, Edinburgh – pleasant enough at street level and above, if a little backward-looking with its ornate wheelbarrow and 'first sod' silver spade on display, but descending into three levels of gloomy basements inhabited, as one resident put it, by troglodytes.

While the new organisation played itself in, no very significant decisions surfaced. Outstanding North British locomotive orders were completed in 1923–4, and a batch of 24 new 4-4-0s to the Great Central 'Director' design (Class 'D11') modified to suit the Scottish loading

Willing Horses – and others

1963 and 1964 saw the swansong of the A4s on the 3-hour Glasgow–Aberdeen trains. As district traffic superintendent at Aberdeen, I was getting quite a lot of flak from the business community about their punctuality, especially the 17.30 from Buchanan Street. After an all-day Headquarters meeting I travelled back on an A4 to weigh up form.

The St Rollox crew got us into Perth on time; it was a pretty ham-fisted performance that would have had L. P. Parker tearing his hair, but at least the clock was satisfied. On came a Perth crew that had better be nameless. As usual we were over time taking water, and set off 4 late. We ambled gently up to Stanley Junction and then, on that more-or-less level racing ground to Forfar, where you had to be doing well over 70 to keep the sharp 32 minute booking, we just loafed, never doing more than 63, and dropped another 4 minutes.

I waited until we were at a stand, then conversationally said to the driver, 'Been working this road long?' 'Oh, aye, some years.' 'On these fast trains?' 'Oh, aye.' 'And do you usually work an A4 this way?' 'Aye, why?'

I blazed: 'Then it's no wonder I'm getting so much complaint from the passengers about the lousy timekeeping. It's men like you causing it. Now you've got an overall limit of 75, so get to it and stay there.'

'But there are speed restrictions . . .' 'Yes, I know what they are, and where, and I shall see that you obey them strictly. Elsewhere it's 75. Now get on and hold it.'

The fireman looked mutinous at the prospect of extra work, but put his shoulder to it. None of the legendary 18 per cent cutoff – it was 25–30 per cent with the regulator out to the stop; with the double chimney the boiler could supply it.

continued overleaf

105

Lightweight 2-6-2. The 'V4' class (two engines only Nos 3401/2) came late in the day, in wartime 1941; no other members of the class were built. Only No 3401 was named carrying smokebox plates Bantam Cock *though the sister engine was unofficially called* Bantam Hen. *Thompson later produced large numbers of general utility 4-6-0s in the 'B1' class and that was that. Both engines worked for much of their lives in Scotland after trials elsewhere and spent a deal of their lives on the Glasgow-Fort William line running there from 1943 to 1949; they were inclined to lose their feet on the hilly sections. Later they moved to other areas of Scotland including Edinburgh, Perth and Aberdeen, mostly on freight workings though in 1954 No 61701* Bantam Hen *was seen on the Deeside branch working a ten-coach special to Aboyne in connection with the Highland Games. World War II and Gresley's death made sure they were only 'two of a pair'. Here No 1700* Bantam Cock *heads a down West Highland line freight near Crianlarich in 1947.*

continued
How that old A4 talked from Forfar to Aberdeen! We made up 5 minutes of our lateness, but as we galloped down from Portle-then white hot embers started to bounce out of the damper doors on to the track. She had burned out several firebars, and the fire was gently subsiding into the ashpan! But by that time we were home and dry. – A. J. Powell.

gauge, arrived in 1924. These did much sterling work in the Forth–Clyde valley and in Fife. The monopoly of ex-North Eastern engines on the Edinburgh–Newcastle expresses was broken when in 1923 three Reid Atlantics were fitted with water scoops to enable them to work south and take water on Lucker troughs. Traffic control, which the North British had brought in at Burntisland to oversee the movement of Fife coal, was extended to other districts. But essentially the first few years saw efforts concentrated in getting back to prewar standards. Traffic was still fairly buoyant, though the General Strike of 1926 left its mark permanently.

On the passenger side, the first noticeable change was the introduction in 1925 of a Pullman service between Kings Cross and Edinburgh serving Leeds and Harrogate en route. It was extended to Glasgow in 1928, by which time it had taken the name *Queen of Scots*. It met an up-market need and with its success new trains of all-steel cars were built in 1928 for it. That year saw other significant developments; in the summer the *Flying Scotsman* started its non-stop running between Kings Cross and Edinburgh, made possible by the corridor tenders built for certain Gresley Pacifics. Haymarket enginemen worked the northern half of the journey. 1928 also saw the first introduction of third-class sleeping cars (to the pre-World War 2 concept of four berths per compartment) on the London–Aberdeen service. The Kings Cross–Fort William sleeper service, which had operated at weekends only since North British days, was put on to a daily basis in 1929.

On the locomotive front, neither Scottish constituent had used six-coupled wheels for a main-line passenger locomotive, sticking to the 4-4-0 (and in the NB case the 4-4-2 also). On some of the severely-graded routes this was a distinct limitation and double-heading was rife. This was first tackled jointly by the locomotive running superintendent and the mechanical engineer, who obtained the transfer of some Gresley ex-GNR two-cylinder 2-6-0s (Class 'K2') from England in 1925 to work on the West Highland line to Fort William and Mallaig. So successful did these prove, raising the permitted passenger train loading from 180 tons for the 'Glen' 4-4-0s to 220 tons, that further engines were transferred in 1931–2, to a total of 13. They were fitted at Cowlairs works with side-window cabs instead of the spartan GNR variety to give the enginemen better protection from the Highland weather, and named after local lochs. In 1930 it was the turn of the Great North line, this time getting ex-Great Eastern 4-6-0s (Class 'B12') to displace the small 4-4-0s from the main Aberdeen–Elgin services. Some ex-GNR Class 'D' 4-4-0s were also drafted in, but found no favour with hard-driving Scots enginemen. There was a continuing need for freight engines, which Gresley met in the 1920s with new Class 'J39' 0-6-0s and (exclusively for the Scottish coal and mineral traffic) Class 'J38s', similar but with smaller wheels. Later newcomers were Class 'D49' 4-4-0s for intermediate passenger traffic and Class 'V1' 2-6-2 tanks which took over much of the Glasgow suburban service.

GN of S freight. One of the class 'D40' 4-4-0s of the Great North of Scotland Railway No 2267, takes a pick-up freight out of Elgin towards Keith on 4 August 1947. Both the 'D40' and the earlier 'D41' classes were used over this section well into BR days almost monopolising the various branches, Speyside, Deeside, Lossiemouth, in the 1950s. No 2267 is clean and sports a somewhat unusual tender cab. Cleanliness on the GN of S section was a watchword even in the difficult war and immediate post-war years.

Latterday Intermediate. One of the mixed traffic versions of the North British Railway Scott class 4-4-0s the 'D33s' were introduced in 1909/10 with 6ft 0in coupled wheels instead of 6ft 6in. NBR No 867 was used in a form of locomotive trial involving a Highland Railway Castle class 4-6-0 No 146 Skibo Castle in 1910 making runs between Blair Athol and Dalwhinnie on the Highland and between Perth and Kinross on the North British. It was reported that the 'D33' gave the better performance. Most of the class worked into Edinburgh in LNER days but they also ran between Glasgow, Fife, Dundee and Perth. No 9894 of 1909 is seen here at Dalmeny Junction in the 1930s.

Scotland especially felt the chill winds of industrial change and depression. With two thirds of costs going on staff, cuts were inevitable. The more feeble branch lines were either totally closed or, more usually, reduced to as-required freight only status; there was no TUCC procedure to be gone through in those days! The Light Railways – Carmyllie, Lauder, Gifford & Garvald – were early victims. The 24-mile Fort Augustus branch, which in traffic terms should never have been built in the first place, closed completely in December 1946 after surviving six years on one coal train a week, increased to daily during the war. Some signal boxes were done away with; a 1936 colour-light signalling scheme at Galashiels, for instance, enabled the adjacent Kilnknowe Junction and Selkirk Junction boxes to be dispensed with. A scheme on an altogether bigger scale was the resignalling of Edinburgh Waverley, in which colour-light signals and electric interlocking enabled control to be concentrated on new signalboxes at the east and west ends. It also came in in 1936. But generally semaphore signals reigned supreme, and some small signal-boxes provided merely to split long sections remained, though they could have been replaced by intermediate block signals. The luxury of two types of brake – both the NB and the GNofS had used the Westinghouse air brake exclusively – could no longer be supported, and removal of air brake equipment was put in hand about 1931. On a more positive note, 1933 saw the first runs of the *Northern Belle* cruise train, which capitalised on the scenic attractions of Scotland.

Economy demanded the elimination of double-heading, and that meant more powerful engines. For the difficult Edinburgh–Aberdeen

main line, infested with slacks and hills, Gresley produced his somewhat revolutionary 2-8-2 *Cock o' the North* in 1934, followed in the next two years by five sister engines. Designed to handle 550 ton trains on this taxing route – and successful in so doing – they certainly did away with the need for assistant engines, but their long rigid wheelbase did not take kindly to the curvature, and they lasted no more than ten years in this form. For the West Highland line, where the 'K2s' were now regularly assisted, six new 2-6-0s were produced in 1937–8. The 'K4s' could be said to put maximum power in the smallest compass, and could take 300 tons unassisted. Perhaps their very power was their failing, for they did not stand the pace in postwar years and were replaced.

The LNER was doing its difficult job in Scotland with evident initiative and improved efficiency when it suffered a serious blow, the appalling rear end collision at Castlecary on 10 December 1937. The 16.03 Edinburgh–Glasgow express ploughed into the back of a standing Dundee-Glasgow train at about 60mph having overrun signals after passing a distant signal showing a false clear in darkness and falling snow. 35 people died, and the locomotive of the Edinburgh train was written off. Inevitably the chief inspecting officer recommended consideration of a system of automatic train control such as was in use on the GWR.

There was a serious scare in September 1939 when a German bombing raid was made on the Forth Bridge, fortunately without damage. The same could not be said of the North Clydeside lines in the heavy raids on Glasgow and Clydebank. At worst, however, services were interrupted for only a few days. The whole pattern of traffic changed; North

Twin K2s at Fort William. The LNER imported several of their successful pre-grouping classes into Scotland, ex GC Director class 4-4-0s, ex GE 'B12s' for the GN of S main line and the 'K2' 2-6-0s for the West Highland often running in tandem with the old North British 'D34' class Glen 4-4-0s. So successful were the 'K2s' that a number of those regularly shedded at Eastfield (Glasgow) and Fort William carried the names of Highland lochs. Here in the sad last grimy days of the LNER Nos 1791 Loch Laggan and 1779 set out from the old Fort William terminus for Glasgow Queen Street.

Scottish suburban service. The LNER ran an intensive service of local trains in and out of both Glasgow and Edinburgh. In some cases ex NBR 4-4-2 tanks ('C16') were in evidence but 'N2' 0-6-2 tanks were far from uncommon even in the 1920s. In most cases the locomotives carried a destination board at the top of the smokebox door. No 2587 enters Waverley station (West end) with a train of NER coaches carrying a 'suburban' headboard, around 1927.

A generation apart. As the order for the production engines was placed with the North British Locomotive Co in July 1947, this made the 'K1' a genuine Thompson LNER design though certain modifications were applied by his successor, Peppercorn. They proved to be versatile and successful engines working anything from colliery trips to express passenger trains, the latter in particular on the West Highland line. So it was no surprise to find No 62012 on Fort William shed over the August Bank Holiday weekend in 1953. The surprise was the discovery of an NBR Glen (one

of the classes to work the route regularly in tandem with the 'K2s' during the 1930s and over the wartime years), particularly as they were being displaced by the growing number of LMS class 5 4-6-0s. In the event the two generations of engine were to combine to haul the morning Fort William to Glasgow train on Bank Holiday Monday. The photograph shows 'K1' No 62012 as train engine (leading as per West Highland practice) and 'D34' No 62482 Glen Mamie as pilot. They make a fine pair running through the Monessie Gorge.

Moved in

Tablets are exchanged manually on the West Highland, often at spectacular speeds.

In steam days the practice was for firemen to hang the tablet carriers by the hoop on the handle of the hand brake while they were in section. There was an occasion when the last train of the day arrived at a signal box on the Moor of Rannoch without a tablet. The driver reported that the carrier had swung off the hand-brake handle with the swaying of the engine and had fallen on to the track. It was a Saturday night and darkness had fallen. The signal-man decided to wait until Sunday when the line would be closed to all traffic and he could stroll up the track at his leisure keeping an eye open for the tablet. When he woke on Sunday morning he found the landscape with an even covering of deep snow! – *The West Highland Railway*, John Thomas.

Sea coastwise shipping was much reduced, and the deep sea fishing industry was affected by the requisitioning of trawlers for naval purposes. Steamer routes on the Clyde had to be curtailed; four of the five LNER ships were taken over by the Navy (of which two were sunk) leaving the 58-year old *Lucy Ashton* to maintain the Craigendoran service alone.

Rehabilitation was a slow business under postwar conditions of shortages of coal, steel and other commodities. But new engines were appearing in the name of Edward Thompson, the CME since Gresley's death in 1941. His Pacifics had few friends, but gradually his Class 'B1' 4-6-0s became commonplace in Scotland, as elsewhere, and his Class 'K1' 2-6-0s, based on a two-cylinder rebuild of a 'K4', took over many of the West Highland duties. To restore prewar standards of service took rather longer, however, and impending nationalisation, with its promised Scottish Region combining LNER and LMS north of the Border, led to a planning blight until the new masters could decide their strategy. Momentum so lost was not easily regained, and the Glasgow suburban services suffered their individual moment of hopelessness – the day all the aged supposedly never-to-be-used steam stock had to be pressed back into service to replace the new blue electric trains and in rush hour Queen Street Low Level was once again never free from smoke. It was 19 December 1960, only six weeks after the blue trains had been ceremoniously introduced at last inaugurating the age of clean suburban travel; traffic immediately shot up 400 per cent, condemnation enough of the discomfort of the old steam service. It took ten months for the serious fault in the electrical transformers to be analysed and rectified.

Named Trains Summer 1939

Coronation	1600 SX Kings Cross–Edinburgh Waverley 1630 SX Edinburgh Waverley–Kings Cross	Supplementary fares All seats reserved	East Anglian	1840 SX Liverpool St–Norwich 1200 SX Norwich–Liverpool St	Limited accommodation
West Riding Limited	1110 SX Bradford–Leeds Central–Kings Cross 1910 SX Kings Cross–Leeds Central–Bradford	Supplementary fares All seats reserved	Scandinavian	1610 Liverpool St–Parkeston Quay Inward service awaited arrival of boat There were a number of alternative paths	Connects with ship to and from Esbjerg conveys Pullman car
Silver Jubilee	1000 SX Newcastle–Kings Cross 1730 SX Kings Cross–Newcastle	Supplementary fares All seats reserved	Hook Continental	2015 Liverpool St–Parkeston Quay 0620 Parkeston Quay–Liverpool St	Connects with ship to and from Hoek van Holland conveys Pullman car
Flying Scotsman	1000 Kings Cross–Edinburgh Waverley 1000 Edinburgh Waverley–Kings Cross	Through carriages to and from Aberdeen			
Scarborough Flyer	1100 Kings Cross–Scarborough 1040 Scarborough–Kings Cross	Through carriages to and from Whitby	Antwerp Continental	2030 Liverpool St–Parkeston Quay 0700 Parkeston Quay–Liverpool St	Connects with ship to and from Antwerp conveys Pullman car
Queen of Scots	1120 Kings Cross–Glasgow Queen St 1015 Glasgow Queen St–Kings Cross	All Pullman cars Supplementary fares	Eastern Belle Pullman Limited	0955 SUO Liverpool St–Clacton 1710 SUO Clacton–Liverpool St Weekdays ran to a variety of destinations advised by handbills.	All Pullman cars supplementary fares
Yorkshire Pullman	1645 Kings Cross–Harrogate 1115 Harrogate–Kings Cross	All Pullman cars including through carriages to and from Bradford and Halifax			
Harrogate Sunday Pullman	1000 Kings Cross–Harrogate 1500 Harrogate–Kings Cross	All Pullman cars Sundays only	Garden Cities and Cambridge Buffet Car Express	0935 1215 SO 1240 SX 1410 2010 2155 } Kings Cross–Cambridge	
The Highlandman	1925 Kings Cross–Fort William and Inverness 1640 Inverness and 1710 Fort William–Kings Cross	Conveys sleeping cars		0925 1230 1525 SX 1530 SO 1725 2210 } Cambridge–Kings Cross	
The Aberdonian	1940 Kings Cross–Aberdeen 1935 Aberdeen–Kings Cross	Conveys sleepers including to and from Lossiemouth			
The Night Scotsman	2225 Kings Cross–Aberdeen (only down train named)	Conveys sleeping cars to Glasgow, Dundee and Perth	Thames–Forth Express	1003 Edinburgh Waverley–St Pancras 0905 St Pancras–Edinburgh Waverley	LMS train ran over LNER between Carlisle and Edinburgh
The Norseman	1200 SO Kings Cross–Tyne Commission Quay 1340 THO Tyne Commission Quay–Kings Cross	Connects with B&N line Bergen ship			
Flushing Continental	1000 Liverpool St–Parkeston Quay 1955 Parkeston Quay–Liverpool St	Connects with ship to and from Vlissingen conveys Pullman car	Northern Belle	Cruise Train Kings Cross 2100 Fridays during June, returning 1045 following Friday	

The interior of Crimpsall erecting shop Doncaster Plant which was built in 1901. This view taken on 20 April 1958 shows ex GN 0-6-0 LNE class 'J6' No 64208 re-assembled after overhaul and immediately behind is class 'K1' 2-6-0 No 62070. The locomotive on the middle road is a class B1 with electric headlamps. This picture shows how untidy railway workshops were with various parts lying around and steps jacks etc. encroaching on the gangways.

A unique colour photograph of class 'A4' No 2509 Silver Link hauling the up Flying Scotsman at Grantham in June 1937 some six months before it was repainted blue. The leading coach is a Gresley full brake in teak with roof nameboard.

Left. Class 'A4' 4-6-2 No 11 Empire of India at the head of the down Flying Scotsman in Newcastle Central station August 1947. Two of the 1920 fire replacement electric stock in blue and cream livery can be seen peeping out behind No 11 probably on a South Shields train.

Right. Although Mallard broke the speed record for steam in 1938 it was not until ten years later that the brass plaques commemorating the event were fixed to the locomotive, no doubt in preparation for the 1948 locomotive exchanges. The LNER only claimed 125mph for Mallard in 1938 and the speed of 126mph if it was reached at all was only a momentary peak.

Class 'B1' 4-6-0 No 1100 in postwar green livery heads the 16.20 to Carlisle in platform 14 at the west end of Newcastle Central station August 1947. No 1100 was built by the North British Locomotive Co, Glasgow in November 1946.

8
THE GOLDEN YEARS OF HIGH-SPEED TRAINS

WHEN memories of slow, dirty and jerky journeys in a rake of six wheelers hauled by wheezing 0-6-0s are forgotten, the image of the LNER of polished blue engines streaking through the countryside at the head of sleek rakes of two-tone blue coaches, or of the *Flying Scotsman* heading one of the periodic new trains of that name comprised of uniform coaches with shiningly-varnished teak, luxurious letterwork and pure white roofs, clearly remains. It was the LNER of the East Coast main line where adventure was mixed with progress and to be a passenger on a named train or Pullman enhanced one's status.

A long shadow had been cast by the 1895 Races to Aberdeen. Though the running was fast by the standards of the time, the start-to-stop average speeds were not very high, in some cases not reaching a mile-a-minute. What they did feature were some examples of extreme recklessness in high speeds on curves. On the last night, 20 August, the North Eastern driver took the reverse curves at Portobello at close on 80mph, depositing the observers in a heap on the carriage floor, while the North British man's speeds on the sharply curved stretch from the Forth Bridge to Burntisland must have struck something like terror in the hearts of his passengers. After that, prestige gave way to pragmatism, and the contestants agreed a minimum eight-and-a-quarter hour schedule between London and Edinburgh by both East and West Coast routes; on the East Coast route this represented an average speed of only 47.6mph nonstop, or less than 50mph with normal stops. The emphasis accordingly changed from speed to increased loads: as engines got larger these were stepped up until the Gresley 'A1' and 'A3' Pacifics were taking well over 500 tons as a matter of course.

The eight and a quarter hour agreement lasted until 1932, only breached by an overnight express in each direction which, from 1923, made the journey in seven and three quarter hours. But times inevitably began to change: on the GWR the train which would become *The Cheltenham Flyer* was accelerated in 1929, to average 66.3mph from Swindon to Paddington, ensuring excellent publicity. By 1932 it was averaging 71.4mph. The LNER was at first slow and half hearted in its competitive reaction. That year by mutual agreement the 1895 agreement was abrogated and the *Flying Scotsman* was accelerated to seven hours fifty minutes. In the summer when the train ran the 392.7 miles nonstop, thanks to Gresley's corridor tenders allowing engine crews to be changed 'on the run', this was reduced to seven and a half hours, but it still represented an average no higher than 52.4mph. In the following year much publicity was directed to the acceleration of the prestige

Luxury

Each of the 1930s luxury trains had its own booklet to aid promotion. Seating plans and schedules were backed up with carefully written text and sound design including colourful covers.

'In the first-class carriages the sections each accommodate four passengers, two at each table arranged on either side of a central gangway. Ornamental screen wings projecting from the partitions give the effect of alcoves for two people. Two swivelling chairs are placed at specially shaped tables, and are so arranged that passengers when dining are facing diagonally towards the windows.' That about the *Coronation*.

'Train attendants' posted letters and telegrams (dining car stewards did that on ordinary expresses), sold postcards and *On Either Side* describing the route, and were generally 'happy to render to the passenger any service which will be helpful in ensuring the fullest possible comfort on the journey'.

Electric cooking, double glazing, sound insulation . . . it all sounds familiar. But first-class dinner at 5s (6d more than third-class) now sounds more than just a bargain.

Earphones

In the early thirties the LNER did everything possible to popularise long distance travel by train. Ahead of the airlines it even rented headphones (a shilling or 5p a journey) plugged in behind the passenger's seat so that he could listen to the radio or gramophone music transmitted from a specially-equipped van. The service was provided in 1932 on the 10.10 Kings Cross to Leeds and the 1730 return and on the 13.20 Kings Cross to Edinburgh and 1405 return.

Experiments were then made showing sound films on a train, and a cinema coach was eventually introduced on the 1010 Kings Cross to Leeds and 1515 return, to be followed for a short time on the 14.05 from Edinburgh to Kings Cross. The vehicle had a sloping floor and was equipped, for about two-thirds of its length, with cinema-type bucket seats. Back projection was used on to the screen at one end. A one hour's performance of news reels and cartoons also cost one shilling. – Frank Harrison.

Short Visit

It was the late Charles Rous-Martin who was travelling from somewhere in Great North of Scotland territory back to London and had a fairly tight connection at Aberdeen into the North British service. His train was running somewhat late, and ran into the main platform just as the guard was flagging the Edinburgh train away from the bay. Rous-Martin flung the door open, sprinted across the platform and just managed to get into the moving train, followed by the loud voice of a porter commenting 'Ye'll no be staying long in the city the day, sir!'

Scarborough Flyer by fifteen minutes; as a result it ran nonstop between Kings Cross and York in 195 minutes – at an average of still only 57.9mph. As late as the summer of 1934, only seven trains on the East Coast main line were booked start-to-stop at 58mph or more, the longest being from Kings Cross to Grantham. The overall standard could only be described as pedestrian.

Behind the scenes, however, something stirred. The LNER Board was impressed by the performance of the German 'Fliegender Hamburger' diesel train and asked Gresley to look at what it could do on the Newcastle run. The calculations were not particularly encouraging, and Gresley was convinced that steam could do every bit as well. On 30 November 1934, it was put to the test. 'A1' No 4472 *Flying Scotsman*, with Bill Sparshatt at the regulator, was tested between Kings Cross and Leeds Central (185.8 miles) on a provisional schedule of 165 minutes each way (67.6mph average) and with 'carte blanche' to run as hard as he liked. The fastest schedule at that time was 193 minutes. Outwards the load was a mere four coaches of 145 tons, and the run was made in 152 minutes. Coming back, two extra coaches brought the load to 205 tons, and the overall time was 157¼ minutes with a momentary 100mph on the descent from Stoke Tunnel – the first 'ton' authenticated by dynamometer car record. Gresley could provide what the Board wanted without the trauma of entering the diesel field.

Having proved that it could be done, the decision was made to introduce a high speed service between Kings Cross and Newcastle in 1935, the Silver Jubilee year of King George V. A further test was made on that route on 5 March, this time using an 'A3' Pacific No 2750 *Papyrus* – nearer to Gresley's concept of the high-speed locomotive already on the drawing board at Doncaster. The train comprised six coaches on a four-hour timing for the 268.3 miles (67.1mph average). Kings Cross driver Gutteridge took it north; it was a sound run without speed exceeding 88½mph, and completed in just over 237 minutes, despite some delays. In the southbound direction, Bill Sparshatt, his nose pointed homewards, was allowed his head after Grantham, and in the course of making a running time of two hundred and thirty one and three quarter minutes, set up a new world speed record with steam of 108mph coming down from Stoke. Three hundred miles in all were run that day at 80mph or more.

Now Doncaster works could get down to work in earnest. The *Silver Jubilee* train was to go into service on 30 September 1935, and four new locomotives and a seven-coach luxury train had to be built. The locomotives incorporated relatively minor changes from the proved 'A3' Pacifics, to increase their potential for sustained high speed; they were streamlined in the Bugatti style and turned out in what was variously described as silver, aluminium or pale grey (for some months there had been an ex GNR tank locomotive shunting in Doncaster works painted in several shades of silver grey to determine the most suitable). The train, articulated in units of two, three and two coaches, seated a maximum of seventy eight first and one hundred and twenty third class passengers and weighed 220 tons; the three coach unit comprised an all

electric kitchen car flanked by restaurant cars for each class. Its exterior finish was in silver coloured Rexine with chromium trim and there was rubber sheeting between coaches to maintain a clean line and deep fairings between the bogies.

A demonstration run was made three days before the inaugural service, with the first 'A4' No 2509 *Silver Link* at the head. Kings Cross driver Taylor succeeded beyond all expectations in a high-speed attempt. On the falling grades from Stevenage, speed was maintained continuously at more than 100mph for twenty five miles with a maximum of 112½mph reached twice. The riding of the coaches left something to be desired on curves, though perfect on straight track; it was an indication of what is now familiarly known as cant deficiency and the need for carefully aligned transitions in running into and out of curves.

The train left Newcastle at 10.00 and from Kings Cross at 17.30, with a stop at Darlington in each direction; the average speed between Kings Cross and Darlington was 70.4mph. A supplementary fare was charged.

The modern LNER. One of Sir Nigel Gresley's garter blue steamlined Pacifics No 4490 Empire of India passes a three aspect colour light signal as it heads the down Coronation towards Potters Bar tunnel on 12 August 1938. Each of the five engines (Nos 4488–92) chosen to haul the Coronation were provided with coats of arms of the countries whose name they carried. This can just be seen below the number on the cabside.

119

In order to give adequate braking distance without moving hundreds of distant signals double block working was specified over longer stretches; on the usual racing ground between York and Darlington where continuous automatic three aspect colour light signalling was installed, it was necessary to impose a 70mph speed restriction for some years until conversion to four aspect. For the first fortnight of the service only one 'A4' was available: indeed *Silver Link* had been built in an incredible eleven weeks and was itself only just available, No 2510 being still at the running in stage, and she handled it unaided. Punctuality proved to be exemplary; in July 1936, for instance, every arrival at Kings Cross was between one and five minutes early. But, by contrast, on 4 September 1936 *Quicksilver* ran hot at York on the up train which arrived in Kings Cross about 25min late behind a GNR Atlantic.

The down train proved very popular with business travellers and often ran with every seat taken, but the departure time of the up train less readily met business needs. Running speeds reached 90mph almost daily, and there were occasional forays into three figures. The coaches themselves, stabled overnight at Heaton, proved highly reliable. In the

Linking the Kingdoms. The up Coronation heads over the Royal Border Bridge at Berwick. Note the beaver tail observation coach (which only ran in the summer), one of two specially built for the train. With late afternoon departures from both London and Edinburgh there was little point in providing such a facility in the dark.

first two years of running, the train was stopped only once en route by a defect – a hot box on one of the coaches – and only three times (including this incident) was the set out of service for a return journey. It ran over 277,000 miles before withdrawal for first shopping in October 1937, when the duty was covered by a spare blue set. The average loading during this period was 145 passengers northbound and 131 southbound. Its initial splendid punctuality record slipped a little as it ceased to be a novelty; 72% (down) and 68% (up) of journeys arrived right time or early, and average lateness was two and a half and one and three quarter minutes respectively. Finally, 61% of passengers took either lunch, dinner or a light meal!

The next logical step was a high speed express to Edinburgh, and on the last Saturday in September 1936 the *Silver Jubilee* stock plus dynamometer car made a test run from Newcastle northwards. The nature of the route precluded sustained high speed, but the 124.4 miles were run in 118 minutes outward and 114 minutes return. Clearly an overall six hour schedule was on the cards.

So it proved. Towards the end of the year it was announced that two new high speed services were to start, the *Coronation* to and from Edinburgh in July 1937 in a six hour timing with a single intermediate stop and a train to and from Leeds in October 1937, taking two and three quarter hours. New 'A4s' began appearing from Doncaster in December 1936 – none of the last minute building which characterised the start of the *Silver Jubilee!* – while the two sets of stock required for the *Coronation* followed in May/June.

The trains were of eight coaches articulated in four twins, plus a novel 'beaver tail' observation saloon at the rear – 312 tons seating 48 first and 168 third class passengers. Meals were served at all seats from two kitchen thirds, the third and sixth vehicles; first class accommodation lay between the two. Pressure ventilation was provided throughout. Five engines to work the train were specially finished in garter blue livery with dark red wheels, while the coaches were in garter blue below the waistline and a light Marlborough blue above.

A demonstration trip to Grantham and back turning on the Barkston triangle, was made on 30 June using No 4489 *Dominion of Canada*. The outward running was restrained with speeds only just into the 90s, but on the return Kings Cross driver Burfoot opened up to reach 109½mph coming down from Stoke Summit. Thereafter the train settled down for public use, leaving Kings Cross at 16.00, with a stop at York (reached in 157 minutes at 71.9mph average), and from Edinburgh at 16.30 with a stop at Newcastle from where Kings Cross was reached in three hours and fifty seven minutes (67.9mph). Supplementary fares graded by distance were charged; between Kings Cross and Edinburgh the addition was 6s first and 4s third class. Kings Cross, Gateshead and Haymarket men shared the working. An interesting item of management attention to detail was that the 0-6-2 tank engine which worked the empty stock from Hornsey into Kings Cross (and which was the first thing that passengers saw when going onto the platform) was kept well cleaned to accord with the ambience of the luxury train itself.

Bathroom B
Catching a fleeting glimpse of the North Sea at dawn and falling back to sleep until the towers of Edinburgh were visible, alighting onto the hubbub of Waverley station but rapidly getting lost trying to find the first of the two lifts to the North British Hotel, and then soaking in the generous bath of one of the bath or dressing rooms . . . it was a familiar pattern for experienced travellers. A fine Scottish breakfast could be charged to Bathroom A or B (the pair were swept away in the 1989 restoration) before facing the day in the city or returning to Waverley to continue the journey north, the station's character changing as the overnight and commuter trains had been dealt with and now family parties and splendidly-dressed Scots ladies were in evidence.

Streamlined to Leeds. The third and final LNER streamlined high-speed train was the West Riding Limited, an eight-coach formation with the 'A4' working only to Leeds although the train itself terminated at Bradford. In 1939 No 4496 Golden Shuttle was one of the regular engines working for fourteen consecutive weeks with only a three-day break. The down train is seen here near Potters Bar.

Hard on its heels came the *West Riding Limited* on 27 September also using 'A4s'. It ran to and from Bradford via Leeds Central providing an evening departure from Kings Cross at 19.10 and reaching Leeds nonstop in two hours and forty three minutes (68.4mph average) and a departure from Bradford at 11.10 and Leeds at 11.31 following behind the *Silver Jubilee* from Doncaster to reach Kings Cross at 14.15 (68.0mph average from Leeds). The train was a repeat of the *Coronation* but without the beaver-tail observation saloon, impracticable because of reversal at Leeds Central. Overall weight was thus reduced to 278 tons. The same blue livery was used. Between Leeds and Bradford the train was handled by a pair of 'N2' 0-6-2 tanks.

The locomotive work involved with the *West Riding Limited* was perhaps the hardest, the timings between Doncaster and Leeds (a section used by many different types of train) proving distinctly tight. Punctuality was not so good, despite valiant efforts by the enginemen concerned: Kings Cross shed used second link men (the 'Leeds' link). There also appeared to be a disproportionate number of engine failures; on at least one occasion a 'V2' 2-6-2 was turned out at the last moment for the 19.10 from Kings Cross – and acquitted itself creditably.

122

In the winter of 1937–8 the overall high speed East Coast services were thus:-

Kings Cross	d/a	16.00	17.30	19.10	↑	14.00	14.15	22.30
Leeds Central	a/d	"	"	21.53		"	11.31	"
Bradford	a/d	"	"	22.15		"	11.10	"
York	a	18.37	"	"		"	"	"
Darlington	a/d	"	20.48	"		10.42	"	"
Newcastle	a/d	"	21.30	"		10.00	"	18.33
Edinburgh	a/d	↓	22.00	"	"		"	16.30

Having established the framework of high speed services they settled down with little change and good reliability. During 1938 the *Silver Jubilee* formation was boosted by an extra third class coach to meet passenger demand, making it an eight vehicle train of 254 tons – still lighter than the *Coronation* and *West Riding Limited*. In the summer of that year, the down *Coronation* was given an additional stop, at Newcastle, without extra time. The very odd occasion when things went seriously wrong stood out like a sore thumb; the day in early January 1939, for instance, when *Golden Eagle* on the down *Coronation* ran hot and had to come off at Grantham. The rebuilt 4-6-4 No 10000 took over and did well to pass Darlington only twenty five minutes late, but itself had to come off at Durham with a hot box. The train was hauled on to Newcastle by the only available engine, an ex North Eastern 'G5' 0-4-4 tank. What a picture that would have made. But the other side of the coin was the record of 4497 *Golden Plover* which worked the *Coronation* on thirty nine consecutive trips during 1939, only marginally beaten by No 4491 *Commonwealth of Australia* which worked forty consecutive trips in 1937.

Trouble at Darlington. A 1939 photograph of an unknown 'A4' being seemingly rescued by an ex North Eastern Railway class 'C7' Atlantic.

Streamlining on the Scotsman. Once in service on a regular basis the 'A4' Pacifics took over the principal express trains on the LNER system. Here No 4482 Golden Eagle in blue livery is seen heading the Flying Scotsman.

There was, of course, a spin off from these high speed services, in the form of a 'creeping acceleration' of the other principal main line trains. The *Flying Scotsman*, re-equipped with new stock in 1938 to a standard fourteen coach formation, and which could load up to seventeen coaches at times, was accelerated to a seven hour timing. It could be tough work for an 'A4' and pilot assistance was not unknown. Several other expresses came into the '60mph or over' category. It all came to a grinding halt at the beginning of September 1939 thanks to Adolf Hitler.

Signalling and Safety

In some developments the LNER led; in others, it lagged well behind, retaining much outworn equipment until the end. A visitor standing in a GN line signalbox would immediately be aware of an ear-tingling jingle-jangle of noise from the telegraph instruments – not the block instruments, for their single needles merely indicated the state of the line, but the ding-dong of morse-telegraph messages on the omnibus circuits of what were called 'speaking instruments'. Looking out of the box he would see signals with centre pivoted arms standing almost vertical when clear – the famous somersaults used by the GN from the late 1870s following the devastating criticism of the slotted-post semaphores at that time which had become frozen in the clear position at Woodwalton during a blizzard in 1876 and were a direct cause of the Abbots Ripton collision when the up Scotsman running under seemingly clear signals hit a goods train setting back into a siding and a down express ran into the wreckage, killing 14 passengers. It also changed from the open block (signals all clear except when specifically at danger such as immediately after the passage of a train) to the system in which each train was offered and accepted and the signals cleared for that movement. Then the GN adopted a green light for clear. Until then green had been for caution, and white for all clear. So were laid the foundations of signalling on the GN which lasted right through the LNER period and survived in places into BR days.

But it was another accident on the GN line in 1935 at Welwyn Garden City when a late night Kings Cross–Leeds train running at about 70mph hit the back of a slow moving Kings Cross–Newcastle train killing 13 passengers, the Welwyn South signalman having forgotten the Newcastle train and thinking that he had forgotten to clear the block indicator for a previous train accepted the Leeds one, that brought further automation.

The inquiry recommended track circuits approaching and beyond the home signal interlocked with the block instruments so that once a signalman had accepted a train its passage had to be proved by occupation and release of the track circuits before another could be accepted. It could not be accepted, moreover, if the home and distant signal arms were clear. 'Welwyn control' became standard over the following decades on main lines in many parts of Britain, but not between Edinburgh and Glasgow in time to prevent what was the LNER's worst accident in terms of fatalities. An express passed a distant signal falsely showing clear at Castlecary in December 1937 and hit the back of a local passenger train, killing 35 and injuring 179.

The LNER did not have the best of records in the matter of collisions – in its last year, it had one in fog at Gidea Park killing seven passengers, one at Doncaster following irregular block working in which 18 died and a derailment at Goswick through excessive speed over a facing turnout in which 28 died. But it also had a remarkable safety record in running the world's most intensive steam suburban service out of Liverpool Street, controlled manually through to BR days. Liverpool Street West Side box was the largest on the GE with 244 levers, with Sykes lock and block operation.

The 1949 resignalling at Liverpool Street and Stratford brought a new concept in equipment and methods for instead of levers large or small there were switches on a panel laid out to represent the track layout. The interlocking was by electric relays, and no longer did bell

After the 1876 collision at Abbots Ripton, the Great Northern Railway adopted the balanced semaphore signal known as the somersault which was a feature on many ex GN lines right through LNER days. GN Atlantic No 4429 heads for Kings Cross through the Northern Heights approaching the London suburbs passing four somersault signals, three mounted on concrete posts.

From the late 1920s the LNER began replacing pre-grouping signals with upper quadrants as here at Newcastle, but followed old operating practices in which the NER used dwarf semaphore shunting signals below the main arm, both arms being cleared for the passage of a through running train. In the background is an original NER lower quadrant gantry.

codes describe the type of train for it was shown on another panel with different spaces representing different parts of the line and the descriptions showing class of train and destination moved from section to section automatically. This was a quantum leap forward, well beyond the widespread colour-light signalling developments on the Southern.

History repeated itself in 1989 with another leap into new technology when Liverpool Street was again re-signalled, this time with computers in the control system.

The GC had made a modest start with three-aspect automatic colour-lights between Neasden South Junction and Canfield Place near Marylebone. Completed just after the grouping in 1923, these were the first main-line colour-light signals in the country. Then A. E. Tattersall, signal engineer for the North Eastern area, pioneered all-electric relay interlocking, getting rid of the mechanical locks between levers that had been an essential feature of interlocking from the last century, and replacing levers by thumb switches. The lever frame was replaced by a track diagram with switches mounted in clusters against each signal position. The turning of one switch checked that the route was free, set the points as necessary and cleared the signal. The first installation at Thirsk commissioned in 1933 was part of resignalling between York and Northallerton and introduced colour-light signals on a much wider scale. The LNER mainly used single-lens searchlight signals, the colour indications

During the 1930s the LNER extended braking distances for its high-speed streamliners by moving distant signals further out from the stop signals to which they applied. This would have meant a hefty pull for a signalman with a wire-worked semaphore and many of the distant signals were converted to colour-lights, like these ground-level searchlight signals between Welwyn Garden City and Hatfield.

Although the LNER used the multi-lens colour-light signal for some installations it made extensive use of the single lens searchlight signal with a moving glass vane carrying the coloured glasses in front of the one signal lamp. These signals at Fenchurch Street also show the practice of the 1930s by providing junction signals with a separate head for each main route before the introduction of the white light route indicator by the LNER in its North Eastern area from 1935. Another feature was the 'S' shunt signals in addition to the disc signals, the latter applying into the loco spurs.

Building on its success with route-relay interlocking in the North Eastern area from the mid 1930s the LNER started the massive re-signalling scheme at York completed in the early years of BR. Routes were set on the one-control-switch system from the panel in front of the signalman while routes set and the position of trains were denoted on the illuminated diagrams.

given by a moving vane carrying the colour filters in front of the lamp. The second light needed for double yellow was mounted in a separate head lower down the post. In this pioneer installation many of the signals were approach lit, with the lamps normally out until a train approached sighting distance.

By the end of the 1930s the LNER had added three more major route-relay interlocking installations at Leeds, Hull Paragon and Northallerton, the latter notable by having white light route set indications on the track diagram. Just one more scheme was completed before World War 2, a tiny and seemingly unimportant one at Brunswick on the Cheshire Lines route into Liverpool. Unimportant? The essential difference from the others was that the operating buttons were placed along the track diagram in geographical fashion instead of control switches mounted in banks beneath the track diagram as at Leeds, Hull, and Northallerton. It was the first entrance-exit panel in the world and it was this style of operation that was installed at Liverpool Street and Stratford in 1949. It was the forerunner of all the major entrance-exit panels in the many resignalling schemes from the late 1950s onwards. In the intervening years the other railways and BR in its early period were still catching up on the technology and it is only now 50 years later that new developments with computers and data transmission are beginning to shape the next revolution in signalling.

There were other ways in which the LNER pioneered, but as stated in the introduction it failed to pursue the pioneer work with automatic train control undertaken by two of its constituents – and accidents which would have been avoided on the GW continued to happen. As the accompanying table shows, there was a rash of serious accidents at the end of the company's life.

Date	Place	Type	Cause	Killed	Notes
14/2/27	Hull Paragon	Head-on collision	Signals restored prematurely and points changed in front of train	12	a
27/6/28	Darlington	Head-on collision	Driver exceeded movement authorised by shunt signal	25	b
15/6/35	Welwyn Garden City	Collision	Irregular block working	13	c
10/12/37	Castlecary	Collision	Distant signal stuck at clear	35	c
10/2/41	Brentwood	Collision	Colour-light signal passed at danger	7	d
28/4/41	Claypole	Fire	Schoolboys playing with matches	6	
30/1/42	Cowlairs	Collision		12	
11/2/42	Beighton	Collision	Train hit displaced load on adjoining train	14	
16/1/44	Ilford	Collision		8	
5/1/46	Ferryhill	Collision		10	
2/1/47	Gidea Park	Collision		7	d
9/8/47	Doncaster	Collision	Irregular block working during resignalling	18	c
26/10/1947	Goswick	Derailment	Excessive speed at turnout to loop line	28	d

NOTES

a   In restoring the signal prematurely the signalman released the interlocking on points which were changed by a second signalman inadvertently in the few seconds before the train reached the locking bar and the train was diverted to the opposite line. Track circuiting would have prevented the accident.

b   The driver's knowledge of the area was questioned; he went beyond the limits authorised by a shunt signal and his shunting move obstructed another line and was hit by an arriving train.

c   After the Welwyn accident the inspecting officer recommended the provision of track circuits approaching and beyond the home signal. Occupation of the berth track circuit (approaching the home signal) would put the block indicator to 'train on line' if it was not already there, and 'line clear' could not be given to the signalbox in the rear if home and distant signal arms were clear. Had 'Welwyn control' been installed at Castlecary, 'line clear' could not have been given to accept the colliding train if the distant signal arm had been wrongly at clear. At Doncaster, resignalling work was in progress and there had been some alterations to electrical controls.

d   AWS would probably have prevented these accidents. At Goswick the driver had not paid full attention to the distant signal.

9
SHEDS AND WORKSHOPS

THE LNER's locomotive running sheds on the company's formation ranged from the Stratford sprawl which was home to well over 300 engines, to remote one-stall sheds at the ends of rural branch lines. Their condition covered the whole gamut from well-maintained to deplorable neglect. In some, preparation had to be done without benefit of a pit; quite a number, operating only tank engines, possessed no turntable. Only two, Stratford and Hull Dairycoates, had progressed beyond coaling by hand; the remainder filled tenders and bunkers by shovel and brawny arms. Ashpit conditions were generally an affront to humanity. At some, locomotive standage space was so inadequate that at weekends they had to be farmed out to traffic sidings. Some were not even *sheds* at all in the literal sense.

The best were probably those on the Great Central's London Extension, built at the turn of the century to a semi-uniform pattern, adequate in size and well equipped by the standards of the time. The North British sheds were not far behind; they were solidly built (which is more than could be said for their wooden coal stages) though gloomy. The worst were often ex-North Eastern depots, old and approaching their end with little in the way of renewal in hand – which was inexcusable for such a wealthy railway. Many Great Eastern sheds were also deplorable, but there at least poverty could be legitimately pleaded. The Great Northern sheds and those of the Great North of Scotland came somewhere in between, usually adequate for the workload.

The general concensus was towards straight sheds, double-ended if the site allowed. By contrast, the North Eastern had hankered for roundhouses at its principal sheds, perhaps a hangover from Stockton & Darlington practice. Hull Dairycoates, with the largest allocation, had no less than *six* of them. Offices and staff amenities everywhere tended to be at best uninviting, and at worst more suited to the Dark Ages. Dormitories for men on lodging turns seemed to be placed in the noisiest proximity to shed yards and offered little privacy. Virtually all layouts had weaknesses in some degree: the important ex-GC shed at Gorton was brought to a standstill more than once a day while a shunt was made from the adjacent works right across the centre of the shed yard.

At least the infant LNER lost no time in getting the measure of its newly-acquired sheds. Sir Vincent Raven, the NER's chief mechanical engineer, was retained for a year to report on the organisation and standard of running sheds and main workshops. Much, he said, needed to be done to bring many of them up to acceptable standards. He also highlighted the number of locomotive overhauls being done at out-

GC Sheds

All the running sheds on the Great Central's London Extension were alike, and a description of Neasden will serve to illustrate them all. Covered accommodation for approximately half the allocation was provided by a six-road shed of the dead-end type sited at some distance from and at an angle to the main line. The running foreman's cabin, the control centre of any running shed was strategically placed about midway down the yard where the six shed roads converged, enabling the foreman to regulate the order of departure of the locomotives, which often left coupled two and three together with the one for the most distant destination in the lead.

Locomotives returning to shed also passed the cabin on their way to the turntable, coal stage and ashpits, and their crews were instructed on which shed road to place them so that each road could be built up in the correct order of departure for the next day's work. Those leaving at nearly the same time were not put on the same road for should the first locomotive fail, it would almost certainly delay the one behind it. The foreman had a shed turner or shunter and a set of shed enginemen to assist in marshalling the shed when the crews could not be used for berthing their charges.

Coaling was done manually from an elevated stage, a massive structure of blue brick supporting the depot's water storage tank of 100,000 gallons capacity. Wagons of coal were propelled up a steeply inclined ramp to the elevated stage and their contents shovelled into steel tubs on wheels, each holding half a ton; these were wheeled on to a kind of chute or drawbridge so contrived as to allow their contents to be tipped into the tenders or bunkers of the locomotives waiting below. – Bill Harvey. See Problems by the North Circular page 142.

Top Shed Kings Cross. Perhaps one of the LNER's best-known depots, Top Shed, was home to thousands of cockney enginemen over the years including such names as Sparshatt and Hoole. It was home too for many famous classes, Ivatt Atlantics, Gresley 'A1s' and 'A3s' and the superb streamlined 'A4s' as well as to more ubiquitous but superbly useful 'V2s'. Here, taken by one of the company's civil engineers, a 'K2' No 4659, 'A1' 2555 Centenary *and the engine of engines, No 4472* Flying Scotsman, *all agleam stand ready for the road.*

station shops attached to running sheds, over 400 a year on the Great Eastern alone. These small shops were usually ill-equipped to do such work economically.

The deficiencies were fully recognised and many acted upon, though under priorities slowed by an acute shortage of money. Shed buildings could usually be left to slowly moulder; there were no wagebill savings in putting new roofs on them. Mechanical coaling plants of appropriate size were financially worthwhile, since coalmen could be dispensed with to justify spending £10,000 for a 300-ton capacity wagon-hoist plant or under £1,000 for a small tub-hoist model. Ashpits clearly needed improvement and could bring savings, but the best means of doing so called for further experiment. Plenty of sheds received water supplies of very poor quality which could only be improved by water softening; this became common in the 1930s. It was also felt that cold water washing-out of boilers was unnecessarily time-consuming and imposed undue stresses in the boilers. This caused strong leanings towards provision of hot water washing plant.

130

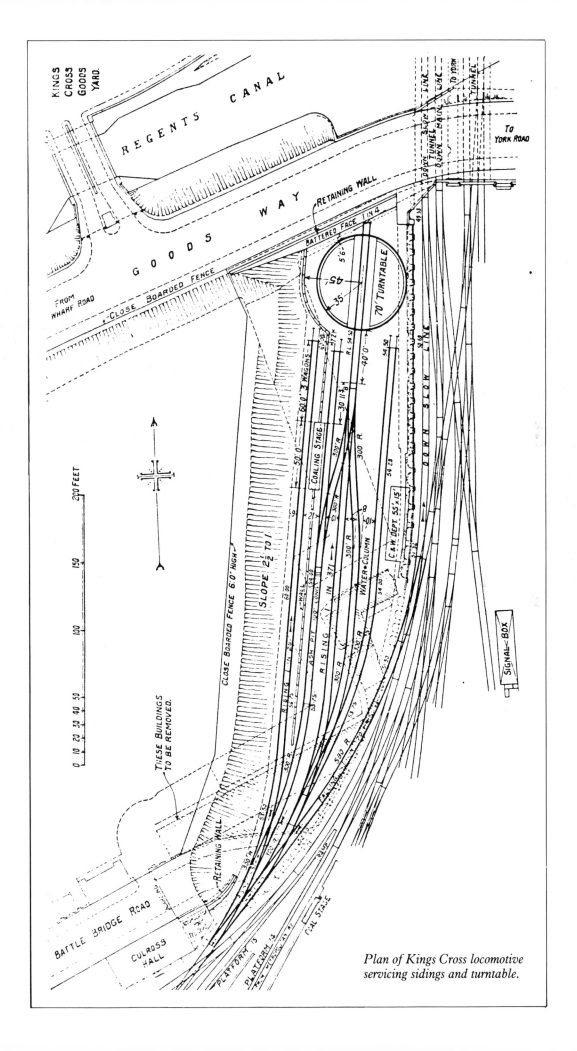

Plan of Kings Cross locomotive servicing sidings and turntable.

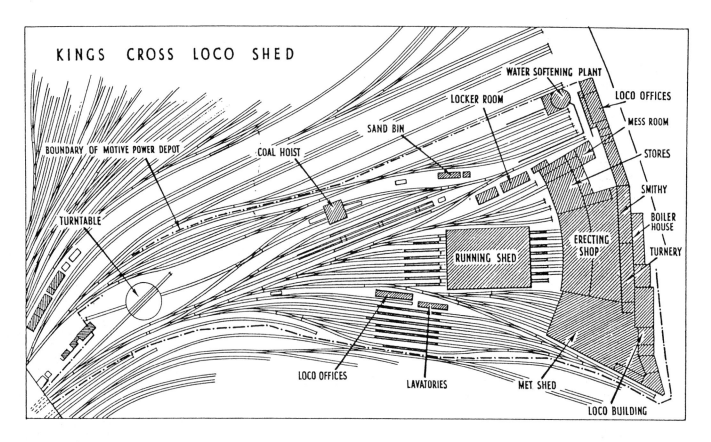

KINGS CROSS LOCO SHED

BOUNDARY OF MOTIVE POWER DEPOT

TURNTABLE

COAL HOIST

SAND BIN

LOCKER ROOM

WATER SOFTENING PLANT

LOCO OFFICES

MESS ROOM

STORES

SMITHY

BOILER HOUSE

TURNERY

ERECTING SHOP

RUNNING SHED

LOCO OFFICES

LAVATORIES

MET. SHED

LOCO BUILDING

Kings Cross Top Shed, the principal London depot for the East Coast route.

North Eastern shed. Gateshead on 1 April 1934. The locomotive to the right is one of the 'D20' class 4-4-0s No 1236 with the class clearly readable on the bufferbeam as was LNER practice. Behind the steam crane is what appears to be a class 'C7' Atlantic.

132

Where history was made. Stockton shed on 5 June 1938 with two of Gresley's ubiquitous 'J39' class 0-6-0s outside. Peeking out from behind the building is a Sentinel railcar in cream and green livery.

One of the first manifestations of such thinking was the erection of a 50-ton capacity coaling plant at Cudworth shed (ex Hull & Barnsley) in 1928. It was only a halfway house, for the wagons still needed to be unloaded manually into a one-ton skip hoist. Almost all subsequent plants were designed and built by specialist firms and were invariably of concrete construction. Both wagon-hoist and skip-hoist designs were used, with attention paid to ways of minimising coal breakage during handling. Early provision for recording coal issues to individual engines was soon abandoned. One depot, Neasden, actually had *two* coaling plants built, the first in the 1930s and the second in 1951 when the first became unworkable due to foundation subsidence! Mexborough, which was first listed for a large coaling plant in 1936 (a dilapidated coal stage had to be supplemented by use of the breakdown crane) finally got it in 1961 – only to see it demolished in 1965 when the shed closed to steam. By 1930 a satisfactory mini-coaler suited to moderate sized depots had also been developed, in which manually-filled narrow-gauge tubs were hoisted and tipped into tenders; this type was quite widely installed.

In the field of ash disposal the LNER inherited the usual crude and labour-intensive arrangements, along with the general practice of full-time firedroppers. The principle of wet ashpits was soon adopted, coupled with the North Eastern system of sunken ash wagon sidings so that at least gravity was on the side of the shovellers where grab cranes were not provided. The basic design went through several development

133

Consultation

After the last carthorse on the streets of Lincoln took it upon itself to kick in the plate glass window of an Italian restaurant, the accident report was duly despatched with the 'Agent's Personal Opinion' paragraph blank. 'Since this type of accident has never happened before, will you please say what made the animal shy', snapped back the district office. The reply: 'I don't know. However I have taken up strongly with the gelding concerned and by the look in his eyes it won't happen again.'

Another example of consultation not going according to the book occurred at Spalding. The original single manning agreement covering diesel shunting engines provided that a man 'in the line of promotion' (ie footplate grade) must ride with the driver if the engine had to go out onto the main line. When the district operating inspector heard that a yard pilot driver would not take a parcels van to a passenger station a hundred yards away because he was 'single manned' he popped down – to tell of the holiday he had just had in Spain. The train from Paris had been about 800 tons, went at about 80mph for about 500 miles without stopping – an electric engine, the driver about five feet tall, in a beret – all on his own. 'Yet you, you great daft b----- won't take one van a hundred yards up the main line.' 'Hang it on' said the driver. – Frank Harrison.

stages in order to give disposal men good access to locomotive ashpans. Two interesting steam cranes for this duty in Scotland were obtained in 1929 and 1932 from Sentinel. That used at Eastfield and Parkhead earned itself the nickname 'Stoorie Annie'. They lasted until 1959.

A handful of completely new sheds was built, either to meet changed traffic requirements or because the existing ones were hopelessly decrepit. First to be opened, in 1932, were Whitemoor (March), to service the newly-mechanised marshalling yard there, and Frodingham, where the expansion of the nearby steelworks had only emphasised the utter shambles which was the single-road Keadby shed, seven miles away. Darlington got a new shed in 1939 on a fresh site to replace a near ruin. It brought a new design of coaling plant in which the coal was stored on an open concrete slope after wagons had been hoisted, traversed over it and rotated. Only one similar (but larger) plant of this type was subsequently built, for the new Thornaby shed in 1958. A new shed at Darnall (an integral part of the Manchester–Sheffield–Wath electrification project) opened in 1943 to replace the disreputable shed at Neepsend. It incorporated all the LNER's distilled wisdom on optimum layout and equipment at the time, a through flow system with 70 foot turntable, 200-ton wagon-hoist coaling plant, wet ashpits with sunken ash wagon siding, ten road through shed with machine shop, electric wheeldrop and hot water washout plant. Probably only Thornaby fifteen years later represented any improvement on it. Wartime conditions also brought the concept of the 'light tunnel', an enclosed through building in which engines could be examined under good conditions; a number were installed. Truly it could be said that the LNER was in the forefront of running shed design in Britain; if only it had had more money to implement the plans.

Ignoring the outstation locomotive repair shops at running sheds (eg Norwich), which were quickly closed or turned over to the running department, the LNER took over some eighteen works. Only two Scottish ones (Cowlairs and Inverurie) and Stratford were integrated works dealing with locomotives, carriages and wagons. Doncaster 'Plant' dealt with locomotives and carriages, Dukinfield built and repaired carriages and wagons, while Walkergate (Newcastle) repaired both (including the Tyneside electric stock). The rest were single-purpose works.

Northwards in order, Stratford was a tight huddle of shops – the 'Hudson' works – on the east side of the main line. The locomotive erecting shop had seriously restricted access via a small turntable; nevertheless it had managed, as a stunt, to build an 0-6-0 in 9hr 47min in 1891. During World War 1 both the locomotive and carriage activities had spread to new buildings around the running shed, including a fine new erecting shop. By 1922 the works had built 1672 new locomotives, but this work ceased in 1924. The bad water throughout the eastern counties gave rise to a good deal of heavy boiler repairs.

At Doncaster the Plant regarded itself as the premier works. It had spread westwards to provide excellent new shops, of which the West Carriage Shop (1898) and the Crimpsall Repair shop for locomotives

134

They are queueing on the ashpit at Norwich shed after coaling and turning. A Britannia, two Sandringhams and a rebuilt Claud undergo servicing in the shadow of the 250-ton concrete coaling plant.

The little two-stall shed at Dereham was home for about a dozen men, and was located within a triangle of lines and dominated by maltings, the main industry of the town. Here an 'E4' 2-4-0 and 'J17' 0-6-0, grubby in the extreme, simmer placidly before their next duty.

Midland & Great Northern as seen by the LNER. Melton Constable was both a shed and locomotive headquarters to the M&GN which suffered many changes of classes after 1936 when the LNER took over responsibility for motive power. M&GN engines were decimated with more modern locomotives (albeit all secondhand) entering the scene. This picture shows such a position prior to the last change in BR days when new LMS class 4 2-6-0s were drafted in and served until the line's closure.

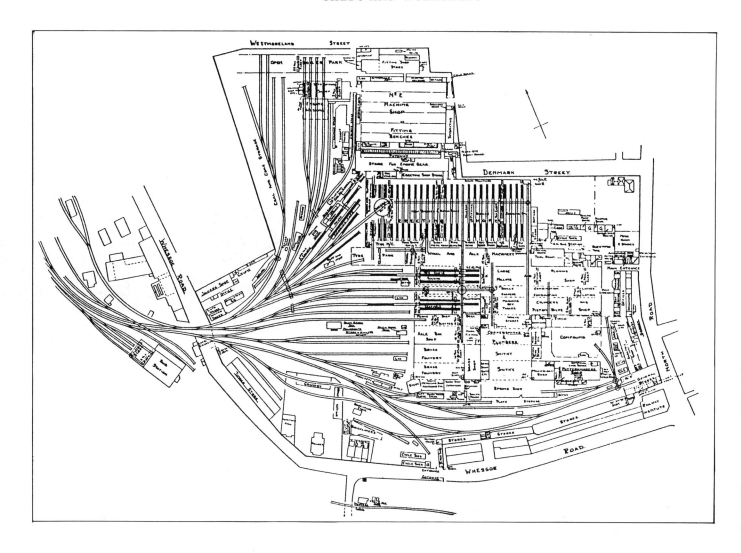

(1901) were the keys. Wagon work had been transferred to the new Carr shops in 1889, making more room for carriage building and repair.

In the Manchester area Gorton 'Tank' (so called because of the high-level water tank which dominated the works), hemmed in between the main line, running shed and housing areas, had been bursting at the seams by the turn of the century. In 1907 the carriage and wagon work was therefore transferred to a new works at Dukinfield, making room for the improvement of Gorton. From this time it had a splendid new 5-bay erecting shop capable of holding about 100 engines. With poor quality water at many Great Central sheds it saw a high proportion of heavy boiler repairs. The minor works at Tuxford (LD&ECR) and Rhosddu (Wrexham, WM&CQR) closed in 1927.

In the North-East, there were locomotive works at Gateshead and Darlington, the carriage works at York in addition to Walkergate (the latter closed in 1964), and wagon works at Shildon and (from 1922) Faverdale (Darlington). Gateshead was a cramped works squeezed on

North Road, Darlington, Locomotive Works, 1954.

Opposite.
A pall of smoke pollution permanently overhung St Margarets shed in Edinburgh, which was surrounded by housing and had an allocation of over 200 engines. Shunting tanks were accommodated in the old works buildings off the picture to the left. The 'K2' is passing on the down East Coast main line, which ran through the middle of the shed yard. There was no coaling plant, only the manual stage on the right.

137

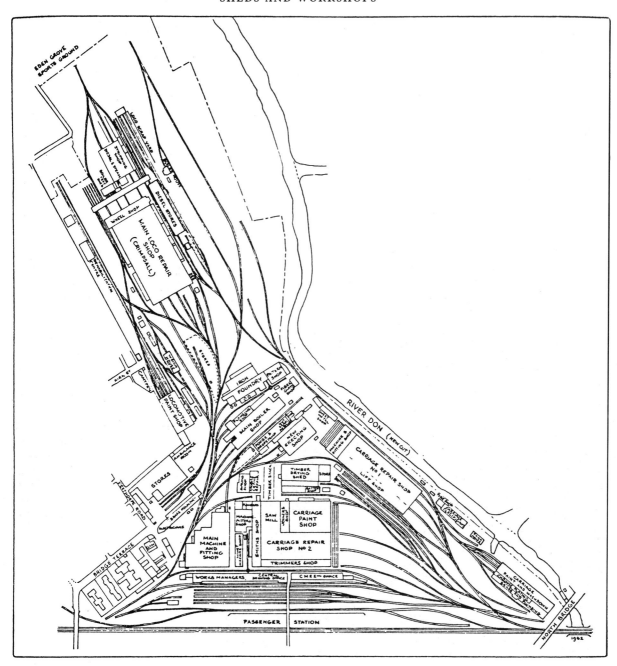

Doncaster locomotive and carriage works.

the south Tyne bank, but until 1910, when all new building was concentrated on Darlington, it had traditionally built the NER's larger locomotives. It was never self-sufficient, going to outside industry for its heavy castings and forgings. Darlington works, dating from 1863, had been extensively modernised before its takeover by the LNER. A new erecting shop opened in 1903, new boiler, tender and paint shops on the Stooperdale site in 1910, new offices two years later and new tinsmiths' and machine shops at the end of World War 1.

The principal Scottish works was at Cowlairs (Glasgow). It could hardly be said to rank with the two 'Ds', and with pure Scottish water its boiler work was comparatively limited. In 1919 it found itself with

138

serious arrears of locomotive repairs, necessitating sending engines to outside contractors for overhaul. Away in Aberdeenshire, the small works at Inverurie led an unspectacular life; it had opened as late as 1901 on a green field site to replace the hopelessly inadequate Kittybrewster. The small repair shops at Kipps and St Margarets (Edinburgh) were handed to the running department in 1925.

The devolved management laid down by the LNER at first saw six (later four) mechanical engineers, of ex-CME or assistant status, installed at the main works. These men could be left to run the works and other activities in their areas under a light rein, with Gresley looking after design, testing and general coordination. As a result there were minor differences in design and works practices between them.

The small outstation repair shops were early victims of Raven's appraisal, and after 1924 new locomotive building was concentrated on Doncaster, Darlington and (spasmodically) Gorton. The depression forced the closure of Gateshead in 1932, though it was resuscitated during World War 2 and did not finally close until 1959. In the retained

Ash Pan Man

One of the dirtiest jobs in St Margarets was that of ash pan man – cleaning hot ashes from underneath the loco's firegrate. Most of the big engines had drop grates and the fierce fire dropped into the ash pan on its way to the ash pit. It hardly seems possible that human beings could survive in such conditions but for years wee Andrew Elder, all five feet of him, went down into that hell umpteen times during a shift and thrived on it. Choking and gasping with the wind blowing the hot muck into his face, Andrew would put his head out between the wheels for a breather and always he was smiling and cracking a joke.

As drivers waited to take the locos on to the shed one might cry out, 'Come oot o'there, ye silly wee so-and-so' and Andrew would cheerfully reply, 'All right – I'll no be long'. Although filter masks were available to protect the air passage, Andrew never wore such things. All the impurities were washed away during regular visits to Jock's Lodge pub immediately above his place of work. There was a well-worn path between the ash lyes and the pub and nobody grudged Andrew or the fire-droppers their ration. – Charles Meacher in *LNER Footplate Memories*.

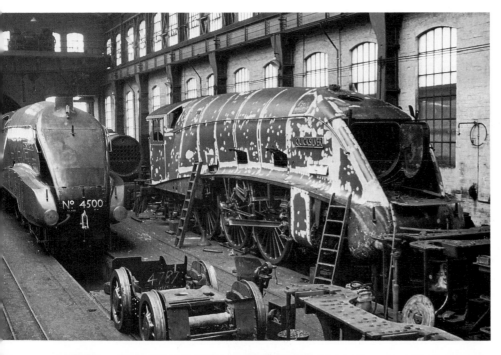

Great Northern works. A corner of Doncaster's Crimpsall erecting shop in 1938 reveals new 'A4' No 4500 Garganey in garter blue, ready to leave while No 2510 Quicksilver, now three years old, is being reassembled after overhaul; valve setting appears to have been completed, though the driving wheel turning device is still in position.

Great Central works. Gorton's splendid erecting shop in 1938, GC Atlantic No 5267, 'Q4' 0-8-0 No 5153 and 'J39' 0-6-0 No 2999 are being stripped for overhaul, surrounded by a seemingly disorderly collection of components ranging from boilers to brake rigging.

North Eastern shops. Darlington works about 1923 or 1924. The 'new' erecting shop built in 1903 with a class 'J27' (NER class 'P3') 0-6-0 on the left. There are some tenders at the end of the shop, one of which appears to be a Great Central design.

works, the old system whereby the complete overhaul of a locomotive was entrusted to one small gang of men had to change under economic pressure to one of specialist groups. This reduced the time in works dramatically; locomotives under and awaiting works repair had fallen from 11½ per cent to 7 per cent by 1930, and general repairs previously taking 60–70 working days were reduced to 23 days. Assisting this improvement was the expenditure in these first eight years of £0.5 million on new machine tools, including £150,000 for 37 new wheel lathes (£4,000 each; what inflation has done for us!) A noteworthy plus point was the capability of the Gorton iron foundry to produce very large, complex items such as the monobloc three-cylinders-and-saddle castings for Gresley's largest engines; those for the 2-8-2 *Cock o' the North* with poppet valves were particularly intricate.

The 1930s saw continuing retrenchment. Gorton had continued a trickle of new building, but even this ceased in 1938–9 (the post-war demand for new locomotives brought building back in the 1948–50 period). Dukinfield ceased carriage repairs in 1939, and but for the war might well have closed soon after. A major disaster overtook Doncaster at the end of 1940, when the Main Carriage Shop (largely devoted to new building) was burned down. It was not back in production until 1949, by that time equipped for building steel-panelled coaches instead of teak.

140

Under BR, and with steam traction still almost universal, the works carried on very much as before, though Gorton in the 1950s was engaged on building electric locomotives for the Manchester–Sheffield–Wath route. But the shadow of the 1955 Modernisation Plan fell over them, and things were never the same again. During 1957 both Doncaster and Darlington ceased to build steam locomotives, and in 1963 Doncaster completed its last steam overhaul, taking on instead the task of building diesel and electric locomotives and repairing diesel locomotives and multiple units. The carriage side there, as at York also, was re-equipped to build all-steel coaches and emus. In 1964 the Main Carriage Shop closed for coach repairs and reverted to wagon repairs with the closure of the Carr. With the completion of diesel locomotive construction, the end came in 1987, though part of the works undertakes wagon work under private enterprise and part is used for the National Parts Store. Darlington produced diesel locomotives in the early 1960s, but with the completion of the Modernisation Plan and the elimination of steam the works closed in 1965 and was sold off. Cowlairs, Inverurie and Stratford closed in 1963, 1969 and 1963 respectively; the Cowlairs site is now covered by a new industrial estate.

So the great works empire which the LNER took over in 1923 is now reduced, after 65 years, to a single BREL works at York, busy turning out emus to feed (mainly) Network South-East. The winds of change have blown through it with a vengeance.

In the shadow of Ben Nevis. Fort William shed on 12 June 1936 showing the two classic locomotive classes of the period, the 'K2' and the 'D34'. Of the visible locomotives only two are identifiable: 'K2' No 4685 Loch Treig and 'D34' No 9035 Glen Gloy.

Problems by the North Circular

LONDON area locomotive depots were unique in their managerial difficulties, particularly during and after World War 2. In large measure these sprang from the acute problem of recruiting – and keeping – suitable servicing and maintenance staff, and to a lesser extent for the footplate grades. Nowhere were these difficulties more manifest than at the ex-GC depot at Neasden.

In 1944 it was just about on its knees. The shedmaster was away a lot through illness, the staff shortage dire. In April, Bill Harvey, then working as a headquarters technical assistant, was told by the locomotive running superintendent to 'put it right'. Some order! The arrival of US Transportation Corps 2-8-0s was seriously aggravating the problems, while weaknesses were also showing up on the British-built WD engines.

Harvey's diary is illuminating. The first dragon to be slain was the grease-lubricated axleboxes and motion of the US engines.

11 July. Post haste to Neasden, 23 engines stopped, 14 US hot.

15 July. Reported to GAM (the LRS) that examiners are misled by high running temperatures of all-bronze bearings into thinking they are hot. Instructed to go to Neasden immediately and examine all 14 US engines stopped – released 5 still warm, remainder after pad and journal exam; GAM delighted.

29 July. Matt (shedmaster) off sick; to Neasden: in hell of a mess, 22 engines stopped, both wheel drop tables broken and less than one day's supply of coal left.

31 July. Acting Depot Supt at Neasden until MDR resumes duty; 30 engines stopped: released 5432 hot box, 1125 middle big end and 2561.

2 August. 27 engines stopped: released 5024 and 4861 spring. Driver Woods refused to take soldier (Canadian Transportation Corps) as fireman – suspended.

4 August. 22 engines stopped; 1st Hospital special 29 mins late away, taking coal – GAM livid.

5 August. 19 engines stopped. Ran out of coal at 04.30, engines on shed without coal. Ashmen (Craddock and Newton) stayed back and filled two wagons from stack – arranged for lifting from stack with steam crane and ash elevator.

7 August. Casual labour picked up 82 tons.

9 August. Coal hopper ran out during night, delays to 06.15, 06.35, 07.05, 07.20 – coal coming in driblets. Lifted 90 tons – Left for home at 19.50.

10 August. Lifted 88 tons. Italian POWs getting difficult.

12 August. Only 4 hours supply of coal left: HQ promises early delivery. 5336 derailed under coaling plant, coaling from one chute.

13 August (Sunday). Hot and sunny – ought to be on river! To shed 09.00 – picked up 71 tons – 28 footplate absentees. Home 14.45 – returned 16.45. Coaling plant stopped, seized eccentric on jigger feed – released it – dep 20.00 hrs.

14 August. Better outlook, 1½ days supply of coal and only 14 engines stopped – spoke too soon! 5369 in collision. Coaling plant now out of action for good. Emergency arrangements for coaling at manual stage.

15 August. Mitchells contacted re plant repair – organising emergency coaling squads (Italian POWs) for old manual stage. Tank engines coaling in London.

16 August. First squad of Italian POWs arrived 18.00 hrs.

19 August. Engine of 1st Ambulance special blocked in by empty coal wagons. Electric coal hoist at Marylebone overran; tub over the top – forget it for a few hours!

20 August. No fireman for 1st ambulance special; 2550 failed with injectors for 09.50 Manchester – fitters taking shelter during air raid; Running Foreman S. Woods lighting up engines on his own.

By November Harvey was back at Neasden, with absenteeism (resulting from long hours) the critical factor.

26 November. Commencement of Sunday night vigils at Neasden to ensure punctual departure of engines working early morning business trains.

13 December. Short of power – Bad position for wash outs. Reprimanded. Italian NCO – very uppish . . .

17 December. OK for power but 01.35, 02.35 and 03.55 trains to Woodford cancelled – no firemen. 5 drivers and 12 firemen absent . . .

23 December. 6338 failed at Northolt on up road; 5276 accidentally or deliberately turned into and collided with North Circular Road bridge – displacing gas main slightly.

11 January (1945). Italian POW Capone Rocco knocked down and seriously injured when an engine collided with ash elevator ('Man dead! Man dead!') – to Park Royal hospital.

18 January. Freezing rain and sleet; K3 No 3814 working 281 special petrol train collided with electric train at Rickmansworth. 50 Italians 'mutinied'.

29 January. Prolonged period (17-29 Jan) of hard frost and sub-zero temperatures; 5505 frozen up in cylinders, wheels skidded when dragged out. 07.18 Denham cancelled, no steam or fire – why?

9 February. 6inch water main to tank burst – put paid to washing out – valve closed. No water available at columns or in shed – can't understand why.

10 February. Mystery solved: Isolated by closure of wrong valve; thought to be the one that isolates No 7 road.

2 March. WD 77364 derailed all wheels at loco inlet points at 13.50. Borrowed Met. 30-ton crane – (Neasden crane in shops). Overload alarm bell kept ringing, driver as nervous as a cat – managed to get ropes off drum. Engine rerailed 21.51, tender 00.18. Last train gone – slept in chair in office.

15 March. Picked up 102 tons coal. Visit from Camp Commandant, appears to think Italians hard done by.

2 April (Easter Monday). Right out of coal; hopper empty at 20.00 Sunday. Dislodged residue from sides of bunker with Mills hand grenade taken from Home Guard stores.

3 April. Special coal train run from Woodford – very satisfactory, only one passenger train cancelled.

There was hope that things could now be kept on a relatively even keel. But four years later, Neasden was again deep in crisis, due to acute shortage of maintenance staff and the heavy workload caused by the dreadful Thompson 'L1' 2-6-4 tanks. But that's another story!

When times were good. A pre-World War II outer suburban train from Marylebone to Aylesbury headed by the then almost standard engine class for the journey – an ex Great Central-designed 'A5' tank No 5024 seen at Chorley Wood on 5 June 1938.

Beccles

Beccles is an excellent example of how many East Anglian stations have changed. Of early construction, it had a red brick main building with a robust wooden structure on the up island platform. Once it boasted five signal boxes, fifty staff. The stationmaster would march down the road to take up his day's duty in his frock coat with fresh buttonhole, looking every inch the pillar of the local community. His big day was when the entire Suffolk Show arrived by rail in 1927.

Now there is but a single track with two-hourly paytrains. But, imagine, an express from Yarmouth South Town is arriving, the coaches from Lowestoft being added to the front, and passengers hurrying over the bridge from the Waveney Valley train in platform 1. Meantime a down local has arrived in No 2, while two locomotives are shunting in the extensive yards and all the signalmen are at attention.

Facing page.
A once busy junction. With the closure of the old GC line as well as the Stratford-on-Avon & Midland Junction route, Woodford (later Woodford Halse) has totally disappeared. This 1930s photograph mentions all the delights but it was a weary journey to Stratford.

Wrexham, Mold and Connagh's Quay. Worked by ex Great Central engines this interloper into Great Western territory remains open. On 4 May 1951 the scene was much as it had been for years with 'N5' 0-6-2 tank No E9289, carrying the early British Railways lettering on its sides, running in with a Seacombe or Chester to Wrexham train. The Great Western General station is in the background.

10
BRANCH LINE MISCELLANY

THE LNER's branch and secondary lines were as varied as the terrain they served, from the Thames to the West Highland, from East Anglia well into North Wales. There were 'penetrating' lines such as that to Silloth on the Solway Firth, joint ventures including the Cheshire Lines Committee, Light Railways, short branches and strings of branches that had been built into some kind of cross-country routes. There were lines that hardly climbed at all such as those in the Fens, branches that took one into spectacular Dales and over the Pennines to Penrith, with some major traffic centres exclusively served by a portfolio of branches.

If there were a special LNER factor it was in the timetabling and general administration of the lines, each of which was viewed as a separate business whose costs had to be controlled as traffic had to be encouraged long before that was generally fashionable. But then the LNER was always hot on paper work and analysis; the traffic apprentices saw to that. Physically the branches might have remained as timeless as those of the Great Western, and undoubtedly the trains themselves remained remarkably unaltered. But the *services* were frequently adjusted. More trains ran on certain days only or for a variety of seasonal periods, and more overall changes were made than elsewhere,

144

often according to the results of experiments. The lowest common denominator service was sparser than elsewhere, and Sunday services especially in winter were very sparingly provided.

Thus the small town railwayman in some distant part might not get quite the glory from the *Silver Jubilee* that the whole of the Great Western enjoyed from Paddington's achievements, but he generally felt his personal efforts counted more, ideas certainly being more welcome. To this Great Western enthusiasts might add that at least tourists could see out of their trains, which was by no means always possible from the grimy LNER secondary stock. Indeed, nowhere was dieselisation more welcome in BR days than on ex-LNER branches, especially in the North East where their availability immediately became a selling point in the region's official timetable.

One of the LNER's curiosities was the large mileage of coastline that could be viewed (if need be through an open window) from its trains. Of branches which have been lost but whose colourful history is still vividly recalled, that between Scarborough and Whitby via Ravenscar immediately comes to mind: a route of vicious gradients, changeable climate and erratic traffic flows. Here indeed the service was constantly being changed, no useful opportunity to add to the coffers being missed, but unnecessary engine mileage (around a pound sterling per ton for coal alone) pruned. Not all seaside railways were as scenic; you could hardly imagine a more desolate place than that occupied by Hartlepool Cemetery North signal box. And in LNER days even the West Highland line lacked much glamour. Not only was vision often restricted by thick smoke and steam of frequently two hard-working locomotives, as well as grime on the windows, but most passengers were workers from the Western Isles not noted for their civilised standards. Many a visitor was

Hiking the West Highland

Locomotives of Great Eastern origin or descent penetrated after grouping to some odd places off their native heath.

It was in Scotland, however, that the ex-Great Eastern was most strongly represented by a batch of the 4-6-0s designed by Holden and classed B12 by the LNER, which on being transferred to the north were nicknamed 'Hikers'.

It was not on the former GNS but over sections of both the Callander & Oban and the West Highland that two of us travelled behind a 'Hiker' – on a Sunday in July 1937. For the modest sum of 5s 6d (27½p) plus high tea at around half a crown (12½p) we covered some 190 miles from the Firth of Forth to the Firth of Clyde and back, through splendid loch and mountain scenery behind both NB and GE locos.

Our light train of five 'Green Goddess' excursion set coaches, 152 tons, was hustled out of Edinburgh Waverley by ex-NB Holmes 'Intermediate' class of 1906, No 9890. She trotted us out to the Forth Bridge in lively style, 65mph after Turnhouse being the highest speed of the day, since the subsequent schedules were planned for the enjoyment of the scenery.

Having reached Stirling via Dunfermline and Alloa, 9890 hooked off, and at the other end there backed down No 8548, a B12 'Hiker', fitted with the ACFI feed water heating apparatus atop the boiler. This gadget attracted the attention of a humorous-minded bystander who asked the driver (now joined by an LMS conductor for the next stage over the 'Caley' to Crianlarich) whether 'yon' contraption was for tea making. Then through Dunblane and Callander to Balquhidder for a brief water stop before tackling the five miles rising continuously at 1 in 60 to
continued on page 148

Typical LNER cross-country services of 1939, including the Grimsby & Immingham electric tramway.

Table 64 GRANTHAM and LINCOLN

Miles	Week Days only	mrn	mrn	mrn	M	S	mrn	aft	H
	London(K C)dep	4 45	7F25	8Z45	10F15	10F15	11K30	4 F 0	5F50
—	Grantham.... dep	7 15	9 41	11 18	12 30	1 23	2 52	6 13	8 3
4¼	Barkston	..	..	..	..	..	Aa	..	..
6½	Honington	7 26	9 52	11 29	..	1 34	3 4	6 24	..
9¾	Caythorpe	7 33	9 59	11 39	..	1 41	3 11	6 31	..
12½	Leadenham	7 38	10 4	11 44	Kk	1 46	3 16	6 36	Kk
16	Navenby	7 43	10 9	11 49	..	1 51	3 21	6 41	..
19	Harmston	7 48	1014	11 54	..	1 56	3 26	6 46	..
20¾	Waddington	7 52	1018	11 58	..	2 0	3 30	6 50	..
24¾	**Lincoln**(LNER) arr	8 0	1026	12 6	1 3	2 8	3 38	6 58	8 37

Miles	Week Days only	mrn	mrn	H	M	aft	aft	aft	S
—	**Lincoln** (L·N·E·R)dep	7 35	8 56	1028	1 26	1 56	4 4	6 22	9 45
4	Waddington	7 43	..	1036	..	2 4	4 12	6 30	9 53
5¾	Harmston	7 47	..	1040	..	2 8	4 16	6 34	9 57
8¾	Navenby	7 52	..	1045	..	2 13	4 21	6 39	10 2
12¼	Leadenham	7 59	Nn	1052	..	2 20	4 28	6 47	10 9
15	Caythorpe	8 5	..	1058	..	2 26	4 34	6 53	1015
18¼	Honington	8 10	..	11 3	..	2 31	4 39	6 58	1020
20½	Barkston	..	..	..	..	..	..	..	..
24¾	**Grantham** 54, arr	8 20	9 30	1113	1 59	2 41	4 50	7 10	1030
130	**London**(K.C.)..arr	1028	11F20	1F15	....	4VF50	6F55	9F25	3 15

Aa Stops when required to take up. F Restaurant Cars between King's Cross and Grantham H Thro' Carr, between King's Cross & Lincoln. K Buffet Car between King's Cross & Peterborough. Kk Stops when required to set down from London (King's Cross). M Mons. only. Nn Stops at 9 13 mrn when required to take up for London (K.C.). S Saturdays only. V Arr. 5 35 aft on Sats. Z Buffet Car. between King's Cross and Grantham.

For **OTHER TRAINS** between Grantham and Honington, see Table 54

Table 71 NEW HOLLAND and IMMINGHAM

Miles	Week Days only	mrn	mrn		aft E	aft S	aft		aft	aft		aft S			
—	**New Holland**....... dep	6 53	8 53	..	1215	1218	1 47	..	3 23	6 9	..	7 30	..	..	..
2¼	Goxhill	6 58	8 53	..	1220	1223	1 52	..	3 28	6 14	..	7 34	..	..	..
5	East Halton............	7 6	9 6	..	1228	1231	2 0	..	3 36	6 22	..	7 42	..	..	..
7¾	Killingholme	7 14	9 14	..	1236	1239	2 8	..	3 44	6 30	..	7 50	..	..	..
9¾	**Immingham Dock**.. arr	7 20	9 20	..	1242	1245	2 14	..	3 50	6 36	..	7 56	..	..	..

Miles	Week Days only	mrn	mrn		non S	aft		aft	aft		aft	aft S			
—	**Immingham Dock**.. dep	8 0	1025	..	12 0	1256	..	2 35	5 18	..	6 52	8 20	..	..	..
2	Killingholme	8 6	1030	..	12 6	1 2	..	2 41	5 24	..	6 58	8 26	..	..	..
4¾	East Halton............	8 14	1039	..	1214	1 10	..	2 49	5 32	..	7 6	8 34	..	..	..
7½	Goxhill	8 24	1047	..	1222	1 18	..	2 57	5 40	..	7 14	8 42	..	..	..
9¾	**New Holland** 69 ... arr	8 28	1052	..	1227	1 24	..	3 2	5 45	..	7 19	8 47	..	..	..

NOTES

E Except Saturdays

S Saturdays only

For **OTHER TRAINS** between New Holland and Goxhill, see Table 68

Table 72 GRIMSBY and IMMINGHAM ELECTRIC RAILWAY

This service is subject to revision. Particulars of any alterations made will be announced locally

Grimsby (Corporation Bridge) to Immingham Dock—7 miles

WEEK DAYS			SUNDAYS
Depart mrn	Depart mrn	Depart aft	Depart mrn
12A50	10 50	6 50	3 0
1A50	11 20	7 20	5 20
3A0	11 50	7 50	7 0
4A15	aft	8 50	8 40
5A20	12 20	9 20	10 20
5A50	12 50	9 50	11 40
6A20	1 20	10 30	aft
6A50	1 50	10E50	1 20
7A10	2 20	11 30	3 0
7A20	2 50	..	4 40
7 50	3 20	..	6 0
8 20	3 50	..	7 20
8 30	4 20	..	9 20
8 50	4 50	..	10 20
9 20	5 20	..	11 20
9 50	5 50	..	..
10 20	6 20	..	..

Immingham Dock to Grimsby (Corporation Bridge)—7 miles

WEEK DAYS			SUNDAYS
Depart mrn	Depart mrn	Depart aft	Depart mrn
12 20	11 50	5B50	12 20
1 20	noon	6B20	3 45
2 20	12S0	6B50	6 0
3 45	aft	7B20	8 0
4 45	12 20	7B50	9 40
5 50	12 50	8B20	11 0
6 20	1 20	9B20	aft
6 50	1 50	10B0	12 40
7 20	2 20	10B20	2 20
7 50	2 50	11B0	4 0
8 20	3 20	11EB20	5 20
8 50	3 50	..	6 40
9 20	4B20	..	8 50
9 50	4B50	..	9 50
10 20	5EB0	..	10 50
10 50	5EB5	..	..
11 20	5B20	..	..

NOTES

The Cars call at the following places: Yarboro' Street, Stortford Street, Cleveland Bridge and Immingham Town, and by request at Jackson Street, Boulevard Recreation Ground, Cleveland Street, Great Coates Level Crossing, No. 5 Passing Place, Marsh Road Level Crossing, and Kiln Lane (Stallingborough). Workmen's Daily Return Tickets, Grimsby to Immingham Dock, fare 7½d. are issued to *bona-fide* workmen by Cars marked "A," available to return by Cars marked "B." On Saturdays only Workmen's Daily Return Tickets are available to return by any Car after 11 0 mrn

E Except Saturdays
S Saturdays only

Table 66 LINCOLN, DUKERIES JUNCTION, SHIREBROOK, and CHESTERFIELD

Miles	Week Days only	mrn	mrn	mrn	mrn	aft S	aft	aft S	aft	aft N	aft S	aft E	aft	aft E	aft S	aft P	aft S	
	Lincoln (L·N·E·R) .. dep	..	..	9 30	From Nottingham (dep 9 46 mrn)	..	1232	..	..	4 25	..	..	6 20	..	..	853	9 20	..
3¼	Skellingthorpe	..	..	9 37		..	1239	..	..	4 32	..	..	6 27	..	..	..	9 27	..
6¼	Doddington and Harby	..	..	9 43		..	1245	..	..	4 38	..	..	6 33	..	..	..	9 33	..
9½	Clifton-on-Trent	..	..	9 49		..	1251	..	..	4 44	..	..	6 39	..	..	..	9 39	..
11¼	Fledborough	..	..	9 54		..	1256	..	..	4 49	..	..	6 44	..	..	..	9 44	..
14½	Dukeries Junction arr	..	..	10 0		..	1 2	..	..	4 55	..	..	6 50	..	..	..	9 49	..
	Dukeries Junction dep	..	..	10 1		..	1 3	..	..	4 56	..	..	6 51	..	..	..	9 51	..
15½	Tuxford (Central)	..	..	10 4		..	1 6	..	..	4 59	..	..	6 54	..	..	..	9 54	..
18¾	Boughton	..	..	1010		..	1 12	..	..	5 5	..	..	7 0	..	..	..	..	..
21¼	Ollerton	..	..	1018		..	1 20	..	..	5 13	..	..	7 8	..	..	927	10 6	..
22¾	Edwinstowe	..	..	1022		..	1 24	..	..	5 17	..	..	7 12	..	..	932	1010	..
—	Mansfield (L·N·E·R) dp	..	..	..	1031	1240	..	..	4 13	..	..	..	..	..	..	..	..	..
27¼	Warsop	..	..	1030	1046	1255	1 32	..	4 28	5 25	..	..	7 20	..	..	..	1018	..
29¾	Shirebrook (North) C arr	..	..	1035	..	1 0	1 37	..	4 33	5 30	..	..	7 25	..	..	..	1023	..
35	Mansfield (LMS) arr	..	..	1052	..	..	4 39	..	..	..	..	..	7 40	..	..	..	1214	..
—	Shirebrook (North). dep	7 15	8 27	1046	..	1 15	1 43	2 13	4 35	..	552	631	7 30	850	9 20	..	1025	..
31½	Scarcliffe	7 20	8 32	1051	..	1 20	1 48	2 18	4 40	..	557	..	7 35	855	9 25	..	1030	..
33¾	Bolsover	7 27	8 39	1058	..	1 27	1 55	2 25	4 47	..	6 4	641	7 42	9 2	9 32	..	1037	..
36¼	Arkwright Town	7 33	8 45	11 4	..	1 33	2 1	2 31	4 52	..	610	..	7S48	..	9 38	..	..	..
39½	Chesterfield F .. arr	7 40	8 52	1111	..	1 40	2 8	2 38	4 59	..	617	652	7 53	913	9 45	..	1048	..

Miles	Week Days only	mn	mn	mn R	mrn	mrn	aft S	aft	aft N	aft S	aft	aft S	aft E	aft E	aft S	aft S	aft E	aft S	aft S
	Chesterfield F ...... dep	..	755	..	1010		1225	1 10	..	230	4 0	520	6 0	7 0	7 0	845	932	10 0	11 0
3¼	Arkwright Town	..	8 3	..	1018		..	1 18	..	238	4 8	528	6 8	..	7 8	853	..	10 8	..
5¾	Bolsover	..	8 9	..	1024		1236	1 24	..	244	4 14	534	614	7 12	7 14	859	944	1014	1112
8	Scarcliffe	..	816	..	1031		1243	1 31	..	251	4 21	541	621	7 19	7 21	9 6	..	1021	..
9¾	Shirebrook (North) C arr	..	820	..	1035		1247	1 35	..	255	4 25	545	625	7 23	7 25	910	954	1025	1121
—	Mansfield (LMS) dp	..	..	..	1028	Nottingham		12S55	..	..	4 10	..	..	..	7 15	..	..	..	..
—	Shirebrook (North). dep	630	..	..	1046	..	..	1 37	1 54	257	4 30	..	..	..	7 30	..	..	..	..
12¼	Warsop	635	..	..	1051	11 0	..	1 42	1 59	3 1	4 35	..	..	..	7 35	..	..	..	..
19	Mansfield (L·N·E·R) arr	650	..	..	..	1115	..	1 57	..	317	..	..	..	..	..	..	..	..	..
16¾	Edwinstowe	734	..	916	1059	To Nottingham (arr. 11 53 mrn)	..	..	2 7	..	4 44	..	..	..	7 43	..	..	..	..
18¼	Ollerton	738	..	920	11 5		..	..	2 13	..	4 50	..	..	..	7 49	..	..	..	..
20¾	Boughton	743	..	..	1110		..	..	Aa	..	4 55	..	..	..	..	..	..	..	..
24	Tuxford (Central)	749	..	..	1116		..	..	2 22	..	5 1	..	..	..	7 58	..	..	..	..
25	Dukeries Junction arr	..	..	..	1118		..	..	..	..	5 3	..	..	..	..	..	..	..	..
	Dukeries Junction dep	..	..	..	1119		..	..	2 24	..	5 5	..	..	..	..	..	..	..	..
28¼	Fledborough	756	..	..	1124		..	..	2 29	..	5 10	..	..	..	8 5	..	..	..	..
30	Clifton-on-Trent	8 1	..	..	1129		..	..	2 34	..	5 15	..	..	..	8 10	..	..	..	..
33¼	Doddington and Harby	8 7	..	..	1135		..	..	2 39	..	5 21	..	..	..	8 16	..	..	..	..
36¼	Skellingthorpe	813	..	..	1141		..	..	2 45	..	5 27	..	..	..	8 22	..	..	..	..
39½	Lincoln (L·N·E·R) 52, 61 arr	819	..	952	1147		..	..	2 51	..	5 35	..	..	..	8 28	..	..	..	..

NOTES

Aa Stops if required
C Sta. for Langwith
E or E Except Sats.
F Market Place
N Fridays only
P Sats. only. Commences 17th June. Thro Train, Cleethorpes (dep. 7 28 aft) and Skegness (dep. 7 38 aft) to Leicester (Cen.) arr 11 9 aft (Tables 57, 70,
R Sats. only. Commences 17th June. Thro Train, Leicester (Cen.) (dep. 7 40 mrn) to Cleethorpes (arr. 11 16 mrn) and Skegness (arr. 11 11 mrn) (Tables 70 and 57)
S or S Saturdays only

Picking up the jam. Tiptree station on the Kelvedon & Tollesbury Light Railway. A mixed train behind an ex Great Eastern Railway '769' class 0-6-0 tank makes ready for departure on 19 August 1950.

continued from page 145
Glenoglehead Summit, 941ft above sea level; our speed on the ascent ranged between 20–23mph, the total time for the 45 miles from Stirling to Crianlarich was 88 minutes.

After an interval to admire scenery (and refreshment) and with 8548 having brought the train round from the Caley station to that of the West Highland and turned, we set off cautiously down the long initial descent to Ardlui with the head of Loch Lomond to our left and thence Loch Long on the other side; beyond Arrochar 8548 tackled the five mile ascent mostly at 1 in 57 to Glen Douglas summit, on which our minimum speed was 21mph. The 36½ miles from Crianlarich to Craigendoran were covered at an average speed, many slacks included, of 32½mph.

Our faithful 'Hiker' came off at Cowlairs West Junction, presumably to retire to Eastfield shed, and was replaced by our friend of the morning, No 9890 for the return to Waverley. – D. S. M. Barrie.

Publicity for famous trains. The covers of booklets presented to passengers on the three LNER streamlined expresses plus a luggage label from the Silver Jubilee *and a set of luggage labels for the* Flying Scotsman. *The booklets, which were issued annually contained timetables, a schematic layout of the train seating, point to point mileages with related speeds (prepared by Cecil J Allen), restaurant car tariff and a map of the route concerned.*

disappointed at the ambiance not to mention the food in the West Highland's restaurant cars, but at least the better off could retreat to the privacy of their sleeping compartment.

The Great Eastern always seemed to be playing hide and seek with tidal water. Between the Thames and Wash it had an astonishing number of termini by or near the sea or estuary. Variety was endless: Hadleigh worked for a time by North Eastern class 'J21' 0-6-0s; Felixstowe Beach where the two drivers did not speak to each other; the freight-only branch to Snape (had this only been preserved, what a way to arrive at the Maltings for a concert!); Aldeburgh with its visits by the *Eastern Belle Pullman* and its neat garden vying with that at the junction, Saxmundham, for perfection; the Air Ministry extension at Pulham Market on the Waveney Valley line particularly for the R33 airship; and the Hunstanton branch where (admittedly in BR days) there occurred what must be the only instance of a steam locomotive being hit by a floating bungalow.

But East Anglia's attractions were not only coastal. Both the Norwich and King's Lynn main lines threw off branches on either side, some combining to form somewhat dubious cross-country routes whose passenger traffic would inevitably become vulnerable to private cars and buses. And competition from pre-grouping days gave rise to anomolies such as the small town of Ramsey being served both by the Great Northern from Holme and by the GN&GE Joint line's only branch from Somersham. But even where there seems to have been duplication, or at least optimism, country stations all had their busy periods, and often indeed became social centres as goods wagons were marshalled at the back of the evening departure (perhaps the first for three or four hours), and last-minute perishables were loaded in the van along with the mail. You could certainly tell the time of year and the state of East Anglia's

"WEST RIDING LIMITED"

THE FIRST STREAMLINE TRAIN

BRADFORD LEEDS LONDON

KING'S CROSS

LONDON & NORTH EASTERN RAILWAY

"The CORONATION"

THE FIRST STREAMLINE TRAIN

KING'S CROSS FOR SCOTLAND

LONDON & NORTH EASTERN RAILWAY

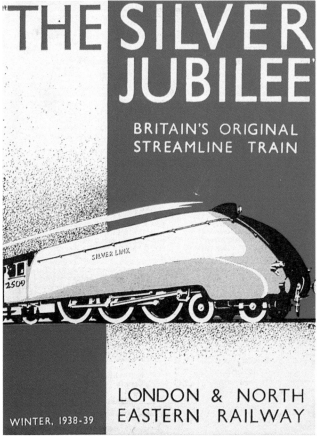

THE SILVER JUBILEE

BRITAIN'S ORIGINAL STREAMLINE TRAIN

WINTER, 1938-39

LONDON & NORTH EASTERN RAILWAY

LONDON & NORTH EASTERN RAILWAY

LONDON

KINGS CROSS

THE SILVER JUBILEE

THE FLYING SCOTSMAN

10 LARGE SIZE 1 d.

LUGGAGE LABELS

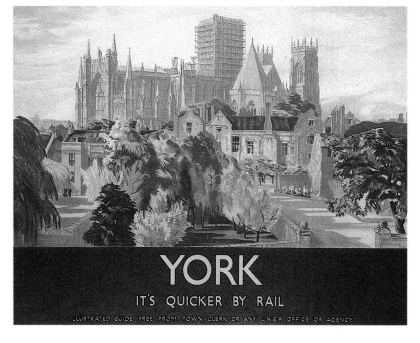

Three pictorial posters showing the delights of Bridlington, London and York. One of the pleasures found whilst station sauntering in pre-grouping and grouping days was the magnificent array of artwork on view both outside and within stations themselves.

It's nice to be beside the seaside. Two east coast holiday posters including the famous energetic sailor at Skegness.

SKEGNESS
IS SO BRACING
Illustrated Guide from Secretary. Advancement Association, Skegness, or any L·N·E·R Enquiry Office.

SALTBURN BY THE SEA

ILLUSTRATED BOOKLET FREE FROM CLERK TO THE URBAN DISTRICT
COUNCIL SALTBURN OR ANY L·N·E·R ENQUIRY OFFICE ⟨LNER⟩

agricultural and horticultural prosperity by what arrived in the form of fertilisers and farm machinery as well as by what was despatched.

Some lines served local industries based on the fruits of the earth – quite literally. For example the sidings at Tiptree for the jam factory; most of the jam left by mixed train. Then the Wisbech, even more 'Light', worked by tram locomotives along the public road, and the mid Suffolk Light from Haughley to Laxfield. With twenty-nine level crossings in nineteen miles, progress of the mainly mixed trains never set out to be other than leisurely. Here as elsewhere the 1939–45 war saw increased freight traffic in connection with nearby airfields. The two branch guards preferred to keep their own brake vans and these were neatly exchanged on a 'meet' at Kenton. One of the drivers came from the footplate of the LNER 2-8-0 + 0-8-2 Garratt locomotive in Yorkshire: quite a change of atmosphere as well as locomotive.

The local lines between Swaffham, Thetford, Bury St Edmunds and Mark's Tey provided a useful link between Norfolk and Essex, the southern section later carrying freight and holiday traffic to and from the Midlands and north west, Clacton trains needing no reversal at Colchester. Between Chappell & Wakes Colne and Haverhill there was the Colne Valley Railway, its shorter route enabling its sparse trains to leave one junction after the departure of the Great Eastern main line train and to arrive before it at the other end. At Chappell, the 'Sudbury train rule' allowed the young porters to take part in Saturday afternoon's football game. On the lowering of the home signal, the half time whistle was blown, enabling the station staff to don uniforms and deal with the two trains. The second half began after the combined trains had left for Mark's Tey.

Facing page top.
Prelude to Preservation. In the spring of 1964 the BBC Railway Roundabout team made a film of 'K4' class 2-6-0 No 3442 (which belonged to the then Viscount Garnock, now Earl of Lindsay) on a trip over the North Yorkshire branch from Malton (Rillington Junction) to Whitby. She is seen here at Goathland, now a station on the North Yorkshire Moors Railway. No 3442 is at present on the Severn Valley Railway.

Facing page bottom.
Enter the new Premier Line. An East Coast main line electrification special returns to Heaton depot, Byker Bridge, Newcastle behind diesel-electric No 47348 St Christopher's Railway Homes.

East Anglian local. Ex Great Eastern Railway 2-4-2 tank as ER class 'F6' No 67221, still with a stovepipe chimney, heads the 09.15 out of Marks Tey en route to Cambridge via Haverhill.

Suffolk cross-country branch. An unknown Great Eastern 'J15' class 0-6-0 leaves Homersfield station with a Beccles to Tivetshall Junction train in 1949.

M&GN station. Cromer Beach on Easter Monday 1952 with 'F2' class 2-4-2 tank No 67225 carrying shed code 32c (Lowestoft) waiting to depart with the evening train for North Walsham.

The year 1944 saw several incidents on the Ely–Ipswich section unique to wartime conditions. The American class 'S160' 2-8-0 was then working in large numbers on main lines here: it was introduced prior to its use on the D-Day landings in Normandy. There were differences from normal practice on these foreigners, one being the fitting of a single reflex type water gauge, showing the water level black on silver, the reverse of what might have been expected. It was also vital to feel the open and shut position of the screw type shut off and drain cocks. Unfamiliarity with this cab layout was the probable cause of three cases of firebox crown collapse, the second occurring near Thurston on the night of 12 January. On 2 June at Soham fire was discovered in a wagon of bombs, part of a loaded munition train. The crew, true heroes if ever there were any, insisted on uncoupling the burning wagon from the train and were drawing it forward when the contents exploded. The George Cross was subsequently awarded to driver Gimbert and, posthumously, to fireman Nightall. It was probably during December that a Claud 4-4-0 No 8894, leaving Haughley on a train from Cambridge, was hit by a 'C47' Thunderbolt plane which was carrying out a simulated 'train busting' attack.

Then there was the Midland & Great Northern Joint Railway, formed in 1893 from an amalgamation of several lines in Cambridgeshire, Lincolnshire and Norfolk. There had been a through service between Cromer and London Kings Cross via Peterborough for a few years before this date, but in 1894, the opening of the Spalding avoiding line and the Saxby–Bourne branch cleared the way for lucrative traffic to and from the Midlands. The M&GN proper made an end on connection with the Midland at Little Bytham Junction at a point almost above the East Coast main line.

The through expresses introduced between Birmingham, Leicester

Last days of the old regime. Melton Constable shed in 1934 shortly before the motive power takeover by the LNER (1936) but nevertheless part of a joint LNER/LMS concern. On the turntable is large Belpaire 4-4-0 No 45 (built Sharp Stewart & Co 6/94) and rebuilt at Melton Constable in 1909 with a new 'G7' boiler supplied by Derby. This became LNER class 'D54'; No 45 was, however, withdrawn in November 1936 and never received the cypher prefix to its number. In the background is 0-6-0 No 70, LNER class 'J40' shown practically as built; it was withdrawn in March 1944 as No 070.

Green Controller

'I'm 'ere' he said 'to get the traffic; and got it I have.' This was my first experience of the M&GN. It was Bob Bennet speaking, the district controller of the LMS at Peterborough. The date was 1935. The subject was cattle from Lynn market. And I, as a new, green chief controller at Cambridge, had been taken along to the meeting by A. H. (Bertie) Wright, my boss. We retired disconsolate.

The next year under a deal with the LMS which did a little to rationalise Joint Lines up and down the country, the LNER took over management of the M&GN and the Western End fell to the Cambridge district. I saw a good deal of Austin Street and stood for the day on August Bank Holiday with John Ellison on South Lynn station watching open-mouthed tiny little engines starting with and panting with twelve or more bogies, packed with sunburnt and crusty kids and parents, up the 1 in 100 to West Lynn Bridge. It was soon obvious that the M&GN was staffed by East Anglians – that is to say, cheerful, humorous, loyal, dedicated, self-reliant, competent, stubborn railwaymen.

Between Spalding and Sutton Bridge the M&GN had several 80-wagon-a-day stations, Holbeach and so on. Elsewhere the old Great Eastern were in all the towns also; Peterborough, Spalding, Lynn, Cromer, Norwich, Yarmouth. And not many of even such towns for 150 miles of railway. The M&GN depended on the traffic the LMS routed to it, freight and passenger. – Gerry Fiennes.

and the east coast were immediately popular, 'The Leicesters' surviving until closure in 1959, the name 'Honeymoon Express' deriving from the departure time from Leicester at about 3.20pm. Similar services were provided for Nottingham and Derby, while in 1923 the LMS introduced an excellent train between Liverpool Lime Street, Manchester London Road, Yarmouth and Lowestoft via Uttoxeter, complete with LNWR twelve-wheeled restaurant car. In due course heavy 'town holiday' and excursion traffic developed, mainly on summer Saturdays taxing the capacity of the line with its many single track sections.

It was indeed in the operation of summer Saturday traffic that the M&GN became notorious. The transfer of single-line tablets from box to box westwards was necessary because of the one way influx of trains passing through Saxby in the early hours. In 1935, the locomotive of the first train dropped and then ran over the tablet – at 1am! Traffic was at a standstill for some hours until the lineman (who had to be got out of bed) had completed repairs. On Bank Holiday Saturday 1936, the 9.35am Birmingham–Yarmouth failed to make its advertised stop at Melton Mowbray and passengers had to be brought on by a Tilbury tank and coaches which just 'happened to be there'. The effects of this one hour delay were widespread, the climax occurring during the afternoon when two trains, each two coaches beyond the capacity of the loop, arrived at South Witham, bringing traffic to a standstill for miles around while one was divided. On this day, nineteen *extra* trains were scheduled to pass Little Bytham Junction eastbound between 1.36am and 11.12am. Trains also came on to the Joint line at Spalding and Sutton Bridge.

On the corresponding day in 1937, Saturday 3 July, it was hoped that lessons had been learned. Not so. The proceedings opened with ex works Midland '4F' 0-6-0 No 4039 dropping its motion near Castle Bytham, followed by the locomotive of a Skegness train failing to 'drop' the tablet at Cuckoo Junction. A search at Spalding station revealed the missing pouch in the leading brake compartment, having been shot through the open window: an obliging porter cycled back with it. Incredibly, Control allowed a repeat of the previous year's crossing episode at South Witham; one train showed evidence of the takeover by the LNER the previous autumn, LMS class '3F' 0-6-0 No 3222 being piloted by LNER class 'J11' 0-6-0 No 6081, running chimney to chimney.

In time, this traffic fell off but significantly on 26 July 1958 in the last summer before closure, eleven extra trains left the Joint line between 12 noon and 4.30pm, destinations including Ambergate, Chesterfield, Kettering and Shirebrook. In the meantime, motive power had graduated through Great Northern, Great Central and Great Eastern designs to the Ivatt '4MT' 2-6-0, whereas, in the opposite direction, the same Fowler '4F' 0-6-0s still reigned supreme. Thus, the Midland & Great Northern achieved the 'distinction' of being the first really long route to be abandoned.

Cross-country routes affording connections with other lines en route included those between Lancashire, Cleethorpes, Hull and Tyneside, worked in part by both LMS and LNER. The Great Central London extension, coming late in the field had few branches, but that between

Almost pre-grouping in Lincolnshire. The station at Louth on the old Great Northern routes from Lincoln and Peterborough to Grimsby; it was the junction for Boston via the Mablethorpe and Sutton-on-Sea loop. Nationalisation came late to Louth as the date is 18 May 1949. In the background is Ivatt 'C12' class ex GNR 4-4-2T No 7359 on a Grimsby local, whilst ex GCR 'A5' class 4-6-2 tank No 9817 (allocated to Boston or Lincoln) shunts in the up main platform. This is a vintage scene none of which is left today.

The Great Northern at Leicester. 'B1' class 4-6-0 No 61142 leaves the old GNR terminus at Belgrave Road at the head of an August Bank Holiday excursion to Skegness in 1961. In LNER days most of the trains over this branch were headed by Ivatt 0-6-0s.

Woodford & Hinton and Banbury conveying vast amounts of freight and long-distance passenger trains between the north east and destinations such as Penzance, Bournemouth, Swansea via Cheltenham and Barry. The Great Northern built a branch to Stafford utilising running powers over the North Stafford there being a healthy milk traffic to Kings Cross. Even in LNER days it was still possible to buy a ticket to London at Stafford LMS station and wander eastwards stopping at every station to the LNER main line before going south to London.

Ex-North Eastern Railway minor routes served both industrialised and remote areas, the Carlisle line with its branches to Allendale and Alston and that over Stainmore certainly qualified as cross country.

Kirkby Stephen, one of the principal towns on the Stainmore route, a cosy market town with a pleasant grey stone outlook, was once like so many other towns an important railway centre. To the east the route served Barnard Castle with connections to Darlington and Bishop Auckland, and to the west lines ran to Tebay and Penrith both on the LNWR main line. The main purpose of the line of harsh gradients was for mineral traffic: coke from the Durham coalfield to the West Coast iron works and haematite ironstone for Teeside in the opposite direction. There was also adequate passenger traffic, including summer services using the through route from the north east to the north west coastal resorts.

At Kirkby Stephen there was a locomotive depot sufficient to accommodate sixteen engines or so; it was well equipped as small sheds

Banking over Belah. A heavy freight makes its way over the spindly viaduct between Kirkby Stephen and Barras on the cross-country route built by the North Eastern to link the eastern coking plants in Co Durham with the steelworks at Barrow and Workington. The date is almost certainly the early 1950s when double heading over the bridge was forbidden. The engines concerned are an ex NER 'J21' class 0-6-0 (the regular performers for decades) and its BR replacement, one of the then new class 2 MT 2-6-0s No 46470 built at Darlington.

went, with a lathe, a forge, a white metalling hearth, a drilling machine and some shear legs essential to lift one end of an engine allowing the removal of one or more sets of wheels when axleboxes had run hot; not an infrequent event on some of the older NE classes.

All freight trains between Tebay, Kirkby Stephen and West Auckland were worked by two engines. In later years, because of weight restrictions on the viaducts at Belah and Deepdale, double heading was not allowed and banking from the rear was the order of the day. In any case it was more prudent to have an engine with brake power at the lower end of the load in case of breakaway – not unknown.

This problem of the viaducts also manifested itself when the breakdown crane was required at Kirkby. This was stationed at Darlington and was a 45 ton steam affair. Its total weight with the relieving bogies was 156 tons. Special instructions required it to be separated from the engine by three empty wagons to cross the viaducts. Also, only the train crew were allowed to ride over the viaduct during the crane's passage. Presumably they were expendable in the event of it falling through!

Kirkby Stephen (NER) was renamed Kirkby Stephen East in BR days to distinguish it from the Midland station on the Settle-Carlisle line. The engine shed housing a number of 'J21' class ex NER 0-6-0s is seen in the right background. The station consisted of a wide island platform with a central stone building with an overall roof extending to the platforms facing immediately adjacent. The two locomotives shown (both 'J21' class 0-6-0s) are Nos 65038 at the head of a Penrith-Barnard Castle train and 65090. The date is August 1953.

Unusual excursion. Ex North Eastern Railway 4-4-0 as LNER class 'D20' No 711 doubleheads 'B16' class 4-6-0 No 1372 at Leyburn on 29 June 1927. They are heading a return special train to London after passengers had been able to see a total eclipse of the sun (the next one is not due until 1999) only viewable within a narrow belt of countryside extending mainly through the counties of Yorkshire and Lancashire. The LNER organised a special overnight excursion from London to Leyburn (one of the suitable spots) showing considerable enterprise.

During most winters the snows came and during heavy falls the cuttings west of Stainmore would inevitably drift up. In order to keep the line clear, light engines were used to run to and fro between Stainmore and Kirkby. Even so the line was blocked completely at Bleath Gill for about six weeks during the snows of 1947 and again for a week or so in 1955.

It was the stationmaster's duty to do the Thursday pay run to the signalboxes between Stainmore, Tebay and Penrith; in the days before motor vehicles were available he would have use of an engine and crew to do this. In those days the paybox contained several hundred pounds which was a great deal of money but there was never a whisper of a problem.

A curious North Eastern station was Elvet at Durham. It lost its regular passenger service in 1931 but received special trains for the Miners' Gala for many years after. Sentinel steam railcars (some named after stage coaches) worked many minor services in the North East.

The North British network of short branch lines survived in the main into nationalisation; these included the Lauder Light Railway which diverged from the Waverley route at Fountainhall Junction. From Hawick one could travel to Newcastle over the Border Counties line from Riccarton Junction to Hexham, while further south, the Port Carlisle branch was at one time worked by horse power.

Aberdeen enjoyed a suburban service provided by the Great North of Scotland Railway; this ran between Dyce on the main line and Culter on the Ballater branch. Smartly worked by Johnson 0-4-4 tanks the schedule included a one minute departure interval as between the Joint and Schoolhill stations, half a mile apart. During a holiday in 1931 there was a child's fare of one old penny return available to one's 'digs' at Kittybrewster. The trip could be made in five minutes, with two stops, a shorter time than that taken by non-stop main line trains. Withdrawal of the service in 1937 precipitated local uproar. On the Ellon Junction to Boddam line, an electric tramway was constructed to convey passengers and luggage between the station and the railway company's hotel at Cruden Bay. Closed to passengers in 1932, freight survived until 1945, the hotel laundry continuing to service the Scottish Region until the end of 1948. Passenger trains on the Fraserburgh and St Combs light railway were worked for many years by Great Eastern locomotives fitted with cowcatchers.

Quite a few LNER branches were closed to passengers in the 1930s, a few earlier, and threats were continually being made of mass closure following the ravages of bus competition. But generally it was felt that running the occasional passenger train for parcels and mail as well as the few people who wished to travel hauled by a locomotive that anyway had to penetrate rural backwaters was better than withdrawal. Unhappy the branchline economics undoubtedly were, solutions to the problem none.

Pre Beeching

In East Anglia, often the road gives a shorter route and in many country districts a service run at regular intervals has advantages over an occasional train service. The bus and the motor coach have created a great deal of new traffic. They have wakened up the villagers and brought fresh interest into many dull lives, not always perhaps to the benefit of the local shopkeepers. But one result is that many railway branch lines are now run at a loss and will soon be closed for passenger traffic. The public cannot expect to travel by private car or bus and still have a train available when it suits their convenience to go by rail. When it is too late some of us may regret that we can no longer view from the train the peaceful stretches of countryside which make East Anglia so attractive. – R. Bell in 1930.

Cruise train. The Northern Belle leaving Glenfinnan viaduct on the West Highland Extension to Mallaig behind double headed D34 class 4-4-0s; the pilot engine is No 9221 Glen Orchy.

Seen at York

Who could resist platform sauntering at York Station? Of course the trains themselves were the real fascination but so much was added by the sweeping curves and that beautiful overall roof. In the days just after the Grouping the variety of colour schemes must have been a sight for sore eyes, green and blue from the LNER constituents, red from the Midland and black from the Lancashire & Yorkshire. But it was the East Coast main line expresses which were the main attraction with only the prestigious *Flying Scotsman* and later the *Silver Jubilee* running through; even the grand *Coronation* halted at York for three minutes, a Garter blue 'A4' at its head. Great green Pacifics were the norm and how magnificent they seemed, big fat boilers, huge sloping fire boxes, miniscule chimneys and above all those names, *The Tetrarch, Gladiateur, Night Hawk, Papyrus* or *Captain Cuttle*; true racehorses all. Even to the men who ran them they were machines which had to be coaxed and carefully handled. But everything did not always run smoothly. W. A. Tuplin, that colourful and controversial commentator on steam, wrote this . . .

It is a busy Saturday afternoon at the north end of platform 9 and succession of northbound trains come in and leave: all take water from the crane. Stopping the train with the back end of the tender opposite the hydrant is not always easy. On engines with left hand drive the driver aims to stop the cab abreast of the top of the ramp. For a man on a right hand drive engine there is no such convenient land mark.

In comes an old 'A1', now converted to 'A3' and although approaching quite slowly, fails to stop at the right place, and the tender filling manhole is out of reach of the hydrant 'bag'. The driver, whose duty finishes here, confers with the Newcastle man who is to relieve him. It is decided that the train must not be set back till all the platform work is done. While the incoming fireman makes his way to the shed to 'book off', his mate

Many a slip. The driver of 'A1' Pacific No 60153 Flamboyant *does not look amused as the wheels spin on starting out of platform 15 (one of the sharper curves) at York with the down 13.41 Newcastle around 1956. No 60153 was delivered new to York shed and remained there for the whole of its working life.*

remains until the starting signal for the train is given on the bell. Then the engine is moved backwards until the tender is in the right place for filling and the brake is snapped on. The momentum of the back end of the train pulls all the couplings tight before it stops. Tender filling begins, continuing with a background of uproar from the safety valves. Three minutes elapse before they are ready to go and then begins a display of the type that York produces on most trains that leave No 9 for the north.

The driver winds the reversing handle to full forward gear; then he tugs at the regulator handle and is eventually only too successful in getting steam into the cylinders. With a fifteen coach train all tight on the curve of No 9 and with the driving wheels standing on rails polished by thousands of slipping wheels, the 'A3' can only do the same. With a violent roar the chimney shoots steam, smoke and cinders skyward. The driving wheels spin round at the equivalent of 60mph each point of contact tearing a flame of sparks from the rail.

As a spectacle it is striking, but how does one stop it? The driver manages to close the regulator at last and the driving wheels quickly come to rest. Just as they do so the engine moves ahead through an inch or two as if anxious to start the train. This is because the friction between wheels and rails increases very markedly when the slipping has almost ceased; the wheels then grip and their momentum urges the engine forward until the straining coupling springs call a halt and pull her back. Correct practice is to open the regulator just before slipping ceases so that at the moment of wheel grip, the cylinders contain steam ready to follow up the forward surge. But on many engines it is impracticable to time the opening of the regulator accurately; the driver is lucky to open it at all.

When he does manage it, the engine moves an inch ahead but the train, tight on the curve, holds like a rock and nothing further happens because a three cylinder engine, with cut off limited to 65 per cent has six almost dead positions in each revolution of the driving wheels. The result is that the starting effort is about a quarter of the nominal amount. This is not enough to start a heavy train on a long curve, and so the engine 'refuses'.

The driver wrenches at the reverse gear handle to make sure she really is in full gear and studies the permanent way intently. No! She won't have it. He proceeds to set her in backward gear. There is no question of spinning the reverse gear handle with a neat wrist action such as suffices on some locomotives. Here you pull back, wrench across, push forward, wrench across, pull back and so on through about ten revolutions. The fireman meanwhile adds a fierce hiss to the safety valve noise by opening the cylinder cocks to let steam out of the places that are correct for forward running but wrong for going back. With the engine at last in full backward gear, the driver opens the regulator again and she pushes the train back a foot or so and then slips thunderously backwards until the regulator is closed. When it is re-opened she fails to move. More winding of the reverse gear handle as the driver sets her in forward gear. Regulator open again and she lurches forward through the foot she had gained by backing, only to stick fast again. The driver waits for a few seconds to give her every chance to go, but she doesn't, she's found another dead point. He makes a gesture of exasperation and once more winds her into reverse with more noise from opened cylinder cocks. This time there must be no half measures and he holds the regulator open until she has run back half a revolution of the driving wheels.

Ahead again! When the regulator is opened she surges forward a foot, stops again at a dead-point while all observers hold their breaths, but after a few moments while pressure builds up in the cylinders, she gets over the hard place and the train moves forward. It is 3ft 6in to the next dead point and in that distance sufficient speed has been attained to overcome it. She passes it, but on a 'good' point beyond it the wheels lose their grip and away she flies on another high speed slip. Regulator shut and opened again as soon as the slip has ceased and, praise be, steam is on again before the train has stopped rolling. With any luck now, she'll get away. She does, very slowly, because every now and then there is a wild slip and speed drops before the wheels regain their grip. This halting progress takes the engine to the Scarborough goods line crossing, fifty yards from the platform and some five minutes after the starting bell first rang. She's picking up now but there are three more slips before she disappears behind the engine shed and the fourteenth coach clears the crossing.

163

11
COACHES: JAZZ QUINS TO CORONATION LUXURY

THERE was nothing quite like an LNER coach of the 1920s and 1930s, with its gleaming varnished teak sides and ends, large bold extended seriffed letters L N E R and running numbers along the side and big 1, 2, or 3 on every door, and a striking white roof, sloping down dome shaped at the ends. At least that was what it was like when it was freshly outshopped, for the smoke, smuts and oil coming from steam locomotive chimneys soon turned the roof grey while the multi-layered mouldings forming the bodyside panels soon gathered dirt which without the benefit of mechanical washing plants soon took the shine off the varnish.

The story is one of remarkable contrasts; the best were head and shoulders above coaches of the other three grouping railways while the worst were not much better than the offerings of the Brighton and South Eastern companies in the last century which without doubt were at the bottom of the comfort league table. As for technical innovation, again there were contrasts with articulation in which coaches shared bogies, electric cooking in kitchen cars and pressure ventilation forming the highlights, against the reluctance to let go of side doors to each compartment in main-line corridor stock and all-timber bodies, while the other railways were introducing steel panels. Timber was cheaper and lighter and the teak sides needed no more than the occasional coat of varnish – even if the coaches tended to break up like matchwood in serious accidents.

Many of those it inherited from the GNR and East Coast Joint Stock already had Gresley's stamp, for from 1905 he was the GN's carriage and wagon superintendent. But in the short space of time between the end of World War 2 and nationalisation Gresley's successor, Thompson, produced a new breed which broke away from most of what had gone before. Though numerically small they became just as much of an LNER hallmark as the Gresley vehicles.

The LNER inherited a high proportion of four- and six-wheelers particularly from the three greats. The Great Eastern six-wheel stock with and without lavatories, and some with clerestory roofs, could often be found on main line services well into the 1930s; a handful ended their days on the Laxfield branch in the early 1950s as the last non-bogie stock to run in ordinary public service. Yet the Great Eastern had started building bogie corridor stock with elliptical roofs from about 1905 and had pioneered dining car services for all classes in 1891 in its Harwich–Manchester North Country Continental train, two years before dining cars were made available to third class passengers on the northern main lines. The GC by contrast was the great social leveller: buffet cars with

What the LNER inherited. The pre-grouping companies passed on to the LNER a wide variety of stock in 1923, some of considerable antiquity and others embodying modern principles. The Great Northern still made use of four-wheel close-coupled sets on many suburban services and some survived almost until World War II; (upper centre) *this gas-lit third-class coach was typical, with narrow compartments and cramped upright seats. The GER, although having some average bogie stock for its main line services between London and Norwich, still used six-wheelers on some services, especially on reliefs and holiday trains;* (top) *this lavatory third was still in traffic in 1938 although by then employed on branch and local work. In contrast Gresley, on taking over as GN carriage superintendent, thought big and for his 1905 Sheffield sets opted for large bogie coaches built to the full height and width permitted by the loading gauge;* (lower centre) *the four-coach trains included this twelve-wheeled composite dining car;* (bottom) *the Great Central introduced some handsome corridor stock around the time of World War I; comparatively spacious, they had timber bodies matchboarded below the waist and long wheelbase bogies.*

164

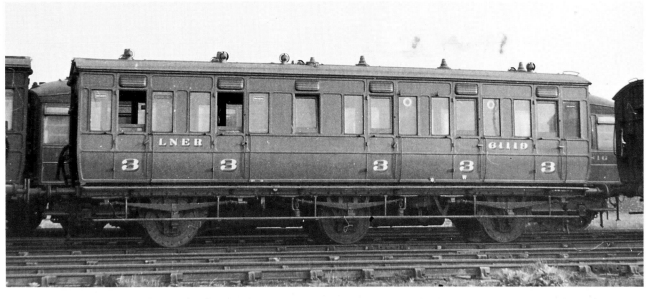

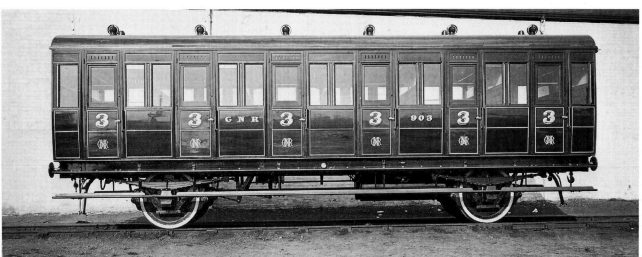

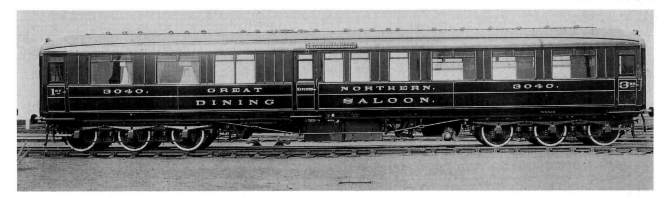

a stand up bar available to all came with the opening to Marylebone in 1899. This pointed the way for the LNER in the 1930s. Moreover the GC passed on two generations of corridor stock, the original low-roof pattern designed for the London opening and the massive matchboarded stock of the years immediately before World War 1 most of which lasted into BR days.

The GN handed on a motley collection of all shapes and sizes, the sets of close-coupled four-wheelers for suburban work, with their low flattened elliptical roofs, contrasting strongly with the massive high-roof with domed ends and full width bodies of the first Gresley corridor stock of 1905. Indeed when the GN built new four-coach trains, including a twelve-wheel dining car, for Kings Cross–Sheffield services in that year they seemed like monsters against some stock no more than 15 years old, mostly short six-wheelers 30ft long and only 8ft wide. In an endeavour to improve riding of the older six- and rigid eight-wheeled stock Gresley experimented in 1907 by rebuilding a pair of six wheelers on bogies, two coaches sharing a centre bogie. This articulation was so successful that more older stock was rebuilt and new high roof 9ft wide articulated twin sets for London suburban trains commissioned in 1911. They were formed as eight-coach trains but after World War 1 further sets were built and the old ones adapted into four-coach units carried on five bogies, the first of the quad-art sets. Articulation was also used for a small number of corridor coaches, mostly brake third/composite twins for selected services, and there was the unique five-coach articulated corridor train for Kings Cross–Leeds duty. It including a centre kitchen car, itself unique in having electric cooking. The *Flying Scotsman* in 1914 was provided with what had become typical Gresley outline stock with domed high elliptical roofs and including NER built all-steel kitchen cars which were thought to be proof against fire from the gas heating and lighting and came from the pool of East Coast Joint Stock financed by the three East Coast partners. The GNR was the dominant partner. There was also a small pool of joint GNR and NER vehicles for specific Kings Cross–Newcastle services which mostly followed GNR styles.

The NE's veering for its domestic coaches was towards the Midland Railway. The combination of domed elliptical roof and round-panel bodysides distinguished the NER corridor product from its Gresley counterpart right through LNER days. The non-corridor versions with clerestory and elliptical roofs, the latter having a certain affinity with LMS stock of the 1920s, also survived into BR.

There was no mistaking a Gresley GN coach, with windows carried right up to the cantrail just below the roof, usually with toplights surmounting quarterlights alongside the doors in compartments, or as ventilator lights in the large windows of open saloons. Windows and body panelling were square cornered, to which the NER objected in vain for East Coast Joint Stock, for it was a source of rot as rainwater was trapped in the corners. A feature which continued right through LNER days was the use of automatic couplers combined with the Pullman style gangway mounted on the bow ends of corridor stock. The bow ended bodies account for the double length dimensions of LNER stock with

LNER suburban. Right from 1923 the LNER had to face the need to renew much of the London suburban stock it inherited from the GE and GN lines. Gresley had already introduced eight-coach bogie suburban trains on the GN, articulated at first in pairs and then in fours. He continued the idea in the 1920s with similar sets for the GN lines where platform lengths, particularly at Moorgate, brought restrictions on carriage and train lengths, and with longer ten-coach trains articulated in fives as quintuplet sets for the Great Eastern suburban workings – the Jazz service – out of Liverpool Street. (top) Gresley brake third of the quin sets; (upper centre) A GN line LNER-built eight-coach quad-art train with GN Class 'N1' 0-6-2T at the head near Potters Bar; (lower centre) for outer suburban and cross-country use the LNER built large numbers of non-gangwayed lavatory coaches, some with internal side corridors so that all compartments had access to the centre toilet compartments as in this lavatory composite; (bottom) the LNER was also involved in suburban electric working expanding the former NER Tyneside system with new trains in 1937, comprising open saloon stock with hand-worked end sliding doors, the coaches being articulated in pairs as two-car units. They were brightly liveried in blue and cream.

166

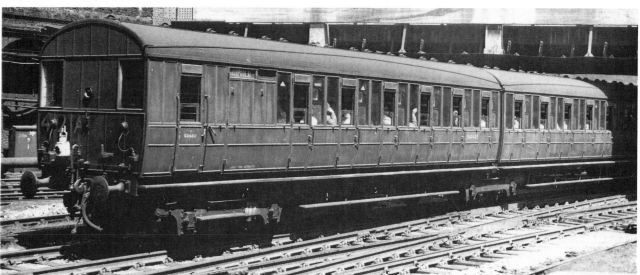

LNER main line. (top right) Teak bodies with beading and mouldings characterised most of Gresley's coaches built until World War II. Most general service corridor vehicles were on 60ft underframes but in the late 1920s Gresley built shorter stock on 51ft underframes for GE section services as for example this corridor composite dating from 1935; (centre right) in 1938 came a number of special sets for named services including one for the Hook Continental which included this brake second with six compartments and still on the service for which it was built twenty-five years later; (below) most notable were the triplet articulated dining sets with first- and third-class cars flanking the centre all-electric kitchen cars; (bottom right) for the shorter distance services requiring catering the LNER built numerous buffet cars capable of serving hot and cold snacks and really the forerunners of today's fast-food buffet.

underframe lengths given over headstocks, and body lengths as over the bow ends, usually 1ft 6in longer than the underframe.

After 1923, for the services from Kings Cross and the City services from Moorgate, Gresley continued to build eight-coach trains in the form of pairs of quad arts. For the former GE 'Jazz' services from Liverpool Street ten-coach trains formed of two five-coach quin arts were produced, a big improvement but still designed for the largest number of commuters in the minimum space. The LMS offered an extra foot between compartment partitions next door at St Pancras and Fenchurch Street. Space was ever at a premium at Kings Cross with its short platforms and at Liverpool Street with its heaviest of all traffic.

For outer suburban, cross-country and some main-line stopping services the LNER made extensive use of non-corridor lavatory coaches accompanying ordinary suburban compartment coaches. Often they were articulated in twin sets with a brake third paired with a lavatory composite. Some of the suburban sets working out of Marylebone and for Cheshire Lines Committee services for which the LNER provided the stock were formed entirely of twinsets of varying combinations. Twin unit electric trains of open saloon pattern with end vestibules and hand worked sliding doors were built for the North Tyneside electric services in 1937.

Four of the constituents (GE, NE, NB and GNS) used the Westinghouse compressed air brake, quicker and more powerful than the vacuum brake used by the GN and GC. But nationally the vacuum was most popular and was adopted (except for some self-contained suburban services) in the interest of flexibility.

The Gresley hallmark already established on GN East Coast stock over the previous two decades was continued on the LNER with timber bodies finished in teak panels with complex three-level construction (the beading below the waist was added on to the bodyside panels while the panels surrounding the windows from the waist to the cantrail were actually recessed so that the add-on mouldings were in the same vertical plane as the bodyside panels below the waist) windows extending from the waist to the cantrail, and domed elliptical roofs curving neatly to meet the bowed ends. There were minor dimensional differences from what had gone before on GN and East Coast stock which meant that the roof line was slightly more gentle and did not appear visually quite so massive as the earlier stock.

Internally Gresley's 1920s corridor stock was laid out largely with individual compartments, eight in a full third, seven in a full first and 3½ firsts and four thirds in a composite. There were three, four, and five compartment variations of brake thirds, and brake composites had four thirds and two firsts. Side doors to each compartment were provided while corridor sides on non-brake coaches mostly had four doors interspersed with large windows. A distinctive detail was the white opaque glass used for obscured windows in toilets, and kitchens of restaurant and kitchen cars. Open stock in the 1920s, while not built in large quantities, appeared in new designs although following much of what had gone before on the GN.

Most spectacular of Gresley's LNER dining cars were the triplet articulated sets first seen in 1924, with a central all-electric kitchen car flanked on one side by an open first and on the other by an open third. The more general introduction of all-electric kitchens on single restaurant cars as well meant that the LNER had to embark on a programme of electric landline installations at stations and yards where the electric kitchens would need to stand during cooking periods. When running, the axle driven dynamos provided power but there were limits on the equipment which could be used simultaneously. Gas cooking still had to be provided between Liverpool Street and Harwich and on some cross-country services going off LNER territory.

The LMS had introduced what it termed 'luxury' stock with end vestibules and wide picture windows in compartments in 1928/30 and from the early 1930s the LNER followed suit, at first for the principal East Coast trains and then with batches for general service. But while the LMS killed the side door to each compartment, the LNER continued to build the type in quantity until World War 2. Greater use was made of open stock, and by the end of the 1930s open thirds formed about one-fifth of the LNER-built standard-length corridor stock. Many of the opens had 'bucket' seats, somewhat akin to individual car seats but in their railway application having a shape bound to induce backache on a long journey.

Specially-built sets of open coaches were used for excursions and Saturday holiday trains; from 1933 a number departed from the usual teak livery by being painted engine green below the waist and cream above. They had plywood bodyside panels and square-ended roofs, and were usually made up into twelve-coach formations with two buffet cars.

The buffet cars, as some now on general service, had a small kitchen for the service of light meals and snacks, and a self service counter for drinks and light refreshments. Most famous of the buffet car services were those between Kings Cross and Cambridge, but others ran between Liverpool Street and Clacton, Newcastle to Carlisle and Middlesbrough, Manchester and Cleethorpes and Hull and Liverpool. The buffets also featured new decor and instead of grained veneers for wall panelling there were coloured rexine finishes trimmed with chromium plate fittings while tables and chairs were of chromium plated tubular style. Some of the LNER buffet cars were long lived and several survived in BR service far from their native territory into the 1970s.

Some LNER variations. (top) Much of Gresley's GN and East Coast stock survived right through the LNER period and this East Coast 58ft 6in corridor third had much in common in general appearance, although not in detail with the standard LNER 61ft 6in version; (upper centre) the mid-1930s tourist stock showed a complete break from traditional Gresley styling with flush-sided plywood bodies on teak frames. Sets were formed of single brake thirds, twin articulated open thirds and buffet cars, all built to a tight budget. Livery was green and cream; (lower centre) in the 1920s the LNER introduced steam railcars in an attempt to cut costs but even with modern steam engine units, as had happened twenty years earlier they were not altogether successful. Some lasted until World War II. All were named, this Sentinel car was called Royal Eagle; *(bottom) for the last few years of the LNER, Thompson was CME and introduced his own designs of coaches including sleeping cars, some of which lasted long enough to carry BR Blue and light grey livery introduced from the mid 1960s.*

170

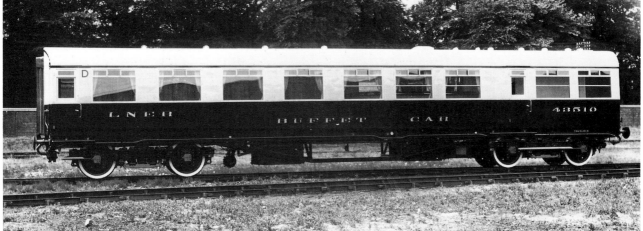

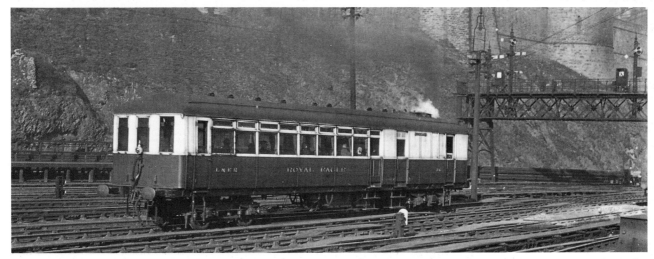

Luxury on the East Coast route. During the late 1930s the LNER went to exceptional lengths to produce a luxury environment in its principal expresses. The Flying Scotsman *lounge bar of 1938, a feature of which was the segregated side corridor avoiding the interruption of passengers passing along the central aisle of a normal open saloon coach.*

Coaches for the high speed streamlined trains and other principal expresses in the mid 1930s offered a spacious luxury unmatched even by Pullmans elsewhere in Britain. The *Flying Scotsman* was given a new set in 1924, partly renewed in 1928 with the triplet restaurant set first-class dining cars sporting what was described as Louis XIV style decor with gracefully painted walls, moulded ceilings, loose individual armchairs and concealed lighting behind curtain pelmets. Two years later two of the first class coaches were replaced by new end entrance firsts with the side corridor compartments seating only four passengers; the coaches had pressure ventilation. The 1935 *Silver Jubilee* between Newcastle and Kings Cross was a short train of seven coaches: an articulated twin brake first and semi-open first on one side of a triplet restaurant set and a twin brake third and third on the other, an extra third soon being added to make it a triplet. The silver grey rexine applied to the external steel panelling had to have special daily cleaning and fairly frequent repainting. Inside, the wall panelling was also in rexine of differing colours with blending curtains and strongly patterned upholstery. There were just four seats in each first class compartment with deep cushions, heavily padded seat backs, head and arm rests, and padded upholstery on side walls. Loose cushions and footrests all added to the drawing room atmosphere. The open saloons had varying seating layouts but from 1938 were standardised at single armchairs on each side of the centre passageway.

The further streamlined trains were formed of twin articulated sets as eight-coach formations – brake third/third, third/kitchen third, twin firsts, kitchen third/brake third, all of open pattern, with two-plus-one in the thirds and one-plus-one in the firsts. All passengers were served meals at their own seats. The LNER recognised that open accommodation was not quite as popular as compartments and divided the first class saloons with partitions between each bay forming four-seat alcoves with a centre passageway. The single armchair seats pivoted to allow them to turn towards the scalloped shaped tables. The third class was partitioned to enclose two bays. Internal decor was in rexine using a grey/green theme with anodised aluminium trim and fittings. Pressure ventilation and heating was designed to avoid having the ventilator windows in the upper parts of the main windows open which with double glazing and bodyside sound insulation helped to reduce travel noise. Outside, the steel panels were painted Garter blue below the waist and the much lighter Marlborough blue from the waist to the roof, divided by stainless steel bands, and with the train name in individual stainless steel Gill Sans letters emblazoned on the coach sides below the windows. In the summer an extra coach ran on the Coronation trains, a streamlined observation saloon with its outer end sloping down over the rear observation window in complementary fashion to the streamlined end of the Class 'A4' Pacific hauling the train. In 1938 yet another train set was built for the *Flying Scotsman* including new longer triplet dining sets. A new feature was a lounge buffet with a side corridor lounge saloon while one of the delicacies served was ice cream!

By 1945 Edward Thompson was in command and produced new

Royal Trains

The last two coaches built for King Edward VII were a combined operation by the East Coast lines in 1908–9, the GN contributing the King's vehicle at Doncaster and the NE that for Queen Alexandra at York. They were so substantially made, on six-wheeled bogies with huge strengthening girders between, that it is doubtful if they would ever have worn out. Apart from a few minor changes they were used for all royal journeys on the LNER, and were loaned on several occasions to the GWR, such as for the funeral of King George V. Nos 395 and 396, they were normally stabled at Hornsey.

After nationalisation the LMS Royal Train was used on numerous occasions on the Eastern Region. LMS Saloon No 799 had hinged buffers which could be made to point down towards the ground when the vehicle was being buck-eye coupled to ex-LNER stock. LNER signalmen had to be specially advised to stop their sending 7 'Stop and Examine' bells when they saw what looked like a buffer falling off.

The train used blocks of wet ice loaded in bunkers under the train for its air-conditioning system. On one occasion a northern district was instructed to obtain a large quantity of ice, which must be in blocks 12×9×9in to fit the bunkers. Although rough ice was available no supplier could be found locally who could cut ice into blocks, so a supply was specially despatched from London on the night goods in two AF containers. In vain, for when the Royal Train arrived, the Wolverton foreman who travelled with it used a crow-bar to break the ice up into small pieces!

designs for post-war stock, slightly longer, with most corridor stock on 61ft 6in underframes and non corridors on 52ft 2½in underframes. The new corridor coaches bore no relation to the Gresley styles. Roofs were square ended and bodies were steel panelled on wood frames. The most notable feature of the Thompson post-war stock was in internal layout where the entrance vestibules were not at the ends but intermediately between groups of compartments, two-door-three-door-two in the thirds and two-door-two-door-two in the firsts and composites. It meant that passengers needed to pass no more than one compartment to reach any seat. A design embellishment which became another hallmark of post-war LNER stock was the oval lavatory windows with the usual white opaque glass. Again in 1948 new *Flying Scotsman* trains were formed using post-war stock which in any case had crept into the formations in previous months, but, other than a lounge bar, internally the coaches were little different from ordinary stock, although the coaches were double glazed and pressure ventilated. The brief luxurious era of the streamliners – and who could miss seeing one of them pass? – had gone with the war and now the emphasis was to be on standardisation.

SOUTH END

63T.7c. — TOTAL 219 TONS 18 CWTS

WEIGHTS~64T.1c.   92T.10c.

390'0" TOTAL LENGTH OVER BODIES

392'0" TOTAL LENGTH OVER BUFFERS

BRAKE THIRD 30 SEATS

CORRIDOR THIRD 42 SEATS

THIRD RESTAURANT CAR 48 SEATS

KITCHEN CAR 120 THIRD CLASS

FIRST RESTAURANT CAR 28 SEATS

SEMI-OPEN FIRST 30 SEATS

BRAKE FIRST 20 SEATS

78 FIRST CLASS, 120 THIRD CLASS = 198 TOTAL SEATS

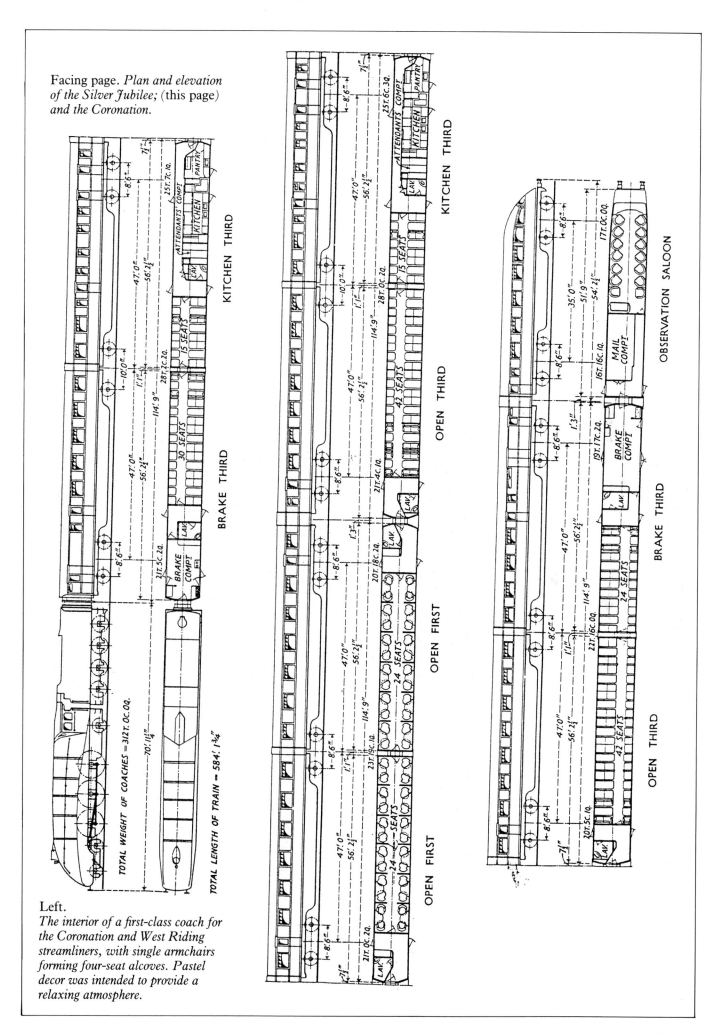

Facing page. *Plan and elevation of the Silver Jubilee; (this page) and the Coronation.*

Left.
The interior of a first-class coach for the Coronation and West Riding streamliners, with single armchairs forming four-seat alcoves. Pastel decor was intended to provide a relaxing atmosphere.

Joint Lines

BEFORE the 1923 grouping there were many joint railways owned by more than one of the pre-grouping companies. At the grouping some disappeared completely into one of the four new main line railways. One example was the Great Northern & Great Eastern Joint Line, an important freight route, which became wholly LNER owned. Some, however, remained jointly owned and the most important in which the LNER was concerned were the CLC and the M&GNJt, which ran their own services. Most joint lines were, however, merely used by both owning companies as routes for their own trains. They owned few miles of track and no rolling stock.

Cheshire Lines Committee (CLC). (Joint LNER/LMS.) 143 route miles. Ran an hourly express service on its 34 mile straight and flat main line between Manchester Central and Liverpool Central. Probably its greatest importance to the LNER was that, by using the connecting line from Godley Junction on the Sheffield-Manchester line (GC), it obtained access to Chester Northgate and its own North Wales and Wirral lines (including the Wrexham Mold and Connahs Quay). It also gave access to Liverpool Central and the docks, including Brunswick and Huskisson Goods Depots. The CLC carried heavy freight. It owned its own passenger rolling stock, including four Sentinel steam railcars but, throughout its joint existence, motive power was provided successively by the MS&LR, GCR and LNER. The popular Liverpool–Manchester expresses in LNER days were worked by ex-GC D9 4-4-0s but some of the 4-2-2s lasted on expresses until 1927. The CLC naturally became part of the LMR after nationalisation.

Midland & Great Northern Joint (M&GN). (Joint LNE/LMS.) 194 route miles. In the last century it formed a penetration by the Midland and Great Northern Railways into the Great Eastern preserve in North Norfolk. It had a long main line forming an end-on junction with the LMS at Little Bytham Junction, immediately to the east of the East Coast Main Line, which ran via Bourne, Spalding and Melton Constable to Yarmouth. A branch from Peterborough and Wisbech joined this line at Sutton Bridge, and two other lines from Melton Constable served Cromer and Norwich. An oddity was that the M&GN Joint half owned, with the LNER, the Norfolk & Suffolk Joint from Yarmouth to Lowestoft. Throughout its life the M&GN suffered from the fact that it served a very sparsely-populated agricultural area. Expresses, by M&GN standards, worked across from Leicester, and Peterborough was also served. The line had its own locomotive fleet, mainly very old Midland style engines of two main types, frequently repaired and modified at the line's own Melton Constable Works. Agricultural produce including sugar beet, and cut flowers from the Sutton Bridge/Spalding area, were cleared by the slow pick-up trains. The whole line was absorbed by the LNER in 1936, quite a liability. It became the first trunk route to fall under the axe after nationalisation.

GN & LNW Joint. (Joint LNER/LMS.) 45 route miles. Ran from Saxondale Junction and Bottesford, on the LNER Grantham–Nottingham line, to Welham Junction, near Market Harborough on the LMS. Its importance to the LNER was that it gave access to its own branch from Marefield Junction to Leicester Belgrave Road, from whence it ran a passenger service to Grantham and many summer excursions to east coast resorts. Even more important was that it tapped the considerable ironstone deposits in the Stathern and Waltham-on-the-Wold areas. It served beautiful, green hunting country. Increase in car ownership and the use of imported high-grade iron ores caused the line's complete closure after nationalisation.

Manchester South Junction & Altrincham (MSJ&A). (Joint LNER/LMS.) A short line from Manchester London Road (now Piccadilly) to Altrincham. A very important suburban line, the first passenger service to be electrified with overhead lines at 1500 V. DC. It still thrives as part of the LMR.

Metropolitan & Great Central Joint (Originally joint Metropolitan and GC.) Formed the ex-GCR's access to London, from Quainton Road to Harrow South Junction with independent GC tracks to Marylebone. It was used by the Marylebone–Manchester expresses. The GW & GC Joint between Northolt Junction and Ashendon Junction provided an alternative route to the north, the GC Main Line being regained by a connecting line from Ashendon to Grendon Underwood Junction. The GC Main Line closure removed the Met & GC's through services, but suburban services are still maintained from Marylebone.

Other Joint Lines. The LNER had an interest in many other joint lines. Some, like the Swinton & Knottingley Joint (S&K) carried a heavy through traffic of express passenger and freight trains. Others, like the Axholme Joint, were sleepy agricultural lines. Many, particularly in the Midland and Yorkshire colliery areas, were built solely to serve the many pits. Among those lines were the South Yorkshire Joint, Mid-Notts Joint, and GC & Mid Joint. It was interesting to see how the two owning companies organised their services to get the maximum tonnage of coal to their own route. It must have been interesting on the SY Joint before 1923, when that line was owned by the GC, GN, NE, L & Y, and Midland railways. What a scramble there must have been!

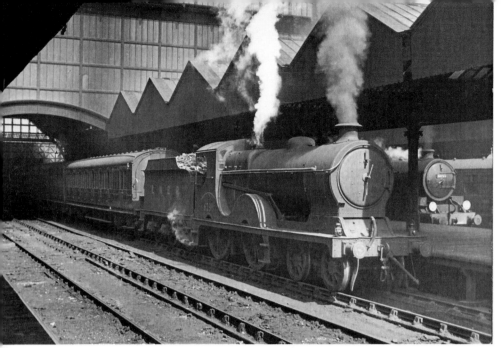

Cheshire Lines train. Manchester Central station on 7 May 1949 with ex GC 4-4-0 'D9' class No 62311 on a Liverpool express (via the CLC line) with a 'B1' class 4-6-0 No 61153 on a Marylebone train in the background – note the disc headcode.

Sutton Bridge, Midland & Great Northern Joint Railway with class 'C' 4-4-0 No 18 leaving the swing bridge, carrying both road and rail, at the head of an up express possibly the Leicester. A genuine joint-line scene with Midland signal boxes at both ends of the bridge controlling Great Northern signals.

Great Central and Metropolitan Joint. Aylesbury station on 2 May 1936 with Jersey Lily Atlantic No 6091 on a GC main line stopping train (the class was then being superseded on the expresses by the new 'B17' class Sandringham 4-6-0s) and Metropolitan Railway 4-4-4 tank No 104 with a Baker Street train – steam to Rickmansworth.

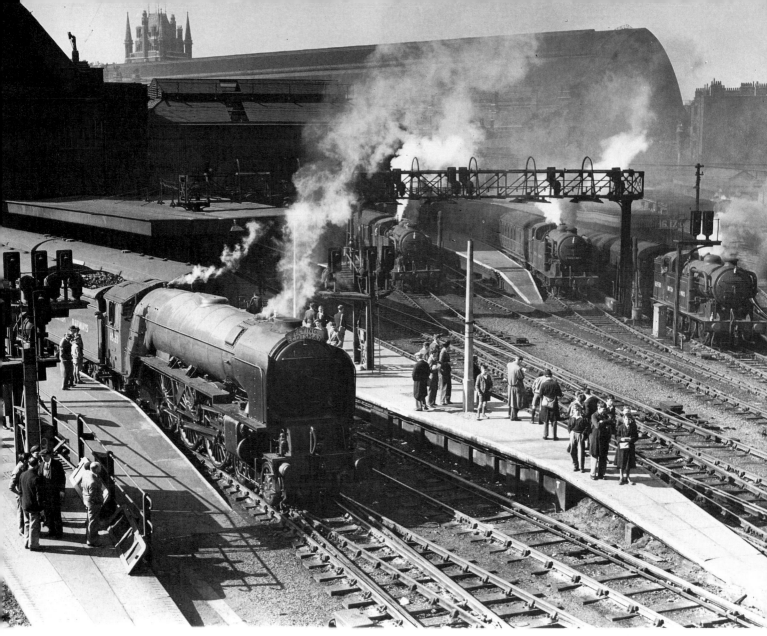

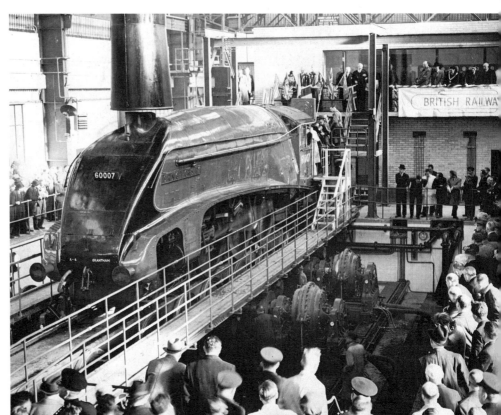

'A4' on test. Not specifically on the LNER but a joint LMS/LNER venture at Rugby, the test plant, though planned in the days of independence, was not opened until October 1948. This was adjacent to the West Coast main line to the south east of Rugby station with access to the LNER via a link to its GC tracks. No 60007 Sir Nigel Gresley was never actually tested on the plant but was the demonstration locomotive (aptly) used for the opening ceremony.

12
LNER INTO BR

THE same basic organisation, the same green livery for passenger engines and varnished teak for carriages, lasted throughout the LNER's quarter century. There was never change for change's sake; much indeed had been achieved through stability. But stability was what nationalisation failed to provide, especially in its early years.

Paying tribute to the LNER's policy of decentralisation, those responsible for the new order divided the system into three: The Eastern Region effectively took over the former Great Eastern and Great Northern systems; the North East was given its independence; and lines north of the border joined those of the LMS in a new Scottish Region. The North Eastern men at York were delighted. After twenty five years of servitude to London, they were free again and quickly despatched an army of painters to spread tangerine over their stations. The Scottish men were rightly fearful that the running in Scotland would be made by the LMS side, though LNER officers took most important posts.

Many penetrating lines initially retained their old allegiances. For example, the Great Central from Sheffield to Manchester remained with the Eastern, and the LMR and ER overlapped considerably in the East Midlands and Yorkshire. The first transfer, on 20 February 1949, was that of the London, Tilbury & Southend, from the LMR to the ER. In April next year the ER gained the ex-LMS lines in South and West Yorkshire and lost the Great Central main line south of Nottingham and also from Woodhead to Manchester. Numerous small joint lines became the responsibility of one region: the Cheshire Lines Committee naturally went to the LMR, the Midland & Great Northern Joint to the ER.

Regional boundaries became tidier, but many railwaymen resented having their allegiance transferred – and the planning of all services from London to the North and Scotland now involved at least two and sometimes three Regions. It was, however, obvious that some adjustments were necessary. Less necessary, and in the long run more harmful, were the changes within the individual Regions, notably the Eastern.

At first the Eastern operated through separate operating, commercial and motive power district offices, but these were sensibly merged under traffic managers covering all three functions, civil and signal engineering remaining separate. It might have been thought that that organisation would last for many years, but no. Sir Reginald Wilson, chairman of the Eastern Region's Board, decided that the Region should also be split into Lines; the LT&S, GN and GE with headquarters at Fenchurch Street, Kings Cross and Liverpool Street respectively, and several

Opposite
The old Kings Cross. Almost unaltered from LNER times this classic Eric Treacy shot shows mid-morning departures in the spring of 1949. On the left is 'A1' Pacific No 60133 (named Pommern *in 1950), one of the Darlington-built engines, in LNER green livery at the head of the Flying Scotsman. On the right in the suburban platforms is a bevy of 'N2' class 0-6-2 tanks which repay a little study. From left to right the first of the three is No 9533 (North British Locomotive Co 3/21) still in LNER livery not receiving its BR number until July 1949; it carries no smokebox destination board and heads an empty stock train. Next is an unknown engine with the legend British Railways on its side tanks and no front numberplate but with a destination board marked 'Main Line.' To the right is BR No 69580 (Hawthorn; Leslie 3/29) fully lettered in the current livery, number on bunker and smokebox doorplate with British Railways in full on the side tanks with empty stock from Moorgate. All the 'N2s' are condensing engines.*

179

Boat train. The Day Continental (with a headboard containing the flags of Holland and Great Britain) waits at Liverpool Street station behind 'B1' class 4-6-0 No 61361 in early BR days. The stock is pure LNER which did not wear the crimson and cream livery at all well.

Station Improvements

In January 1946 the Station Improvement Committee produced a comprehensive *Stations Improvements Booklet*, extolling the need for neatness, cleanliness and brightness (day and night) and laying down standards for platforms, waiting rooms and even lavatories ('separate lighting should be arranged for the WC cubicles').

Fluorescent lighting would give a daylight effect in enquiry offices 'for the purpose of reading timetables, handbills &c' while in concourses 'sufficient spill should be available to make the roof visible'. No longer was it sensible to think of lighting as detached from the structure and decorative work in a station. Especially should the LNER lantern be illuminated.

Groups of buildings might be simplified, obsolete equipment removed and approach roads improved by 'the planting of trees and shrubs or the formation of gardens. The Engineer will supply concrete curbs, flower pots &c, and also when possible will supply labour to assist in fixing them, but it should be understood that the station staff will thereafter have to maintain.'

The new Pacific. One of the first routes to receive Robin Riddles' new Britannia class 4-6-2s was the old Great Eastern main line from Liverpool Street to Norwich. The engines replaced the 1930s-built 'B17' Gresley three-cylinder 4-6-0s and proved to be popular with the crews who drove them. No 70012 John of Gaunt is seen at Brentwood with the up Norfolkman in July 1951.

district boundaries were changed. Within a short time the Lines had disappeared and the districts had become a smaller number of larger divisions.

After splitting into the Eastern and North Eastern Regions in 1948 they were remerged in 1967 as the new Eastern Region with headquarters at York, a massive upheaval. Since then there have been many changes. Many titles which had been used for well over a century disappeared. Porters became 'railmen', platelayers 'trackmen' and stationmasters 'station managers'. Responsibility for several stations was then given to area managers, answerable to the divisional managers. The areas themselves have been constantly subject to mergers and then the divisions were abolished. Now in 1988 the old Great Eastern Line has re-emerged as the new Anglia Region. In the meantime, of course, the directors of Inter-City, Provincial, Freight and Network South East cover all BR regardless of Regional boundaries. The Regions may have been quick, in 1948, with their cans of paint but they had nothing on Network South East more recently, spreading red paint over the suburban areas of four – now five – different Regions. The corporate identity of which BR was so proud has suddenly gathered almost as many different liveries as there were prior to 1923.

Anyone who has lived through several reorganisations will know how impossible it is to prevent some square pegs landing in round holes, and how much energy is diverted from the basic task of running the railway. As Gerry Fiennes said: 'When you reorganise you bleed.' What a bleeding time it has been since 1948! Even now someone, somewhere may be thinking up the next instalment.

In Scotland, the LNER's merger on an end-to-end basis of the North British and Great North was administratively easy. Pooling these with the LMS ones on which former rivalries were yet alive was altogether more tricky; many were the local disputes and angers. LNER men started by being unhappy about the choice of the LMS's Glasgow offices as HQ, but LMS men were even more upset that the first head man was the LNER's T. F. Cameron – especially as he continued to live in his flat in the North British Hotel at Edinburgh and commute by official car. His successor, and the next three after that, were all LNER men. They were successful ultimately in carving out a Scottish identity, though the Scottish Region went through horrible internal administrative changes similar to those on the Eastern. Never, for example, was it easy for MPs and captains of industry to keep in touch with key men for they and their duties changed too rapidly.

In Scotland as well as in England, it was naturally the development of the East Coast route that was most in the news. As soon as possible after the war, the LNER resumed fast running. The large fleet of Gresley Pacifics and 'V2s' had been joined by 'A1' and 'A2' Pacifics designed by Thompson and Peppercorn. The 'A4s' frequently ran at very high speeds when regaining time, without publicity. However, it took ten years before main trains were booked at average speeds in excess of 60 mph. The *Flying Scotsman* recommenced non-stop running in summer 1948, the year when numerous bridges were washed away north of

180

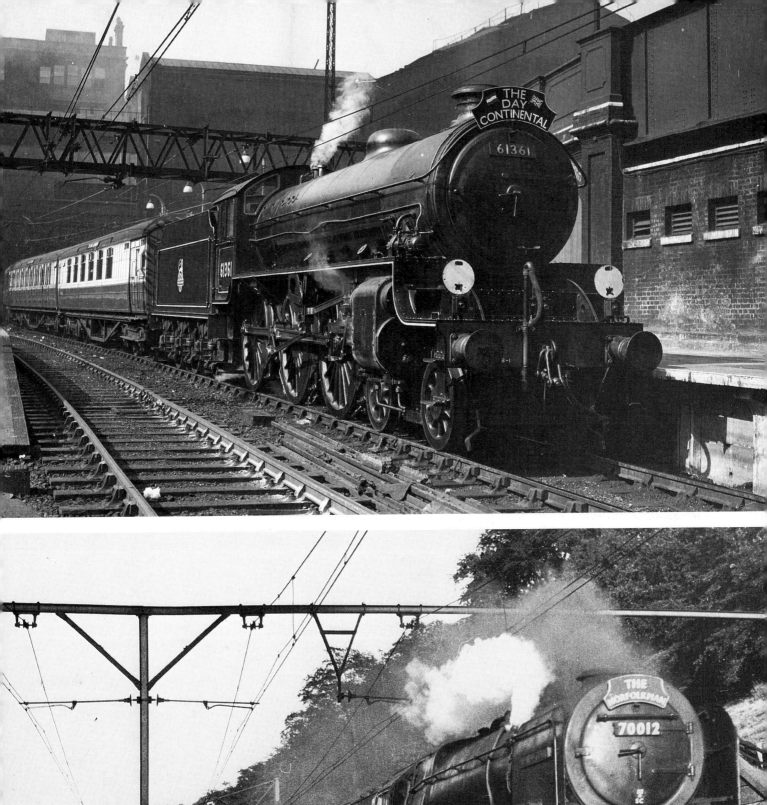

On trial in foreign parts. The 'V2s' were some of Gresley's most successful engines and as such were given a thorough going over in early BR days. Here No 60845 is undergoing trials out of Swindon in late February/early March 1953; the train is a heavy one made up of twenty-one coaches and the old GWR dynamometer car. The station is Badminton.

The end of an old era. The Western portals of the old and new Woodhead tunnels just at the end of the steam era in 1954. The twin bore ex MS&L tunnels, which were true hell holes for enginemen, were replaced by a single-bore tunnel and the route electrified to Sheffield and Wath on Dearne. A very much-needed modernisation which at the time revolutionised this original MS&L main line. Sadly the capital expenditure was scarcely in the loan columns when the route was declared redundant. A London-bound express approaches the tunnel drawn by a 'B1' class 4-6-0 whilst an 'O4' class ROD type 2-8-0 leaves with a long coal train.

Berwick, causing diversions from Tweedmouth via Kelso to Edinburgh. A few 'A4' drivers managed to run non-stop for 408.6 miles, a world's record for steam engines; this involved close watch on the tender water over the 92 miles between Lucker troughs and Edinburgh. In 1949 the non-stop working was transferred to a new train, the *Capitals Limited*, which was renamed *Elizabethan* in 1953. The timing was reduced to 6hr 30min in 1954, and the 'A4' class proved they had lost nothing over the years. On a special train from Doncaster to Kings Cross in 1959, *Sir Nigel Gresley*, driven by Bill Hoole of Kings Cross, achieved 112mph on the falling gradient from Stoke Tunnel towards Peterborough.

In May 1961 the first of the 3300 HP 'Deltic' diesels arrived, the total fleet eventually amounting to twenty-two. Eight were allocated to Finsbury Park depot, six to Gateshead and eight to Edinburgh Haymarket. The Eastern engines followed tradition and were named after racehorses, the NE and Scottish ones bearing the names of regiments. Considerable accelerations were made and high daily engine mileages achieved. Increased business caused the immediate post-war service of five Anglo-Scottish trains per day to be increased to nine. By 1973 the timings had been reduced to 3½ hours to Newcastle and 5½ hours to Edinburgh. When the 'Deltics' were withdrawn they had each run over two million miles. The High Speed Trains were introduced in 1978 and, in the following year, Newcastle was reached in under three hours and Edinburgh in 4½ hours. Any enthusiast of steam who had ridden up Stoke bank on a steam engine due for shops with a driver who was not inclined to make the best of it, struggling over the top at 30 mph, was sold on dieselisation when he rode with the driver of an HST and felt the brakes go on at the top to honour the 100mph restriction down to Grantham.

The great improvements in service were, of course, mainly due to the changes in motive power, but improvements to the infrastructure also played a great part. Re-alignment of Offord curve, requiring diversion of the River Ouse, raised speed from 70 to 100mph. At Grantham North the speed went up from 70 to 95mph, and work at Bawtry viaduct permitted 80mph. Improvements were also effected at many other locations including Shaftholme Junction, Aycliffe, Durham and Newton Hall. The construction of three new tunnels between Potters Bar and Greenwood removed the notorious Potters Bar bottleneck in the GN suburban area. Major works were carried out in the reconstruction of Peterborough North station eliminating the 20mph restriction. Recently the Selby restrictions have been by-passed by the new route between Doncaster and York. Many more improvements were made over the years, including upgrading most of the route to 125mph for the HSTs. In LNER days there were a great number of manual signalboxes on the East Coast main line as elsewhere; trains are now signalled by Kings Cross, Peterborough, Doncaster, York, Newcastle and Edinburgh.

The route is now being electrified and will be worked by Class 91 electric locomotives on passenger trains and Class 90 on freight. They will, no doubt, live up to their predecessors, the Stirling Singles, Ivatt Atlantics, Gresley Pacifics, Deltics and HSTs.

Bulk freight with steam. One of the Consett iron ore trains in the days of 'Q7' operation. The 56-ton bogie hopper wagons had air operated doors for rapid discharge and the locomotives allocated to this service carried a Westinghouse pump on the right-hand side. The train is shown here between South Pelaw Junction and Annfield Plain being banked by a second-class 'Q7' 0-8-0.

Whilst these improvements were being made on the main line different changes were taking place on the branches. In the 1950s arrival of the diesel multiple-units, initially serving Leeds, Bradford and Harrogate, permitted withdrawal of large numbers of small, old steam engines but, unfortunately, even the cheaper method of operation could not save many of the lines. Branches in East Anglia, Lincolnshire, Yorkshire, the North-East and Scotland were slashed. The old M&GN Joint serving North Norfolk disappeared almost completely, northern East Anglia suffering especially severely from closures. Main lines which had been transferred to the LMR were closed, including almost the whole of the ex-GC main line. The Woodhead route, electrified at 1500 volts DC overhead after the war with a new three-mile long tunnel, is no more.

Scotland also suffered severe branch and secondary line closures, the whole of the once-proud 'little and good' Great North being swept away apart from the single route from Aberdeen toward Inverness and the Dufftown branch, though the more publicised loss was that of the Waverley line from Carlisle to Edinburgh along with its once-numerous connections. But the LNER route was chosen in preference to the LMS for the Glasgow–Aberdeen traffic and Edinburgh–Aberdeen is now seen as part of the East Coast main line with record levels of service.

Built-in obsolescence. Temple Mills new hump yard as seen in August 1959 showing the modern mechanised marshalling of wagons. The control tower and hump with secondary retarders in the foreground are viewed from the top of a lamp standard. Unfortunately, this view is now history as BR, contrary to mainland Europe and other western countries, has abandoned the traditional freight train and wagon load freight in favour of bulk freight, mineral and container trains.

The GE, LT&S and GN London Suburban services have of course, been electrified. The GN services from Finsbury Park to Broad Street and to Moorgate via the Metropolitan Widened Lines ceased to operate, and were replaced by the take-over from London Transport of the GN&City Line, permitting GN suburban trains to reach Moorgate via Drayton Park. This involved production of the first dual-voltage overhead line/third rail trains. The GN had lost the High Barnet, Edgware and Alexandra Palace branches. The GE lost the Woodford, Hainault, Epping and Ongar services to the Central Line of London Transport.

On the freight side the MGR coal trains started to run in 1964. The Eastern Region includes a large number of pits supplying the new super power stations at West Burton, Cottam, High Marnham, Thorpe Marsh, Ferrybridge, Eggborough and Drax, replacing the many trains to more-distant small power stations. Coal to gas-works and virtually all domestic coal disappeared. In the early years after the war operations had been improved by closing many small marshalling yards, in most of which flat shunting took place, and opening very large mechanised Hump yards equipped with mechanical retarders. Yards were opened at Ripple Lane and Temple Mills in East London, at Healey Mills in the West Riding, Tyne and Tees in the north-east, and Millerhill and Thornton in the ex-LNE part of the Scottish Region. The last modern marshalling yard to be opened was at Tinsley, near Sheffield, in 1965, equipped with the revolutionary Dowty system of retarders and booster-retarders. They were too late – overtaken by changing traffic flows and the arrival of Freightliners from 1965.

HST for London. Edinburgh Waverley station on 29 May 1988 with HST power car No 43116 City of Kingston-Upon-Hull at the head of the 17.00 for Kings Cross.

Common Owners
Nationalisation changed people's (or at least Southern people's) views of ownership . . . now everybody owned everything. So there was little that Kings Cross division could do except express irritation when 'South Lines' transfer trips that went out with a solid LNER 'Queen Mary' brake (which of course everybody loved) came back with an SR affair.

But who would have guessed that when a 'B1' locomotive went missing for a month, and despite daily enquiries had seemed to disappear off the face of the earth, its whereabouts would be publicly reported in *Trains Illustrated* as the first to turn up in that part of the Southern Region!

185

Quick and Dead
Yesterday I happened to get in the brake of a Shenfield electric going to work and in it was an old, a very old, retired driver, whom I knew. And I said to him because he is an old boy who likes a compliment, 'Tom, you had a name for losing very little time in fog. How did you do it?' He only said one thing. 'I never lost my way.' That was an exaggeration, of course. There can be no driver living or dead who can always have been sure of his position in fog. The ones who crawl and find out in fog are the living. The ones who don't, are the dead. – Gerry Fiennes in a BBC talk.

The Network System. A scene on Bethnal Green Bank on 10 January 1989 showing the newly electrified East Anglian lines with class 86/2 No 86260 Driver Wallace Oakes GC at the head of the 12.35 Network Express from Liverpool Street to Kings Lynn and 315 emu No 315814 on a Hertford East-Liverpool Street train.

After the transfer of the lines in South and West Yorkshire from the LMR to the ER and NER, many steps were taken to eliminate the dual serving of pits from ex-LMS and ex-LNE branches. Many routes and small yards were closed, and much freight-train mileage eliminated. Within a short time the bringing into service of the new power stations and transfer of most of the traffic to MGR trains caused more closures. Concentration on the larger new pits resulted in many closures in once extremely busy areas such as Barnsley and Mexborough. This also caused the closure of the first hump yard at Wath. The run-down of heavy industries such as steel, heavy engineering and shipbuilding has also reduced the tonnage of freight carried by rail.

With electrification to Leeds in 1989 and to Scotland in 1991 and the second generation DMUs on the remaining branches, together with the new cheaper methods of signalling those lines, the future should be bright. If only the infrastructure, motive power and rolling stock improvements had been available with the traffic levels of yesteryear. Did investment have to go along with nationalisation, and did national ownership have to mean such perpetual upheavals?

The disappearance of the huge if slow flows of traffic, especially down the main arteries toward London, would seem as shocking to those who worked in LNER days as would a return to the conditions then prevailing to today's younger railwaymen. And while many passengers may hanker after the 'golden' days of railway travel, incredulous would they be if they had to ride in four-wheeled suburban trains whose compartment dividers scarcely reached to the tops of the heads of taller travellers squeezed into the six seats a side.

Publicity and Public Relations

Looking at a wide spectrum of LNER publicity, from colour posters, through press releases to exhibits it would be difficult for an observer to get a true picture of the balance of the railway's real functions. Large gleaming passenger engines, an emphasis on speed, glamorous continental travel, sunny resorts crowded with beautiful young people and authentic locals, glorious rural areas just waiting to receive rail-borne hikers who never appear in hordes. Of course it was not the duty of any Publicity Department to advertise the sometimes rather down-at-heel trains, only a comparatively few of which ran at express speeds. In the high summer the busy resorts, Clacton, Skegness, Cleethorpes and the like were chock-a-block, offering accommodation ranging from grand hotels to rather grim lodging houses. But the advertising to relate industry to rail haulage was quite low-key, even though it was the very lifeblood of the railway.

Yet publicity is the art of persuasion and if the commuter half poisoned by Gasworks Tunnel, squashed shoulder to shoulder in his Gresley articulated coach caught a glimpse of the northbound *Silver Jubilee* at Finsbury Park, then was faced with a wall of colourful posters as he stepped out of the train at Potters Bar, he might yet identify with the glamour image rather than

Open day at Stratford. Of all the grouped railways the LNER was at the forefront when it came to the public relations exercise of shed open days when the public were admitted and allowed a good look round. In some cases they were even treated to an aerial view by being hauled up in a wagon by the depot's steam crane, an exercise scarcely commending itself to today's Health & Safety Executive! This photograph shows two particularly interesting locomotives 'B12/3', No 8579 newly rebuilt in May 1932, plus a Sentinel shunter, its peculiarity explained by clear and simple wording on a notice fixed to the bunker side.

the grimy reality, go home and leaf through the thousand plus pages of the LNER Holiday Guide purchased for 6d and book a holiday in Scarborough.

The LNER was run on a shoestring, yet it projected an image that got it known world-wide as a high-speed railway, as an engineering innovator and transporter of royalty to Balmoral and Sandringham. The Press office releases concentrated on speed, the opening of new facilities such as Whitemoor Yard or the new suburban stations. What we would now call a corporate image was also pioneered early by the LNER with its Gill Sans typeface and elliptical logo. Certainly the post-grouping pauper had style.

187

The advertising manager of course had to relate to the fact that the LNER conglomerate sold rail passenger and goods transport, but also owned a large chain of hotels, ran ports, steamships, waterways, a large fleet of delivery wagons, catering services and also a number of bus services in its early days. There were many more alternative opportunities in the inter-war years to spend spare cash than there had been in the pre-war years. There was competition from road services, a host of new consumer products and services, new suburban houses, but also longer holidays, more and longer commuter journeys and higher expectations, so the LNER did battle for its share through publicity.

Posters were a major tool. Well-known artists of the period were commissioned to extol the virtues of beauty spots, resorts and aspects of railway and industrial life. By the late 1920s a poster exhibition could be held to celebrate an art form in which Tom Purvis's Seaside series vied for attention with Frank Mason's Lighthouse series, Fred Taylor's evocation of historic cities served by the LNER or H. J. Gawthorn's industrial paintings. Some sixty or so large posters a year were produced, many now treasured collectors' pieces, some of the best of their genre. They could be bought direct from the LNER, thus helping defray the cost to the railway.

The Bill Room of the advertising department at York despatched posters far and wide, to the continent as well as to the furthest points on the LNER system. They also handled a vast array of booklets, handouts and other publicity materials. Booklets were produced to back up the improving services of the 1930s. *On Either Side* was distributed on request to travellers on principal Scottish expresses for a shilling, a price which stood comparison with similar booklets issued by its rival the LMS. It was a rolling map of what to see on the long journey, items of historical and railway interest were highlighted. Its companion *Notes for LNER Passengers* included a 'Streamline Commentary' by the popular writer Kenneth Matthews . . . most impressed by the smoothness of the new trains which allowed him to write his article without it being a 'succession of jabs and slashes on the paper'. Praise of the double glazing, buckeye coupling and ventilation followed, although modern readers would have been put off by the sound-proofing achieved by asbestos spraying! Those half-dozen super trains were a tonic for the system after the depression and the publicity men made the most of it. They had souvenirs, cards and books produced for sale including Cecil J. Allen's *The Coronation*, a paper-weight of *Silver Link* sold at 2s 6d, whilst a set of six souvenir dessert plates showing cathedrals served by the LNER and made by Wedgwood could be obtained for 12/- (60p). Even in the depths of the war George Dow produced *The First Railway in Norfolk* to celebrate a local centenary in 1944.

Triplets out of Harwich. A poster showing the Amsterdam, Prague *and* Vienna *used on the overnight journeys connecting with the boat train services in and out of Liverpool Street. From 1932 to 1939* Vienna *was used for weekend cruises to continental ports, and after war service was requisitioned as a troop carrier for the Ministry of Transport which duty it carried out until 1960.*

THREE NEW LUXURY SHIPS
HARWICH-HOOK NIGHTLY SERVICE
The Largest Vessels in regular service between England and the Continent
FULL INFORMATION FROM CONTINENTAL TRAFFIC MANAGER L·N·E·R LIVERPOOL STREET STATION LONDON. E.C.2.
OR HULL. PRINCIPAL L·N·E·R OFFICES, STATIONS AND AGENCIES.

13
PRESERVATION

THE LNER was more interested in its history than any other of the grouping companies. Events such as the centenary of the Stockton & Darlington were celebrated on the grand scale, a procession including several complete trains of various vintages and the company's own York Railway Museum was established . . . primitive maybe by today's standards but a vital start, the only one of its kind. But LNER exhibits came only from the North Eastern and Great Northern, the fact that all the North British Atlantics went for scrap being especially regrettable. Most famous of the LNER constituents locomotives on view was Patrick Stirling's GNR single-wheeler No 1, though Henry Ivatt's small Atlantic No 990 *Henry Oakley* was also much viewed – along with the two strangers, the GWR's record-breaking *City of Truro* and the LBSCR's 0-4-2 *Gladstone* purchased from a friendly Southern Railway by the Stephenson Locomotive Society.

The National Railway Museum at York is now one of Britain's premier tourist attractions, but for a time the attention moved south, the Transport Commission opening the short-lived museum in an old bus depot at Clapham in the nick of time. A number of classes had already bitten the dust, but a GC 'improved' 'Director' 4-4-0 No 506 *Butler Henderson* was secured in 1961. It is at present on loan to the Great Central Railway at Loughborough where it has been restored to working order – a very appropriate piece of private enterprise. From the GE came a 'J17' 0-6-0, a 'J69' 0-6-0 tank and the last 2-4-0 to see active service on British rails, one of Holden's 2-4-0s, ex 'E4' No 490. John Scholes, the curator, also collected an 'O4' 2-8-0 of Robinson's Great Central design and one of the Wath electric locomotives was claimed by the NRM. From pure LNER stock the only locomotives to enter the collection were the record-breaking 'A4' No 4468 *Mallard* and the 'V2' 2-6-2 No 4771 *Green Arrow*.

Two other classes escaped the scrapman and are on static exhibit at Glasgow's Transport Museum: North British 'D34' 4-4-0 No 256 *Glen Douglas* and GN of S 'D40' 4-4-0 No 49 *Gordon Highlander*. Both were used on special excursions in Scotland between 1959 and 1966.

There was no Barry scrapyard on the LNER's old territory and only one engine, a 'B1' 4-6-0, made the acquaintance of Dai Woodham, scrap man extraordinary. While there are not so many LNER as GWR and even SR preserved locomotives, individual preservation did come to the scene quite early with a number of small tank engines, a couple of GE section tender locomotives, a 'J15' class 0-6-0 and a reboiled 'B12' 4-6-0. Most of these have seen work on preserved railways in recent years.

But the first prize must be awarded to Alan Pegler in his acquisition of 'A3' Pacific No 4472 *Flying Scotsman*. It is easy enough to say 'well done' in hindsight but Alan Pegler was certainly wise not only in his selection of the engine but also in getting his solicitor to draw up a contract covering its operating rights over BR. While all other steam was banned, *Flying Scotsman* kept the flag flying.

Five other 'A4s' were rescued for preservation, one (No 60010 *Dominion of Canada*) going to Canada, one (No 60008 *Dwight D. Eisenhower*) to the USA, with three to run in the United Kingdom, though the only major contender for main-line running in very recent years has been No 4498 *Sir Nigel Gresley* which has been seen almost countrywide and has been an excellent performer. The Earl of Lindsay (then Viscount Garnock), whose family has long been associated with the Western Highlands and who is himself a great enthusiast, purchased one of the 'K4' 2-6-0s specially built for the Fort William line: No 3442 *The Great Marquess*. It has worked a number of main-line specials since its withdrawal in 1961 and overhaul at Cowlairs works. It has just undergone a heavy repair on the Severn Valley Railway at Bridgnorth.

Sections of various types of line have been preserved. The main line is represented by the Great Central Railway based on the GC's Loughborough (a typical GC island station). The seaside railway comes to life again at Sheringham on the North Norfolk Railway, part of the M&GN. And dramatic scenery and preservation come together on the North Yorkshire Moors line based on Pickering but with a long section of the North Eastern branch toward Whitby. At its Grosmont locomotive headquarters the North Eastern Locomotive Preservation Group have an ex-NER class 'P3' (LNER 'J27') 0-6-0 and a class 'T3' NER 0-8-0 as well as the BR built 'K1' No 2005 (62005). The latter has made its debut on BR's own steam excursions now run regularly between Fort William and Mallaig, where again steam and scenery combine. Scotland has its own piece of railway preservation at Bo'ness which houses another ex-LNER class, the 'J36' 0-6-0 from the North British Railway named *Maude* – not as one might first assume a lady's name but rather a commemoration of a World War 1 General recalling the engine's service with the ROD.

It is of course not only on the West Highland that BR has cashed in on the enthusiasm for steam. Several seasons have seen popular steam runs to Scarborough, while LNER engines also appear on steam specials elsewhere. *Mallard* and *Sir Nigel Gresley* as well as *Flying Scotsman* have been seen by greater numbers of people than in their ordinary working days.

One further item of LNER interest has caught the preservationist's imagination, the Gresley buffet car. Many examples of this useful vehicle lasted into the early 1970s and they can be found not only on their old company sites but also at other tourist attractions like the Severn Valley Railway and the Birmingham Railway Museum. And two of the coaches preserved by this book's publisher in Devon are Gresley's, a corridor third rebuilt as an engineer's coach and a pigeon carrier full brake.

The old museum. The LNER was the only member of the Big Four, or indeed the only British railway company, to set up its own museum open to the public. This was almost adjacent to the station at York in Queen Street and it housed a number of historic items including NER No 1621, a survivor of the 1895 Races to the North and a competitor to the LNWR's Hardwicke, *also preserved; and two Great Northern Atlantic classes, the original Klondyke in* Henry Oakley *and the superheated No 251. Somewhat generously the museum was also home to an old LB&SCR engine, the 0-4-2* Gladstone *and the Great Western's* City of Truro. *Seen here in the 1960s are No 251, NER 2-4-0 No 1463 and the NER 2-2-4 tank* Aerolite.

The Plant Centenarian. To celebrate a hundred years of Doncaster works the Eastern Region of BR arranged a special train hauled by veteran Great Northern Railway Atlantics from Kings Cross to Doncaster with a return trip at express speed behind an 'A4' Pacific. Sunday 20 September 1953 was a true red letter day for any LNER enthusiast. The special train which left Kings Cross at 10.40 was hauled by 'C2' No 990 Henry Oakley *piloting 'C1' No 251, driven respectively by drivers Hailstone and Hoole; it is seen here climbing Holloway Bank. Since that time* Henry Oakley *has been steamed on several occasions and has been a working exhibit at Shildon in 1975 and on the Keighley and Worth Valley Railway, but No 251 has remained a static exhibit.*

191

An Ivatt survivor. One of the very early arrivals in the preservation scene was Capt Bill Smith's 'J52' class 0-6-0ST No 1247. Now in the National Railway Museum at York it spent some years on the North Yorkshire Moors Railway where it is seen near Beckhole on 22 August 1976 with the Sundays-only 14.00 from Grosmont to Goathland – diesel from there on because of fire risk.

Twin Scotsmen. For the summer timetable of 1938 the LNER introduced two completely new trains on the Flying Scotsman *service. To publicise them a press run was arranged on 30 June 1938. From Kings Cross to Stevenage Great Northern Railway 4-2-2 No 1 hauled a train of vintage six-wheeled coaches. Here passengers transferred to the new train for a high-speed run to Barkston, north of Grantham, where the whole train was turned on the triangle. The return journey was non-stop to Kings Cross. Here GNR No 1 and class 'A4' No 4498* Sir Nigel Gresley *are standing at Stevenage. Both locomotives are preserved, No 1 in the National Collection and No 4498 privately.*

Station Interludes

Cambridge

Cambridge was the largest of the Eastern Counties original stations to survive into the LNER period. It was by then unique with its long single main-line platform facing east. At each end were pairs of bays. That at the south end was used by ex-LNWR engines on maroon trains from Bletchley and Oxford, often headed by minuscule Webb 2-4-0s or Whale and Bowen-Cooke's demoted express engines. At the north end an ancient ex-Midland 2-4-0 creaked in from Kettering with a short and often near empty train. The ex-GNR had a buffet car express service from King's Cross and from 1936 it was often headed by Ivatt large Atlantics on a smart rake of teak coaches, its buffet car seemingly permanently occupied by undergraduates.

The station offices and bookstall faced the arriving passenger, who must often have wondered why the train did not get to the platform before it had gone half the length of the station and clacked noisily across the crossover. If bound for ex-GER territory the passenger would be faced with elderly GER coaches, clerestories, sometimes six-wheelers or early bogies painted in coprolite brown and hauled by Intermediate 2-4-0s for Colchester, Mildenhall or March via St Ives. Claud Hamilton 4-4-0s took trains on to King's Lynn and Peterborough where sometimes the brightly polished green royal engines performed on humbler trains.

The glorious exterior was always thronged with cabs and omnibuses. The long *porte cochere* was badly needed as the somewhat exclusive undergraduate and academic clientele had up to two miles to travel into town and they did not take kindly to sharing buses with the lower orders. The engine shed at the north end was the most easily accessible in East Anglia, a veritable museum to be savoured.

Leeds

The Southerner's perception of England north of the Trent tends to be of a foreign land, of satanic mills, cloth caps and clogs . . . So it was perhaps unfortunate that those who ventured north to Leeds, cosseted in a prestige service from Kings Cross should arrive at Central. Not to put too fine a point on it, the station was a dump. Bishop Eric Treacy might concentrate on impressive steam locomotives from carefully chosen standpoints, but always in the background was a gloomy station, smoke-blackened, with narrow platforms under a low roof, its unattractive buildings tarted up unconvincingly with Gill Sans. Central it was not! And if you were going on to Bradford, the short journey over the alps was likely to be in a grubby and sour-smelling compartment coach under the pall produced by a hard-working 'N1' tank.

The Beer Train. A Kings Cross buffet car express so nicknamed by undergraduates leaves Cambridge behind a superheated Ivatt Atlantic in 1933.

Cambridge today. Two trains for Liverpool Street wait in today's modern station. On the right is the 17.05 fast headed by 86/2 class No 86256 Pebble Mill *whilst emus Nos 305 515 and 305 519 make up the 17.25 stopping service. The date is 19 February 1988.*

Leeds Central. A multi-railway joint station but principally LNE group, in early BR days. Not the most architecturally elegant building, now gone completely. Class 'V2' 2-6-2 leaves on an up express, possibly a relief, as the usual power was class 'A1' or 'A3' 4-6-2s. On the right a 'J39' 0-6-0 is backing onto its train.

A quarter of a mile down Wellington Street, things were rather better arranged, particularly after 1938 when the LMS's Wellington Station was rebuilt and combined with the joint 'New' through station to form Leeds City, fronted by the imposing new Queens Hotel. The rebuilding provided an elegant concourse with high ceilings and a line of amenities and shops, the main entrance being direct from City Square as if to tempt the Black Prince off his plinth to take the train for France and war.

But if the LMS did, then BR undid. After less than thirty years of rebuilt life, the Wellington platforms were turned into a parcels depot and car park. The concourse, where once tykes met passengers arriving from London, Edinburgh and Glasgow, little more than a passage is now closed off.

Leeds City east end with class 'C7' 4-4-2 No 2193 in wartime unlined black with NE on tender on a local train possibly to York or Hull.

Aberdeen

Among Aberdeen's long-enduring reputations is its early railway cussedness: the Great North of Scotland was wont to start its trains from the Waterloo station just before passengers arriving from the south at Guild Street could rush the half mile that separated them; to be followed by the increasingly deplorable first joint station. But by LNER days, Aberdeen had a thoroughly modern second joint station of glass and sparkling grey granite, well matched to traffic needs. Its platform layout only dated from 1907–8, its main buildings from 1914. Though it matched the LNER's keenness to enhance its reputation principally as the operator of services from the south, it was only joint by virtue of absorbing the GNSR!

The station's modest splendour centred on the spacious circulating area. You came through one of the two passages from the booking hall, to be faced by the bookstall and above it a train indicator of admirable clarity if of undoubted Caledonian origin. In the wings of the main building were all the appropriate facilities on a generous scale; refreshment and dining rooms – in the latter a long-standing delicacy was skink soup – waiting rooms, and elaborate toilet facilities with hairdresser and bathroom (just the thing after an overnight journey from London). The whole area, under a lofty glass roof with glazed end screens at the bay platforms, was light and airy and had a *thought-out* look.

During the day there was a steady trickle of trains, though with the demise of the Culter–Aberdeen–Dyce suburban service in 1937 this was thinned out to the point where two through platforms were superfluous. But with the departure of the second London sleeper train soon after eight, and the arrival of the evening Edinburgh and Glasgow expresses, the station fell into almost uninterrupted slumber until next morning.

Norwich Thorpe

Excepting only Liverpool Street, Norwich was the crowning glory of the old GER. The six-platform station was built on a new site in 1886. Its red brick exterior was dressed in creamy Bath stone and the impressive frontage crowned with a silvery dome, covered with fish-scale zinc plates. The ironwork surrounding the forecourt was impressive and the same pattern was repeated in the screen to the platforms. From the end of the platforms the steam depot and works dating from the 1840s was close at hand, activity always highly visible as the GER never had many of its engines under cover on shed.

The dining room was lace-curtained and discreet, used to refreshing the county folk before they ventured into the void beyond Norwich, fortifying them with Bullards Beer and filling dishes. In LNER days 'B12' and later 'Sandringham' 4-6-0s were seen on the London trains, 'Claud Hamilton' 4-4-0s did the honours on trains to Wells, Cromer and to Cambridge, Peterborough and King's Lynn, whilst fussy little 'Gobbler' 2-4-2Ts chuntered in and out with Yarmouth and Lowestoft trains. In the goods yard 'J69' 0-6-0Ts were in evidence and the pilot was often an even tinier 'J65'. Reliable old 'J15' and 'J17' 0-6-0s clanked in and out with pickup goods from the country.

As a terminal, Norwich Thorpe was comparable in size with Charing Cross and seemed as busy on summer Saturdays. Its choked approaches and cramped yard added to the impression of perpetual motion, teak coaches, goods wagons, black engines and the occasional green one all visible with the turn of the head and dominated by the pumping of Westinghouse brakes. It was a unique terminal right at the hub of what in effect, was a cartwheel of routes to the coast and inland towards the Midlands and South.

Norwich Thorpe station on the formation of the LNER. A view taken by the official photographer showing the impressive terminus much as it is today except for the removal of platform canopies and the addition of overhead wiring.

GN of S main line. Two typical locomotives head a Keith and Elgin train at Aberdeen on 4 April 1947; 'D40' class 4-4-0 No 2275, very much a native, and an imported ex Great Eastern Holden 4-6-0, LNER class 'B12' (nicknamed Hikers) No 1513. The GN of S engine would be in unlined black and the 'B12' in apple green.

continued opposite

14
BRITAIN'S NEW PREMIER LINE

AT 12.15 on 11 August 1988 – what were you doing at the time? – history was being made. The very first electric train rolled into Leeds, precursor of a full Kings Cross–Leeds high speed electric service to start in October 1989 and a similar service from Kings Cross to Edinburgh two years later.

The West Coast route from Euston through to Glasgow finally came on stream with 25kv traction on 6 May 1974. It brought the fastest timing down to five hours. At this time the East Coast rival, thanks to Deltic diesel locomotive haulage and steady infrastructure improvement achieved the first five and a half hour timing from Kings Cross to Edinburgh, but there was inevitably talk about concentrating traffic on the electric route and maybe closing Newcastle–Edinburgh. Since then, the relative positions of the two routes has changed utterly. On the East Coast the hard worked and weary Deltics were displaced by InterCity 125 High Speed trains with a new timetable effective from August 1979. Edinburgh was reached in under 4hr 40min – improved on until by the winter of 1988/9 a service of fifteen day trains averaged 4hr 43min with a best time of 4hr 26min. On the West Coast, the next leap forward was tied to the APT, supposed to bring the journey time down to 4hr 10min with the 1981 timetable. It of course failed to enter commercial service, and the stop-gap solution has been stop gap indeed. Despite a relaxation for 110mph running, because of recovery times and extra stops the Glasgow service has from (1988) become little better than a semi-fast series of six day trains averaging 5hr 36min (the kind of relegation accorded the Great Central route ahead of its demise). London to Glasgow via Edinburgh is just as quick.

Into this situation was tossed (in February 1981) a joint Department of Transport/British Railways *Review of Main Line Electrification*, looking at the financial returns from various electrification options, including the East Coast main line, building on the revenue growth from the HSTs. The suburban electrification from Moorgate and Kings Cross to Welwyn Garden City and Royston (linked with the resignalling Kings Cross–Sandy) had meanwhile come into operation from October 1977.

By the early 1980s it was becoming apparent that, despite their commercial appeal, the HST sets would not last for ever, or be able to cope with increasing demand. Pressed into ever greater mileages their reliability was declining. So work began on planning electrification of the East Coast main line to Edinburgh and the Leeds spur at 25kv. BR's submission, at an overall cost of £306 million (1984 prices) was authorised in July 1984. The submission anticipated a saving of 60 per cent on train maintenance and of 25 per cent on fuel. Benefits included a major improvement in reliability and a small increase in revenue. It set out a timescale for a three stage introduction of electric services, to Peterborough in May 1987, to Leeds in May 1989 and to Newcastle and Edinburgh in May 1991.

On the 44½ mile route from Hitchin (the limit of suburban electrification) to Peterborough wiring could proceed quickly with few overbridges needing raising and extensive slow lines to minimise traffic disruption. The main need here was to get the four additional class 317/2 emus delivered for the new service. The next 109½ miles to Leeds involved rather more infrastructure work to provide electrical clearances, including a potentially difficult operation on a bridge at the south end of Doncaster station. On this predominantly two-track section rather more reliance had to be placed on diversionary routes at night and at weekends. Little track rationalisation was needed, but a number of small schemes have raised permitted speeds, particularly on the approach to Leeds. The critical element here was to get sufficient of the new class 91 locomotives and associated coaches delivered and safely through a stringent programme of high-speed testing. The final stage, the 237 mile route between Doncaster and Edinburgh, while needing further deliveries of locomotives and stock, hinges almost entirely on major track rationalisation and associated resignalling in the York and Newcastle station areas, with lesser work at Darlington, Durham and Edinburgh. At York, for instance, major simplification of the approach tracks at each end of the station permits an increase of speed through connections from 15 to 50mph. A particularly difficult element of the York work was the raising of Holgate Road bridge at the south end of the station; until this was done the track rationalisation in the vicinity could not be completed. At Newcastle the provision of a new island through platform will permit the decimation of the famous (but costly) diamond crossings at the east end of the station.

Apart from the emus for the Peterborough trains, the submission provided for 31 electric locomotives of class 91, with 225kph capability, 21 class 90 locomotives mainly for freight traffic and 31 sets of Mk4 coaches. The York, Leeds and Newcastle resignalling schemes were not included since these would stand on their own feet. When completed, over 30,000 masts will have been erected together with enormous mileage of fibre optic telecommunications cabling and extensive immunisation of existing signalling equipment.

In previous overhead electrification schemes it has been the practice to provide concrete foundations for the masts, an operation needing two-line occupation for their erection and a minimum of two weeks for the concrete to cure. But on the East Coast main line, where ground conditions permitted, a new system of tubular steel piling, vibrated into the ground and to which the masts are bolted, has been used. Erection can be done in a single occupation at a rate in excess of six an hour. In fact, this system was pioneered by the LM Region at the time of the extensive Crewe rationalisation.

Naturally the main focus of interest will be the trains themselves.

continued

answer. 'I can't hear you, sir; I shall have to change the headset,' was the plea to give more time.' When communication was resumed the boss fired the first shot: what had the district officer's assistant told him?

In the war most control offices were transferred to country stations; the office which replaced Doncaster can still be seen on the down side at Bawtry. An engine and saloon – always known as 'The Dido' – sometimes provided a link with a city (such as Lincoln) and the temporary office (Blankney).

After nationalisation the Lines or Regions had conferences with their Divisions and BRHQ had conferences with Regions. It was then usual for the conference to be delegated to operating assistants at divisions or freight or passenger officers at regions.

Taking the morning conference at Division could be tricky. The GN Line had a freight officer who used to count brake vans seen from passenger train windows, and on his way to work counted the freight trains in the 'cab ranks' approaches to Ferme Park Yard. He was never short of talking points and often complained about a fast freight being delayed by a stopping passenger. But if the passenger officer took it, the complaint would be about passengers being delayed by freight. Frank Harrison.

In the making. Class 31/4 No 31441 passes through Doncaster station on 17 November 1988 with a southbound electrification train consisting of concrete mixers and a brake van.

When the Kings Cross–Leeds service opens, it will be the third express service in which push-pull mode has been employed. The draft timetable for the East Coast line indicates that about 80 per cent of the train mileage will be with normal daytime formations, and only 20 per cent with overnight sleeper or other coaching trains. There is virtue, therefore, in keeping the majority of the class 91 locomotives semi-permanently attached to their trains, only uncoupling for maintenance. It has proved an entirely satisfactory means of working at speeds exceeding 100mph, and the technique of controlling a locomotive from the other end of the train by Time Division Multiplex (TDM) over two train lighting control wires is now firmly established. However, in the case of the Mark 4 coaches the two-wire RCH cabling is replaced by International Union of Railways standard data quality wiring.

The class 91 electric locomotives are very much state-of-the-art machines; the specification called for the ability to haul/propel 520 tonne trains at up to 140mph and to haul 750 tonne sleeping car trains unaided over Shap and Beattock Banks should the design ever be used on the West Coast main line. Produced by GEC with mechanical parts and final assembly at BREL Crewe, they have a continuous rating of 6075hp (4530kw) on an all-up weight of only 81.5 tonnes. The four traction motors are mounted on and below the body, with shaft drive to gearboxes mounted on the bogies and linked to the axles by flexible

200

drives: this limits the unsprung weight which can be so punishing to the track. Gone are brake blocks acting on the wheel treads. Down to a moderate speed, braking will be rheostatic, the heat being dissipated in fan cooled resistance banks. At lower speeds, the automatic air brake progressively takes over applied through a disc brake unit on each motor shaft. The power is controlled by thyristor converters controlled by a microprocessor system to give extremely fine control of traction power, including 'creep control' to maximise power to match rail condition and thus avoid slipping. Following trials it proved necessary to put the early locomotives back into Crewe works for fine tuning of the electronics before they could enter service.

Given the decision to go push-pull, the external styling of the class 91 locomotive needs to fall into line. A streamlined nose is desirable at both ends of high-speed trains but a locomotive with two such noses (as the single class 89 electric) would leave an untidy gap ahead of the first coach. The class 91s therefore have a blunt end next to the train, matching the coach end. However, it contains a second cab for the overnight services, speed then being limited to 110mph. At the far end of the standard daytime trains, the driving cab will be incorporated in a driving-van trailer. In between will be eight Mark 4 coaches; built by Metro Cammell at Birmingham, these are 76ft 9in long over gangway faces and to a new profile, more restricted at cantrail level in order to provide for tilting – as was done with the ill-fated APT – should this be required in future. (The locomotive will not tilt.)

Progress with electrification as far as Leeds has been so far advanced

New at Kings Cross. Following the naming ceremony carried out by the Prime Minister Margaret Thatcher on 16 January 1989, class 89 No 89001 Avocet *leaves the station at the head of the 12.05 special train for the Royal Society for the Protection of Birds' headquarters at Sandy, Bedfordshire.*

that the first class 91 worked electric trains were able to start at the end of 1988, before the delivery of any of the new coaches. As an interim measure therefore, random services started with InterCity 125 trains of Mark 3 coaches with one power car replaced by the electric locomotive and the other serving as an unpowered driving trailer, the engine running only to provide power for lighting and air conditioning. By full service introduction to Leeds with the October 1989 timetable, sufficient Mark 4 coaches – including the driving-van trailers – were available to allow the Mark 3 coaches with power cars to be dispensed with.

For freight traffic and some passenger trains the class 90 locomotives, similar to those working West Coast services, are an update of the proven class 87s with thyristor control, creep control to avoid wheelslip, 'cruise control' as applied to some cars and TDM remote control.

And the end product of all this expenditure? Perhaps the first thing will be the greater reliability of electric traction. Then there will be the improved ambience for travellers in terms of cleanliness and quietness, particularly at stations. An important plus for many, especially the business community, will be improved timings; the word is that Kings Cross–Edinburgh timings of four hours or slightly more will be the norm, and even figures below four hours have been mentioned. This may well depend on agreement for a modified signalling system; for 140mph trials the signalling between Peterborough and Stoke Summit was modified by addition of a flashing green aspect to give, in effect, an extra signal section for braking purposes.

Some questions remain to be answered. What is clear is that the East Coast main line with its splendid views of a whole series of cathedrals and of North Sea cliffs and beaches will continue to play a vital role for decades to come.

Train of the future. The 12.38 test train from Kings Cross to Doncaster passes Sandy at speed on 10 August 1988 powered by GEC class 91 electric locomotives No 91004.

LNER Chronology

1922 Shadow board meetings held to decide structure. Hull & Barnsley Railway voluntarily merged with the North Eastern.

1923 1 Jan. LNER formed with Whitelaw (NBR chairman) as chairman and Ralph Lewis Wedgwood (NER general manager) as chief general manager.
1 Jul. Colne Valley & Halstead Railway absorbed. East & West Yorkshire Union Railway absorbed.

1924 21–29 Jan. ASLEF strike causing major disruption.
23 Apr.–1 Nov. British Empire Exhibition, Wembley. Class 'A1' 4-6-2 locomotive No 4472 *Flying Scotsman* exhibited.
24 Apr. Harwich–Zeebrugge train ferry service inaugurated by the Great Eastern Train Ferry Co Limited.
1 Jul. Mid Suffolk Light Railway absorbed.
Birthday Honours List. R. L. Wedgwood knighted.
Grant of Arms by College of Arms (one of only three railways plus the British Transport Commission to be granted).

1925 9 May–31 Oct. British Empire Exhibition to Wembley. Class 'A1' 4-6-2 locomotive No 4472 *Flying Scotsman* and Class 'K3' 2-6-0 No 200 exhibited.
1-14 Jul. Stockton & Darlington Railway centenary. Exhibition at Darlington.
2 Jul. Stockton & Darlington Railway centenary. Procession of old and new locomotives and several complete trains along part of route of Stockton & Darlington Railway.

1926 4–12 May. General Strike.
10 May. Up *Flying Scotsman* maliciously derailed (by miners) at Cramlington.

1927 1 Jan. Zeeland Steamship Co service to Vlissingen transferred from Folkestone to Parkeston Quay, Harwich.
29 Jun. Total eclipse of the sun. Special excursions to Leyburn, Richmond and West Hartlepool. A total of 37 trains was run, including two sleeping car trains, carrying 16,488 passengers.
20 Aug. Temporary loudspeaker system first used at York for the direction of passengers.

1928 1 May. First non-stop runs by *Flying Scotsman* between Kings Cross and Edinburgh and vice versa made possible by the introduction of corridor tenders.
24 Sept. Third class sleeping cars introduced (four berth with rugs and pillows).

1929 29 Mar. New Hump Yard at Whitemoor, March, brought into use, the first in Great Britain to be equipped with hydraulic wagon retarders.

1930 SSs *Vienna* (1929) *Prague* and *Amsterdam* entered service on Harwich – Hoek-van-Holland route.
Jun. Four cylinder compound 4-6-4 locomotive

No 10000 entered traffic fitted with 'Yarrow' water tube boiler working at 450 psi.

1931 11 May. Electrification of Manchester South Junction & Altrincham Railway (1500v dc) jointly with LMS.

1932 Summer. Weekend cruises to Belgium and the Netherlands by SS *Vienna* commenced.

1933 Jun. *Northern Belle* land cruise introduced to give a week's tour over scenic lines in England and Scotland. (Ran each June until 1939.)
Jun. Camping coaches introduced at selected stations in the North East.
19 Nov. Thirsk signal box opened, the first controlled by thumb switches and relay interlocking. The area covered was 4½ miles, then largest in the country.

1934 1 Jan. Gidea Park – Shenfield widening completed; also colour-light signalling and burrowing junction at Shenfield.
May. Class 'P2' 2-8-2 locomotive with rotary cam poppet valves No 2001 *Cock o' The North* entered traffic, built specifically for the Edinburgh–Aberdeen line.
4 Oct. New fish dock at Grimsby opened with 37 acres of enclosed water.

1935 7 Jan. Shildon–Newport electrification discontinued: due to decline of coal traffic the renewal of overhead not justified.
30 Sep. *Silver Jubilee* streamlined express between Newcastle and Kings Cross and vice versa in four hours introduced. Four new class 'A4' 4-6-2 locomotives built specially.

1936 Liverpool Street–Shenfield and Manchester, Sheffield, Wath electrification schemes authorised.
Jun. Class 'V2' 2-6-2 mixed-traffic locomotive No 4771 *Green Arrow* introduced.
1 Oct. LNER took over operation of Midland & Great Northern Joint Railway including 85 locomotives.

1937 3 Jul. *Coronation* express introduced between Kings Cross and Edinburgh and vice versa in six hours with 'Beaver-tail' observation car during summer months. Five class 'A4s' painted blue for the service.
27 Sep. *West Riding Limited* introduced between Bradford, Leeds and Kings Cross.
1 Nov. LNER took over from London Transport the working of passenger trains north of Rickmansworth and all freight services. Eighteen former Metropolitan locomotives added to stock.
10 Dec. Company's worst accident (Castlecary) killing 35.

1938 14 Mar. Newcastle–South Shields line electrified.
3 Jul. World speed record for steam of 126mph claimed by class 'A4' No 4468 *Mallard* down Stoke bank between Grantham and Peterborough.

203

30 Sep. William Whitelaw, chairman, retires; Sir Ronald Matthews appointed.

1939 Mar. Sir Ralph Wedgwood, chief general manager retires; C. H. Newton appointed.

3 Sep. Streamlined trains (last ran on 31 August) withdrawn on outbreak of war.

1940 17 Nov. Eric Gill sculptor and designer of LNER's own 'Gill Sans' typeface died.

1941 Class 'V4' 2-6-2 locomotive No 3401 *Bantam Cock* (Sir Nigel Gresley's last design) entered service.

5 Apr. Sir Nigel Gresley died age 64. Edward Thompson appointed.

1942 Dec. Class B1 4-6-0 locomotive introduced.

1943 C. H. Newton, chief general manager knighted in Birthday Honours List.

1944 10 Aug. Fitzherbert Wright was appointed director in January 1944 and class 'A4' 4-6-2 4486 photographed successively as Nos 1928 *Brigid*, 1931 *Davina* and 1934 *Bryan* being the names of his daughters and son and their years of birth.

1945 First post-war corridor carriages produced with centre doors and transverse passages in lieu of end doors.

1946 May. 2000th locomotive built at Doncaster works. (Class 'A2/3' 4-6-2 No 500 *Edward Thompson*.)

Jun. Edward Thompson, chief mechanical engineer, retired, A. H. Peppercorn appointed.

1947 Three serious accidents in final year killing 53 people.

May. SS *Arnhem* entered service on Harwich–Hoek-van-Holland route.

Jun. Sir Charles Newton, chief general manager, retired, Miles Beevor, chief legal advisor appointed acting until end of year.

Aug. M V *Suffolk Ferry* entered service on Harwich–Zeebrugge train ferry.

1948 Directors refused compensation for loss of office. Hugh Dalton speaks of 'poor bag of assets' inherited from the railway companies. LNER split between Eastern, North Eastern and Scottish Regions of BR.

Royal train engine. The Royal train carrying HM King George VI and Queen Elizabeth passing Hadley Wood in 1938. The engine is Super Claud No 8783 – the normal locomotive for such duties, and always kept in pristine condition. Note the special headcode.

ACKNOWLEDGEMENTS

In this fourth and final volume on Britain's four 'great' railways, we have once again been fortunate in having the help of professional railwaymen for whom the LNER was very much part of their lives. Add to this the advisory team who have kept an eagle eye on our progress and the LNER jumps into perspective. The stalwarts include John Powell, a Derby apprentice rising through the ranks (after war service in the Royal Engineers) to traction and train crew manager at the BR Board, and John Edgington who worked in LMS Control and the LMR PR department prior to joining the National Railway Museum in 1975. Newcomers were Frank Harrison, who joined the LNER as a clerk, returned after the war as a traffic apprentice and rose to operations manager at the Board, and Richard Joby with a wealth of knowledge of things Great Eastern. This corporate knowledge has proved invaluable. Then there has been some evocative writing from the pens of Richard Hardy and Bill Harvey, both ex-LNER men whose names are almost household words to the knowledgeable enthusiast.

As in the companion volumes, many friends have searched their memories and notebooks and to those not mentioned by name we say thank you. Material from many sources has been added for balance and character. In particular we would like to thank Richard Hope, the editor of *Railway Gazette International* for permission to use line drawings and material from that publication and the *Railway Magazine* for similar permission. *Meccano Magazine* also proved a useful source, as of course did the *LNER Magazine*. Last, we must thank the preservationists, who have saved not only locomotives and rolling stock, but whole stretches of the railway as well.

We have been lucky with photographers too: Dick Blenkinsop, the late Eric Treacy, C.R.L. Coles, E.R. Withersett, H.C. Casserley, P.M. Alexander, Jim Jarvis, Brian Morrison, A.W. Flowers and many others. They and the National Railway Museum have been able to work wonders alongside the L&GRP and Millbrook House collections, and George Heiron has, of course, painted another jacket for us.

The main chapters are based on material supplied as follows:

Introduction	David St John Thomas
Freight	Frank Harrison
An Observer Remembers	Frank Harrison
Stations	J. Brodribb
East Anglia	D. Walsh
Locomotives	John Powell
Scotland	John Powell
The Golden Years of High Speed Trains	John Powell
Sheds and Workshops	John Powell
Branch Line Miscellany	H.N. James
Coaches: Jazz Quins to Coronation Luxury	Geoffrey Kichenside
LNER into BR	Frank Harrison
Preservation	P.B. Whitehouse
Britain's New Premier Line	John Powell

Fillers between chapters are based on material supplied by: Richard Joby and John Edgington (Tree of Growth and Chronology and Named Trains); John Powell (Working the Fish, LNER Personalities – with Richard Hardy – and Station Interludes); D.S.M. Barrie (Soldier Enthusiast in Wartime East Anglia); Frank Harrison (Peterborough and Joint Lines, with Peter Baughan); Geoffrey Kichenside (Signalling and Safety); Bill Harvey (Problems in the North Circular); Dr W.A. Tuplin and P.B. Whitehouse (Seen at York); Richard Joby (Publicity and Public Relations, plus the Tree of Growth with John Edgington). The Railway Correspondents and Travel Society's *Railway Observer* produced the Locomotive and Stock Allocations.

Black and white photographs are by: J.H.L. Adams (86, 135 *lower*, 155); P.M. Alexander (10, 28 *upper*, 64, 72, 133, 136 *upper*, 144, 155, 177 *upper*, 182 *upper*); D.S.M. Barrie (8); R. J. Blenkinsop (4); British Rail (158, 178, 184); British Steel/ Richard Joby (19); W.A. Camwell (141); H.C. Casserley (66, 132, 160, 177 *lower*); C.R.L. Coles (16, 33, 46, 50, 52 *both*, 58, 71 *both*, 90, 97, 109, 180 *both*, 187, 204); Basil Cooper (83); J.C. Flemons (191); J. Edgington Collection (161); A.W. Flowers (61); W. Leslie Good (9, 17 *upper*, 22, 23, 51 *lower*, 75, 102 *upper*, 176 *centre*, 195 *lower*); W. Leslie Good (9, 17 *upper*, 22, 23, 51 *lower*, 75, 102 *upper*, 176 *centre*, 195 *lower*); R.G. Jarvis (94 *upper*, 100 *four*, 102 *lower*, 196); G.M. Kichenside (127 *both*, 165 *four*, 167 *four*, 168, 169 *three*, 171 *four*, 172, 174); G.D. King (157 *lower*, 192 *upper*); L&GRP (6 *upper*, 15 *lower*, 31, 88, 89, 145, 148); Millbrook House Collection (6 *lower*, 17 *lower*, 49 *upper*, 51 *upper*, 60, 69, 123, 128); Brian Morrison (185, 186, 194, 200, 201, 202); National Railway Museum (15 *upper*, 20, 29, 35 *lower*, 39, 56, 83 *bottom*, 91, 92 *four*, 93, 94 *four*, 101, 103, 104 *both*, 106, 110, 122, 130, 139 *both*, 140, 183, 188, 192 *lower*, 193, 197); A. Scotland (89, 125); Eric Treacy/Millbrook House Collection (Frontispiece, 65, 67, 96, 98, 124, 126, 136 *lower*, 162, 178, 190, 195 *upper*); Dr W.A. Tuplin (63 *both*); P.H. Wells (159 *upper*); E.R. Wethersett (21, 76, 108, 119, 120); and P.B. Whitehouse (35 *upper*, 73, 74, 111, 135 *upper*, 154 *both*, 159.

Colour photographs are credited to the following sources: J.H.L. Adams (152 *upper*); Colour Rail (77, 80 *upper* and *lower*, 114 *upper* and *lower*, 116); Colour Rail/J.M. Jarvis (44); G. Harris/Millbrook House Collection (115); G.F. Heiron (41); Robert Humm Collection (149 *luggage label* and *badge*); Brian Morrison (152 *lower*); National Railway Museum/Millbrook House Collection (150-1); W. Potter (113); and P.B. White-house (78-9, 149 *leaflets*).

INDEX

Names of trains and illustration page numbers are in italics

Abbots Ripton collision, 125
Aberdeen: fish market, 40
   station, 67, *196*
   suburban service, 161
Aberdonian, The, 18, 112
accidents, 125, 128
Aerolite, 191
American: class S160 2-8-0, 155
Anglia Region, (BR), 180
Annesley: marshalling yard, 30
APT, Advanced Passenger Train, 198, 201
ashpits: Norwich, *135*
   wet, *133*
Atlantics, *9*, *16*, 46, *125*
   Ivatt, *8*, *89*, *193*
Avocet, *201*
Aylesbury station, *177*

Ballater station, 67
Bantam Cock, *106*
Bantam Hen, *106*
Barnard Castle station, 66
Barrie, D. S. M., 54
beaver tail observation saloon, 121, 122
Beccles: changes at, 144
behaviour: on trains, 70
Belah viaduct, *158*, 159
Bell, William, architect, 64
Berwick, Royal Border Bridge, *120*
Beyer Peacock & Co., 94
Birmingham Railway Museum, 191
Black Pig, *100*
boat trains, 48, 53, 181, 188, 205
   see also Continentals
Border Union Railway: 'Waverley' line, 21
BR: *see under* locomotives and separate regions
Bramham Moor, The, 92
branch lines, 144–63
   closures, 161, 184
   freight on, 153
   locomotives on, 48
Britannia, *135*
Brocklesby station, 61
buffet cars, 170, 191, 205
Bury St Edmunds station, 68

Calder, James, 105
Caledonian Railway, 67
Callander and Oban Railway, 145
Cambridge station, 68, 193, *194*
Capitals Limited (later *Elizabethan*), 183
Castlecary collision, 109, 125
Castle Hedingham, *71*
Centenary, *130*
cheap day: to London, 53
Cheltenham Flyer, The, 117
Cheshire Lines Committee, 16, 23,

37, 144, 168, 176, 177, 179
City of Kingston-Upon-Hull, *185*
City of London, *94*
City of Truro, 191
City of York, *89*
Cleethorpes, 48, 50
coaches, 164–78
   finish, 168
   Green Goddess, 145
   open, 170
   quad art, *166*, 168
   quin art, *166*, 168
   through, 8
   triplet articulated, *169*, 170
Cock o' the North, *91*, *92*, 109, 140
Colchester station, 68
Colne Valley & Halstead Railway, 73, 153
Colwick: marshalling yard, 30
Commonwealth of Australia, *123*
Continentals: *Antwerp*, 14, *15*
   Day, *181*
   Flushing, 14, 112
   Hook, 14, 57, 81, *169*
   North Country, 23
   Scandinavian, 14
Coronation, *13*, 21, 117, *120*, 121–3, *149*, *162*, *175*
Cowlairs (Glasgow) shed, 138–9, 141
Cromer beach, *154*
Cubitt, Lewis, architects, 59
Cudworth shed: coaling plant, 133

Darlington sheds, 138, 139, *140*, 141
Dereham shed, *135*
diesel electric locomotives, 97
   conversion to, 145
   Deltic, 183, 198
   multiple-units, 184, 186, 205
Director class, 85
Dobson, John, 62
docks: LNER, 189
   ownership, 13
   Tyne, 13
Dominion of Canada, *121*
Doncaster, 7
Doncaster shed, *134*, 137, *138*, *139*, 140, 141, *190*, *200*
drivers: experience of, 36, 37
   Henson, 93
   rivalry of, 45
   Walls, 95
Dukeries Junction, *28*
Dukinfield shed, 140
Dundee Tay Bridge station, 66, 105
Durham viaduct, *9*
dynamometer car: use of, 121

Earl Marischal, *98*
East Anglia: branch line closures, 161
   freight traffic, 38
   ports, 189
   wartime railways in, 54–5
East Anglian, *13*, 14, *75*
East London Railway, 70

Eastern Belle Pullman, *75*, 148
Eastern Belle Pullman Limited, 48
Eastern Counties Railway, 14, 24–5
Eastern Region, BR, 179
Eastern Union Railway, 25
Edinburgh & Glasgow Railway, 21, 64
Edinburgh: St Margarets shed, *137*, 139
   Waverley, *8*, 21, 64–6, *67*, *104*, 108, *110*, 121, 145, 198
earphones: on trains, 118
Elder, Andrew: ash pan man, 139
electrification, 11, 20, 70, 183, 184, 186
   of East Coast line, 198–202
   suburban, *166*, 168, 185
Elvet, Durham, 160
engine: changes, 47
   efficiency, 95
excursions, *160*
   Bank Holiday, 157
   coaches for, 170
   evening, 56, 57

Faringdon, Lord, 82
Fay, Sir Sam, 18, 82
Felstead, *92*
Fiennes, Gerry, 30, 180
films: shown on trains, 118
fish: freight of, 29, 39–40
   ports, 39–40
Flamboyant, *162*
Flying Fox, 7
Flying Scotsman, 7, *8*, 12, 18, 39, 53, 106, 112, 117, *124*, *130*, *162*, *178*, 180, 191, *192*
   coaches, *166*, *172*, *173*, *174*
   at Kings Cross, 45, *60*
   poster for, 55
   at 100mph, 118
Football class, 51, *52*
Forth: Bridge, *21*, 109
   Firth of, ports, 189
freightliners, 185
freight traffic, 29–44, 47, 53, 57, 74
   agricultural, *16*, 32, 153
   on branch lines, 153
   coal, 18, 19, 28, 29–30, 38, 61, 107, 185–6, 189
   engines for, 86, 159
   fish, 29, 39–40
   and food preservation, 33
   general merchandise, 30–1
   iron ore, 30, *183*
   milk traffic, 34
   mineral, 19, 30, 107, 157
   at Peterborough, 69
   pigeons, 32
   receipts, 38
   sugar beet, 34, 74
   timings, 32
   vegetables, 32–3
   war traffic, 38, 81

Garden Cities and Cambridge Buffet Express, 14
Garganey, *139*
Garratt engines, *94*
Gateshead running shed, *132*, 137, 139
Geddes, Sir Eric, 82
Gladiator, *63*
Gladstone, 189, 191
Glasgow: Queen St Low Level, 112
   station, 22, 66, 198
   Transport Museum, 189
   see also Cowlairs shed
Glenalmond, *61*
Glen Gloy, *141*
Glen Mamie, *111*
GN & GE Joint line, 53, 176
GN & LNW Joint line, 176
Golden Eagle, 123, *124*
Golden Plover, *123*
Golden Shuttle, *122*
goods: depots, 31, 59
   stations, 38
Gorton, 47
   Tank shed, *136*, *139*, 140, 141
Great Central Railway, GC, 11, 18–19, 47, 54–5
   coaches, 164, *165*, 166
   standards of, 8
   steamers, 189, 205
Great Eastern Railway, GER, 11, 14, 16, 25
   branch lines, 158
   coaches, 164, *165*, *167*
   Jazz service, 67, 70, *166*, 168
   stations, 67–8
   steamers, 189, 205
Great Marquess, The, 191
Great North of Scotland Railway, 11, 22–3, 40, 87, 107
   branch lines, 161
   stations, 67
Great Northern, 88, 96
Great Northern Railway, GNR, 11, 16, 18, 24
   coaches, *165*, 166, *167*, *169*
   cross-country lines, 47–8, 158
   stations, 61–2
Green Arrow, 21, 29, 189
Gresley, Sir Herbert Nigel, 12, 82, *83*, 84, 87, 88, 90–1, 93
   buffet cars, 191, *205*
   coaches, 164
   as engineer, 95
   Pacifics, 7, 18, *60*, 85
Grimsby fish docks, 39, 61
Grey of Falloden, Viscount, 82
GW/GC Joint line, 53, 176

Halesworth station, *75*
Harrison, Herbert, 57
Harwich: port of, 24
   train ferry, 7, 205
Henry Oakley, 189, *190*, 191

high speed services, 117–28
  coaches for, 170, 173
  see also HST
Highlandman, The, 112
Holcroft, H., 87
holiday: coaches, *171*
  traffic, 75, 153, 156
Homersfield station, *154*
Hoole, Bill, 183, 191
horse-drawn drays, 35, 38
HST, High Speed Trains, 183, *185*
Hull: port of, 20
Hull & Barnsley Railway, 20
Hull Dairycoates running shed, 129
Hull Paragon, 64
Humber estuary ports, 189, 205
hump yards, *184, 185*, 186
Hurworth, The, 45
Hush Hush, *94*

Immingham: and coal shipment, 29
  docks, 61
infrastructure: improvements, 183, 198
Inter City 125 High Speed trains, 198, 202
Inverurie (Aberdeen) shed, 139, 141
Inyala, 96
Ipswich & Bury Railway, 68
Ipswich station, 68
Ivanhoe, 21
Ivatt, H. A., 82
  Atlantics, *8*, 16, *89*, 130

John of Gaunt, 181
joint lines, 176

Kelvedon & Tollesbury Railway, 73
King George V, 9
Kings Cross, 57–9 *passim*, 178
  bombing of, 20
  coupon, *149*
  Flying Scotsman at, 45
  Leeds HS electric service, 198–202
  loco shed, *132*
  memories of, 7
  Top Shed, *130, 131*
  traffic volume, 18, 81
Kirkby Stephen, 158, 159

Lancashire, Derbyshire & East Coast Railway, *28*, 48
Lancashire & Yorkshire Railway, 82
land cruising, 48
Lauder Light Railway, 160
Laxfield station, 74
Leeds Northern Railway, 19
Leeds stations, 193, *194, 195*
Leeds United, 94
Leicester station, *157*
Lincoln, 48, 61
Liverpool Street, *56, 57, 59, 71*
  exit from, 14
  hotel at, 81
  memories of, 7
  signal controls, 125–6
  traffic volume, 18
livery, 173, 179
Loch Laggan, 109
Loch Treig, 141
locomotive: classification, 85
  nicknames, 85
  preservation, 189–91
  stock, of LNER, 1947, 99–104
  BR: emus, *194*, 199
  4 2-6-0, 136
  5 4-6-0, 110
  24 0-4-0T, 189
  25 0-4-0T, 189

2 MT 2-6-0, *158*
4 MT 2-6-0, 156
3F 0-6-0, 156
4F 0-6-0, *156*
31/4, *200*
86/2, *194*
89, *201*
90, 202
91, 200–1, *202*
0-4-0, 73
0-4-0T, 189
0-6-0, 73, *157*
01 2-8-0, *101, 182*
A 4-6-0, *15*
A1, 7, 37, *60, 86*, 97, 117, 130, *162, 178,* 180
A2, 180
A2/2 2-8-2, *98*
A3, 7, 40, *92*, 118, 130, 162, 191, *194*
A4, 31, 37, *65, 83*, 91, 92, 105–6, *124*, 130, *139, 162, 177*, 180, 191
A5 4-6-2, *103, 143, 157*
Britannia 4-6-2, *181*
B1 4-6-0, 95, 96, 106, 112, *157, 177, 182,* 189
B2 4-6-0, 97
B3/2 4-6-0, *50*
B4 4-6-0, *52*
B7/2, *100*
B8 4-6-0, *61*
B12 4-6-0, 14, 48, *51, 71,* 76, 107, 145, 196
B12/3 4-6-0, *72,* 187
B16 4-6-0, *10,* 160
B16/2 4-6-0, *63*
B17 4-6-0, 14, 48, *52,* 68, *71,* 76, 81, 90, *94,* 177, 196
B17/5, *94*
Claud Hamilton, 4-4-0, 14, 48, *135,* 196, 193
C 4-4-0, 177
C1, 8, *63,* 190
C2, *195*
C4 4-4-2, *23, 51*
  Jersey Lily, 48, 53, 85, *177,* 205
C7 4-4-2, *39, 63, 123, 132, 195*
C11, *22*
C12 4-4-2, 48
C12 4-4-2T, *64, 157*
C16 4-4-2, 110
D1–3 4-4-0, 48
D2 4-4-0, *16,* 48
D9–11 4-4-0, *63,* 100, 105
D11/1 4-4-0, 53
D20 4-4-0, *102, 132, 160*
D29 4-4-0, *21*
D33 4-4-0, *108*
D34 4-4-0, 109, *111, 141*
D40 4-4-0, *107, 189*
D41 4-4-0, *87,* 107
D49 4-4-0, 20, 45, 90, *92,* 107, *177*
E4 2-4-0, *73, 135, 193*
F2 2-4-2, *154*
F4, 71
F5, 71
F6 2-4-2, *153*
Garratt 0-8-2, 30
GC 4-6-0, *39,* 48
GWR Great Bear, 46
G5 0-4-4, *9*
G7 4-4-0, *155*
Holden 2-4-0, 189
Holden 4-6-0, *196*
H2 4-4-4, *103*
Johnson 0-4-4, 161
J5 0-6-0, *49*
J11 0-6-0, *100,* 156
J15 0-6-0, *6, 31, 73, 74, 154,* 189, 196

J17 0-6-0, 135, 189, 196
J20 0-6-0, *33*
J21 0-6-0, *66,* 148, *158, 159*
J27 0-6-0, *140*
J36 0-6-0, 105, 191
J37 0-6-0, 105
J38 0-6-0, 90, *91,* 107
J39 0-6-0, *49, 67,* 90, *94,* 107, *133, 139, 194*
J40 0-6-0, *155*
J52 0-6-0ST, *192*
J69 0-6-0, *189, 196*
J72 0-6-0, *65*
J83 0-6-0, *104*
K1 2-6-0, 111, 112
K2 2-6-0, 36, 48, *90, 107,* 109, *130, 136, 141*
K3 2-6-0, 39, 48, 88
K4 2-6-0, 93, 109, 191
L1 2-6-4, 95, 143
N1 0-6-2, 66
N1 0-6-2T, *167*
N2 0-6-2, *20, 46,* 66, 110, *178*
N5 0-6-2, *145*
N7 0-6-2, 66
Pacifics
  Gresley, 7, 89, 180
  Super, 7, 91, 92
P1 2-8-2, *35*
P2 2-8-2, 21, *92,* 98
P3 0-6-0, 191
Q4 0-8-0, *139*
Q7 0-8-0, *183*
Raven, 87, 88, 89
Reid, 22, *102,* 105, 106
Riddles 2-8-0, *35*
Robinson 2-8-0, *28,* 85, *100*
  Director, 4-4-0, 68, *100*
ROD 2-8-0, 30, 85, 100, *182*
Sentinel shunter, *187*
V1 2-6-2, *104,* 107
V2 2-6-2, 13, 21, *29,* 63, 93, 122, 130, 180, *182, 194*
V4 2-6-2, 93, *106*
LMS: and BR, 179
  coaches, 170
  drivers, 45
  and freight, 29
LNER: chronology, 203–4
  criticism of, 13
  cross-country trains, 23
  farewell to, 14
  magazine, 10
  management, 13, 82, 84
  mechanical engineers, 139
  modernisation, 11
  revenue of, 10, 13
  transfer to BR, 179–88
LNWR, 68, 69
London: depots, 142
  termini, 12
Louth station, 157
Lowestoft, 54, 67–8
luggage labels, *149*
luxury: coaches, *170, 172*
  on trains, 117

Mablethorpe, 48, 50
Mallard, 9, 53, 84, 191
Malton & Driffield Railway, 19
Manchester, Sheffield & Lincolnshire, 18, 60–1
Manchester South Junction & Altrincham Railway, 176
Manchester stations, 57, 61, *177*
Marks Tey junction, *72,* 73, *153*
marshalling yards, 30, 36–7, 38, 69, 185
Marylebone station, 38, 57, 59–60, 64

Master Cutler, 8, 19
Matthews, Sir Ronald, 82
Melton Constable shed, *136, 155, 176*
Metropolitan & Great Central Joint Line, *52,* 176, 177
Metropolitan Railway, *177*
Metropolitan Widened Lines, 67
Mexborough coaling plant, 133
Midland & Great Northern Joint, M & GN, 16, 40, 54, 69, 74, *136,* 155–6, 176, 177
  closure, 184
Mid-Suffolk Light Railway, 73, *74*

nationalisation, 14, 21, 81, 97, 157, 185, 186
  and freight, 29
Neasden running shed, 129, 142–3
  coaling plant, 133
Network System, 186
Newcastle Central station, 62, 65
Newton, C. H., 82
Night Scotsman, The, 112
Norfolk & Suffolk Joint Railway, 25, 54, 176
Norfolkman, 181
North British Railway, NBR, 11, 21–2, 105
  branch lines, 160
  hotels, 21, 22, 121
  stations, 64–7
North East Region (BR), 179
North Eastern Railway, NER, 11, 13, 16, 18, 19–20
  coaches, 166
  depots, 129
  stations, 62
  swing bridge, *10*
North Norfolk Railway, 191
North Yorkshire Moors Railway, *192*
Northern Belle, 48, 108
Northern & Eastern Railway, 24, 25
Norseman, The, 112
Norwich: shed, *135*
  – Thorpe station, 68, 196, *197*
  in wartime, 54
Nottingham Victoria station, 60, *61*

Pacifics, 13, 46, 53
Papyrus, 53, 118
Parker, Leslie Preston, 84
Parnwell, Sidney, 82
passengers: East Anglian, 72, 153
  express engines, 86
  volume of, 64
Peppercorn, Arthur, 97
Peterborough, 62, 69
Peterborough, Lynn & Sutton Bridge Railway, 69
Pommern, 178
Pom-Pom, 100
posters, *188*
PS Lucy Ashton, 112
PS Waverley, 22, 48
public relations: booklets, 188
publicity, 187–8
Pullmans, 75, 106, 205
  Clacton (Eastern Belle), 75
  Harrogate, 16, 18, 112
  Yorkshire, 18, 112

Queen of Scots, The, 8, 18, 106, 112
Quicksilver, 120, 139

Ramsey branch line station, 148
Raven, Sir Vincent, 82, 129
reorganisation of LNER, 179–88
road competition, 74

Robinson, John G., 82
Romford, 18, 75
routes: scenic, 145, 202
Royal Sovereign, 97
Royal trains, 173
Rugby Central station, 68

safety: on railways, 59
St Combs Light Railway, 67
Sandringhams, 47, 48, 51, 52, 86, 97,
    135, *177*
Scarborough Flyer, 20, 112, 118
Scotland: railway closures, 108, 184
    suburban service, 110
    Western, harbours, 189
Scotsman, 30
Scottish Region (BR), 179, 180
Scottish Railway, 11
Scottish Union, 37
Severn Valley Railway, 191
sheds, 129, 134
    light tunnel, 134
Sheffield Special, 19
Sheffield Victoria station, 61, *63*
signalling, 46, 74, 125–8
    centralised, 183
    colour light, 75, 126, 127
    electric, 74, 126, 199
    at Peterborough, 69
    Welwyn control, 125
signals, *9*, *10*, *16*
    entrance-exit panel, 128
    searchlight, 46, *127*

semaphore, 46, 108
somersault, *125*
    upper quadrant, *126*
Silver Fox, 16
Silver Jubilee, The, 7, 12, *16*, *92*, 112,
    118–23 *passim*, *149*, 162, 173, *174*
Silver Link, 12, 53, *92*, 119, 120
Sir Nigel Gresley, *178*, 183, 191, *192*
Sir Ralph Wedgewood, *83*
Skegness, 48, 50
Skibo Castle, 108
South Eastern & Chatham Railway,
    87
Southwold Railway, 54, 75
Sparshatt, Bill, 118, 130
Spearmint, 46
specials: St Leger Day, 23
speed: of trains, 117–28
stations, 57–69
    coastal, 148
    country, 148
    improvements, 180
    staff, duties of, 53
steam railcars, *171*
Stephenson, Robert, 25
Stockton & Darlington Railway, 19,
    189
Stockton shed, *133*
Stratford on Avon & Midland
    Junction Railway, *144*
Stratford running shed, 129, 134, 141
    open day at, *187*
Sunderland, *52*

Sutton Bridge, *177*
Sweedie Junction, Thetford, *73*
Swinton & Knottingly Joint Railway,
    23, 176

tablets: changing of, 112, 155
Talisman, 30
Tattersall, A. E. T., 126
Tay Bridge, 22
TDM, Time Division Multiplex, 200,
    202
Temple Mills hump yard, *184*
Thompson, Edward, 96–7, 112
    coaches, 164, *171*, 173–4
Thornton, Sir Henry, 70, 82
timetables: of branch lines, 144–5,
    146–7
    of East Coast line, 200
traffic control, 198, 199
travel: cheap, 21, 72
Tuplin, W. A., 162
Tweeddale, 102
Tyne docks, 13
    boat trains, 205
Tyne & Wear Metro, 62

viaducts, *158*, *159*
volume: of passengers, 64

Walter K. Wigham, 37
warflat trains, 54, 55
wartime traffic on LNER, 13
Wath: marshalling yard, 30

Watkin, Sir Edward, 60
Waveney Valley Railway, 54, 144,
    148
Wedgwood, Sir Ralph Lewis, 13, 82
West Highland Railway, 47, 93, 107,
    109, 112, 145–6
    Hikers, 145, 148
    stations, 66–7
West Riding Limited, 112, 122, 123,
    149
    poster for, 55
Whitelaw, William, 10, 12, 82
Wilson, Sir Reginald, 179
Wisbech & Upwell Tramway, 73, 74
    freight on, 74
Woodford (Halse), *144*
Woodhead tunnel, 50, 61, *182*
World War II: and GER, 54–5, 81
    at Kings Cross, *20*
    and locomotive depots, 142
    services in, 109–10
Wrexham, Mold & Connagh's Quay
    Railway, *145*, 176

Yarmouth, 24, 40, 54, 67
York, 19, 20, 45, 162–3
    carriage works, 137, 141
    Eastern Region HQ, 180
    National Railway Museum, 189,
    190
    station, 62, 63
York, Newcastle & Berwick, 19
York & North Midland, 19